MS. MENTOR'S
new and ever more
IMPECCABLE
ADVICE FOR
WOMEN and men
IN ACADEMIA

MS. MENTOR'S
new and ever more
IMPECCABLE
ADVICE FOR
WOMEN *and men*
IN ACADEMIA

Emily Toth

PENN

University of Pennsylvania Press

Philadelphia

Published by
University of Pennsylvania Press
Philadelphia, Pennsylvania 19104-4112

Printed in the United States of America on acid-free paper

10   9   8   7   6   5   4   3   2   1

Library of Congress Cataloging-in-Publication Data

Toth, Emily.
   Ms. Mentor's new and ever more impeccable advice for women and men in academia / Emily Toth.
      p.   cm.
   Includes bibliographical references and index.
   ISBN 978-0-8122-2039-1 (alk. paper)
   1. Women college teachers—United States—Miscellanea. 2. Women graduate
students—United States—Miscellanea. 3. Women college teachers—United States—
Social conditions. 4. Women graduate students—United States—Social conditions.
5. Women college teachers—United States—Conduct of life. 6. Women graduate
students—United States—Conduct of life. I. Title.
   LB2332.3.T683 2009
   378.1'2082—dc22   2008022362

To B.T.

Contents

Preface

The fledglings of academe floundered and whimpered. They panted. They trembled. They were sure there was some homework assignment they'd failed to turn in.

They knew not why they had made enemies, nor how they had been sentenced to meetings that seemed to be nothing but peacocking and frothing. They wanted to respect their elders, but often found them ponderous, mysterious, or inane. They wanted their students' respect, not "I wasn't in class. Had to go skiing. Did I miss anything?"

Among themselves, newbies would marvel, sigh, and moan. And sometimes weep.

And then Ms. Mentor arose to rescue them from their backwardness and confusion. From her ivory tower, she would dispense her impeccable wisdom to the huddled masses. Eyes would be opened, ears would be cleaned, and careers salvaged.

Ms. Mentor began with ladylike unobtrusiveness, with a tiny 1992 advice column for *Concerns*, the newsletter for the Women's Caucus for the Modern Languages. From the beginning she dwelled in her ivory tower, from which she channeled her perfect wisdom through Emily Toth (rhymes with *both*), professor at Louisiana State University. They are not the same person, for Ms. Mentor is much taller, has a deeper voice, and is a heavy metal fanatic.

An early column with a controversial stance on fashion ("frumpy sells better than chic") led to a guest appearance in *Vogue* and then to a 1997 tome, *Ms. Mentor's Impeccable Advice for Women in Academia*. Then Ms. Mentor infiltrated the Internet, when her monthly "Ms. Mentor" column made its maiden appearance on the *Chronicle of Higher Education*'s Career Network site in August 1998. In 2000, *Content Spotlight* named her one of "The Net's Hottest Columnists."

There have been dissenters. During her first five years online, Ms. Mentor often got a blunt evaluation from a retired widow who would write: "Ms. Mentor: You are still full of shit." Once Ms. Mentor's column began appearing in print as well as online, in 2003, the irascible widow's messages stopped. Ms. Mentor does not know why.

Two years later, there was a tragic loss. When the Hurricane Katrina flood swept through and destroyed Emily Toth's apartment in New Orleans, hundreds of Ms. Mentor's letters were washed away into the Gulf. (Maybe there are eager readers in Mexico still drying and perusing them.)

Throughout her incarnations, Ms. Mentor has insisted on confidentiality for her flock. Letter writers' names are instantly removed from her files. No readers' real names are ever revealed in her column, and identifying details are always scrambled. Sometimes there are sex changes; often there are geographical ones. The law school dean who once convened his faculty to harangue them ("Who wrote this to Ms. Mentor? I'll have your brain!") was barking up the wrong banister. The original letter writer was a chemist in Calgary (or maybe not).

Readers, it seemed, hungered for the blunt inside knowledge, the rants, and the gossip that Ms. Mentor disseminated. The column soon had more than 15,000 hits a month. Ms. Mentor herself received some fifteen to fifty e-mails a month (ms.mentor@chronicle.com) and quickly realized that she could not answer them all. (Ann Landers had a staff of a dozen people; Ms. Mentor has two cats, one of whom is very grouchy.) Very few queries could be handled in the column, with its maximum of fifteen hundred words.

Nor could Ms. Mentor publish the best, smartest, and weirdest rejoinders—until this volume.

She had been able to summarize some letters in her "Sage Readers" section, and correspondents were also directed to "Career Talk" and other columns on the site. Others simply had to languish, although the *Chronicle Forums*, expanded in 2006, unleashed thousands of academics to communicate their questions, woes, scurrilities, and joys to one another under screen names ("monikers"). Some of them even rudely trashed Ms. Mentor. ("Youth," she sighs.)

When Ms. Mentor asked her flock to e-mail her and identify themselves as regular readers of her "Sage Readers" section, hundreds did—perhaps spurred by the offer of extra credit, which always entices the honor society types who populate academia. Some fussed over whether "I read Sage Readers" is past or present tense. Put two academics in a room, Ms. Mentor knows, and you will have at least four interpretations, followed by seven pedantic quibbles that will keep everyone's faces flushed and arteries pulsating with life.

The self-identified Sage Readers were not just the usual suspects, the newbies. They were from thirty-one American states, five Canadian cities, and one large city in Italy. Many were graduate students or adjuncts, but there were also artists, grants officers, bookstore managers, librarians, publishers, marketers, novelists, and one wine maker. Some of them felt they were special and wanted double extra credit for introducing their friends to Ms. Mentor, or for working really, really hard.

After a dozen years as a "crusty doyenne" writing in "third person haughty" (according to early reviewers), Ms. Mentor remains convinced that the academic world can be improved, and that she and her readers must continue to tote their loads, take up arms, bear their burdens, clear the trenches, ponder quaint and curious volumes of forgotten lore, and . . . stop when they've rattled on for too long.

Ms. Mentor trusts that this tome, full of her impeccable wisdom, will move the world of academe—indeed, the universe itself—toward greater perfection.

She is also sure it will get an A.

A Note for the Prurient

This volume contains some material that could not be published in the *Chronicle of Higher Education*'s Career Network, for reasons of taste or language. One such issue came up with Ms. Mentor's May 2005 column on dysfunctional departments. There was some distress over her quoting the title of a special issue of *Granta*, the British literary magazine: "The Family: They Fuck You Up."

But Ms. Mentor's column is most apt to be expurgated if her short question-and-one-word-answer bits concern bodily functions or sexuality, or are deemed to be likely fakes. And so, for the delectation of readers of this tome, and to speed their way into the rest of the book, she gives them one of the expurgated questions. Readers are free to determine their own answers and send them to her in care of her channeler at etoth@lsu.edu. There will, of course, be extra credit.

The Unexpurgated Question

Question (from "Agatha Aghast"): My history professor insists on wearing a kilt to teach his "Practices of the Victorian Era" class. While I am all for authenticity, it has become apparent to all of the students that "Professor McShameless" does not wear underwear while he teaches. This, combined with his penchant for "swordplay demonstrations," has left all too little to the imagination of those of us sitting in the first three rows. My fellow students and I have discussed how to approach the professor about this. We are reluctant to report his behavior to the administration but are anxious that he start to adopt decorum more appropriate to a true Victorian. What would Ms. Mentor suggest?

The Petty and the Profound
What They Write to Ms. Mentor

Why Won't He Erase the Blackboard?

Q (from "Lee"): I have another item of ridiculous pettiness to lay at your feet.

I teach at a small liberal-arts college where most people are collegial and friendly—except for a psychology professor I'll call "Dr. Territorial Marking," because that's what he does.

Dr. Marking precedes me in one classroom. From the very first day of class, I have come in to the room to find the blackboard covered with his psychoanalytical squiggles. Erasing the board for him is a small thing, but it annoyed me.

I didn't think it would be a problem, so I left a note on the board asking him to erase it. He apparently erased the note and left the squiggles. So I left a note on the lectern. Again the note disappeared and the squiggles continued. Next, I mentioned politely to a mutual acquaintance that I would really appreciate it if he could erase the board. Nothing. Finally, I sent Dr. Marking an e-mail directly, apologizing for the inconvenience, but asking that he erase the board.

No response.

At each point, I expected the whole thing to be over. By now, I'm starting to feel insulted, like he feels he's so far above me that he doesn't even have to obey a common rule of classroom etiquette. Would it be wrong to send him a gift-wrapped, engraved eraser and an elbow brace for Christmas?

A: Even Ms. Mentor, ever patient and tolerant, thinks you sound a little neurotic.

Many, indeed, are the provocations and small ignominies that academics mete out to their fellow sufferers ("colleagues") in this vale of tears. Young faculty members are routinely assigned to teach squirming freshmen at 8 A.M. or sleepy socialites at 4 P.M. Full professors commandeer the best classrooms and bore the young with tales of the good old days when parking was readily available. Copy machines break down; superb administrative assistants decamp. Someone has to serve on the Faculty Senate's Committee on Committees.

Ms. Mentor knows it does little good to urge people to be kind and selfless, unless they are untenured. But she urges all to cultivate a sense of humor, to try to laugh rather than gnash or spit at the abounding sillinesses. For Ms. Mentor is not without experience in the eraser wars.

Long long ago, Ms. Mentor was plagued by "Zizi," a hyperactive teaching assistant who would zoom into Ms. Mentor's classroom at the official moment that classes ended and furiously erase Ms. Mentor's blackboard while our heroine was still completing her last, most brilliant peroration. Once Zizi appeared, all attention was gone, and nearly half the students— to judge by their final exams—ultimately failed to grasp the meaning of life as explained by Ms. Mentor.

But Lee needs practical answers now, not the maunderings of his elders.

What, for instance, might Dr. Marking's squiggles mean? During the Cold War, he might have been suspected of transmitting CIA secrets (but of course no one does that anymore). Or now he might be suffering from "dysgraphia" (formerly known as "bad handwriting"). Maybe he does have an entitlement mentality and feels that erasing the board is for lesser beings, not high-status professors.

O, the temptations when one tries to analyze a psychology professor . . .

Perhaps Dr. Marking resents having to use a blackboard at all, since most institutions have gone on to PowerPoint. That is excellent for the sciences, where precise drawings and figures are essential—but Ms. Mentor deplores the use of PowerPoint in other venues, where most presentations are canned and overscripted. She wishes the presenters would just write significant words on the board and talk about them with wit and perspicacity. PowerPoint is robotic and unromantic, and when it becomes universal, there will be no more heartrending country songs like "My Tears Have Washed 'I Love You' From the Blackboard of My Heart."

As for Dr. Marking: Perhaps he has become unhinged and separated from reality by the demands put upon him in academe. And so he behaves forgetfully and rudely, like those who forget to put the lid down or flush.

Of course, psychologists know that "there are no accidents" and that "forgetting" always has some other meaning.

Maybe Dr. Marking just hates you.

Ms. Mentor agrees that you have done all you can to stop this extravagantly selfish behavior. One might say that you have been gentle and polite—or that you have behaved like a nagging and passive-aggressive mom. ("It would make me so happy if you would just clean your room. I ask so little of you.") You've probably triggered the inner rebellious child that lies snarling within all of us.

Ms. Mentor is starting to feel unhinged about all this.

What to do?

In the "Real World" outside of academe, you could put in a grievance, try to get Dr. Marking reprimanded, recommend him for counseling, outsource his job to India, incite whispering campaigns, or take a sledgehammer to the offending blackboard. ("If I can't have it, no one will!")

If you do decide to buy Dr. Marking a symbolic holiday gift, Ms. Mentor suggests you do a little research first on exactly what to get. Write it down in your journal, download all the sites where it is sold—and then give the money to something useful, such as Habitat for Humanity.

After that you should congratulate yourself for being in academe. You are in the only profession that pays you to think out loud and to put your musings on the blackboard for a captive audience.

Most marvelous for you, though, is that whatever happens in a class—and however unruly or spectacular a course turns out to be—it's over at the end of the term. After December, unless your school is extremely tiny, Dr. Marking won't be teaching in the classroom ahead of you, fouling your mood and your blackboard. You can simply count the days until he'll be somewhere else on campus.

And then you can start each class with what you most deeply crave.

A clean slate.

Should I Stay or Should I Go?

Q (from "Isabelle"): Although I come from more cosmopolitan roots, I'm loving my tenure-track job in the rural Midwest. The problem is my very disgruntled spouse ("Peter") who really, really, really hates it here and, no matter how much he loves me, can't stay. (He also can't make a living here doing the kind of work he enjoys.)

If I walk away from this great job without another one in hand, I may never get back into academe, and I fear that I will come to resent my spouse. But I can't inflict any more misery on him. We're considering commuting, but that's expensive, difficult, and not a long-term solution. I also can't think of any other career I would like as much as this one that would allow us to live where he wants. In all your wisdom, what do you suggest?

A: If Peter must pout, perhaps you want out.

Ms. Mentor, who has observed many a scenario like yours, can imagine your life. On campus, you enjoy your colleagues, energize your students, and feel productive, valuable, and smart. And then you go home to a brooding, melancholy presence. You work to draw him out and share the happiness of your day. But he gets up from the dinner table, slams doors, and growls, "You brought me here to this Godforsaken place." Your sex life is dying.

You'd like to include him in university social gatherings, but you can't rely on his behavior. He may disparage "the idiocy of rural life," or insult the provost, or refuse to dress for the occasion. Your colleagues may find him so unpleasant that they wonder about granting you tenure. You're intelligent and collegial—but would they be stuck forever with Petulant Peter?

Perhaps Ms. Mentor is being melodramatic. Yet she knows that even in these enlightened times, attention-seeking husbands have been known to sabotage their wives' careers. "Bill" picked a fight just before his wife's dissertation defense, so that she arrived at her oral with shaking hands and a tear-stained face. "Bob" flew into a rant about their messy house the night before his wife's first conference presentation. "Arthur" told his wife's new colleagues that as soon as they got settled, "I want her to have a baby. That matters more than a job." And "Paul" chose the night before his wife's first on-campus interview to tell her that he might be in love with someone else.

Presumably, Peter was not always difficult, and Ms. Mentor wonders what he gave up to go with you to the Midwest. Surely, as a youngish person, he can find something to do with his talents. Can he teach? Write? Do computer work? Since you seem to be supporting him, can he offer his full time in schools, hospitals, museums, homeless shelters, or political causes? (With so much U.S. money sunk into Iraq, home-front good deeds are desperately needed.) Can Peter run for office, research zoning and legal issues, tutor illiterate adults, offer himself as a consultant, build houses, repair musical instruments, be a chef for Meals on Wheels for elderly and disabled people, or start a much-needed local business?

He doesn't have to get rich, does he? Can't he make something valuable of his life in the Midwest? Except for actors and musicians, few people have to work in specific geographical areas. The feeling of being "exiled to the provinces" is mostly a problem of attitude. With a cushion—your income—Peter can indulge his curiosity, try different jobs and roles, and expand his imaginative horizons. He can make himself an entertaining, lively partner in your life.

Or he can be a Mr. Pitiful and destroy your career.

Ms. Mentor congratulates you for describing your dilemma clearly. You would probably have trouble finding another tenure-track job, let alone one that you loved. Moreover, your leaving a job because your husband is grumpy will make it easier for employers to tell themselves, "We hired a woman, but she didn't work out. We won't make that mistake again."

Ms. Mentor, if she were truly ice-veined and immune to the charms of romance, might also offer a cold and rational calculation: The average American marriage lasts about seven years, and half of marriages end in divorce. But a career continues, and you'll be spending more than thirty years in the labor force. Which part of your life will have more long-term impact on your comfort and happiness? Those new, cold-blooded economists who study social choices would also point out that your odds for getting a new spouse are much better than the probability of getting another good job.

What to do?

Ms. Mentor believes that you should keep your Midwest job and try a commuter marriage. Peter may find that his perfect job does not exist, or you may discover than he is a hopeless malcontent. You will certainly find your job easier and more pleasant if anger and withdrawal aren't waiting for you at home. Ms. Mentor recommends adopting a dog or several cats.

You and Peter will have breathing space or, if need be, a soft road leading to the end of the relationship. Sacrificing your career for someone who says he loves you is a very nineteenth-century thing to do, but unbecoming in the twenty-first. If you cannot both be happy, and if Peter refuses to support you in your joy, what is he contributing? Or as Ann Landers used to say, "Are you better off with him or without him?"

Ms. Mentor suspects you already know the answer.

And Then?

Ms. Mentor knows what happened to "Lee." After the "Blackboard" column (2005), he wrote to say that he was embarrassed but also rather honored to be known to the world, under a pseudonym, as "a little neurotic." Other scholars, as readers will soon see, sympathized with Lee, diagnosed Dr. Marking, and chortled happily at the minor follies and eccentricities of academic types.

Ms. Mentor does not know what happened to Isabelle and the troubled marriage she shared with Peter in 2003. Ms. Mentor destroys all identifying details and has not heard again from Isabelle—whose version of "the two-body problem" was causing such grief and pain. Isabelle and Peter's struggle is the most common and most wrenching knot in academic lives today—and Ms. Mentor's answer brought her some praise, but also unprecedented waves of fury.

Contrary to popular opinion, academics are not passionless people.

For Lee, Ms. Mentor's flock had sweet reason and comic irony.

Some correspondents thought Dr. Marking was "an exhibitionist, leaving his droppings" and wanting his work complimented. "My guess is that if Lee had made a remark praising Dr. Marking's squiggles, he would have more readily consented to erase the board." (This consultant, like most, assumed that "Lee" is female—although, of course, Dr. Marking could be flirting in his somewhat deranged way with anyone of any gender.) Another writer ("Jim") tattled on himself. Even when the previous teacher did erase the board, it was never done to Jim's satisfaction, "So I always bring my own bucket and squeegee."

Others debated whether not erasing the board is worse than not flushing or not cleaning the lint trap—but still others saw it as a teachable moment. Several cited *All I Really Need to Know I Learned in Kindergarten*, by Robert Fulghum: "Clean up your own mess." One clever scientist asked the nonerasing party before her not to "leave ideas that have been discredited for seventy-five years on the board. It so confuses my students." That problem was solved.

—

Readers were much testier with Isabelle and Peter, and Ms. Mentor became the messenger-target of their wrath.

The question, as everyone seemed to understand it, was this: Should Isabelle give up her hard-won tenure-track job to move to a city that Peter prefers?

"You have some nerve telling them to get a divorce," wrote several correspondents. (Readers will note that Ms. Mentor did no such thing. Anger distorts perceptions.)

"The wife needs counseling," wrote others. "She needs to learn to compromise. What about her biological clock? What if her husband is clinically depressed?"

"The most important thing is family," wrote another, "and no sacrifice is too great. If you quote my letter, don't use my name."

And another, after a brutal dissection of small towns and their lack of "amenities necessary to life, such as opera and museums and French food," concluded: "You know nothing about marriage, Ms. Mentor, and you are clearly too selfish to consider giving up something for someone else. No wonder you're a Ms."

Another diagnosed Ms. Mentor: "You are clearly sociopathic."

As Ms. Mentor licked her wounds, she noted that these attack letters were almost all signed by men. Hmmm.

Another stack praised Ms. Mentor. "Dump the grump!" wrote the correspondent of greatest brevity. Others pointed out that Peter had already made up his mind to leave Isabelle: "He's putting place above partnership. Why is that considered OK when a man does it?"

Those "Go, girl!" epistles were almost all from women, as were the true stories from women who had put their husbands' careers first, had given up their own degrees and the lives they wanted, and now regretted it very much. The women did not spout overarching principles ("family first" or "career first"), but gave details—the money they lost, the bitter custody fights, the lifelong sense of resentment and betrayal.

Then, some four years later, in the *Chronicle* forum, Ms. Mentor saw a posting from a wife ("Nancypants") with two small children, several post-doc positions, but an increasingly older Ph.D. and no tenure track job because the husband refused to consider living in any but a few of America's most popular cities. "He can't see moving for a job that I might like."

Several respondents again wondered, "Why is it up to the woman to sacrifice?"

Ms. Mentor hastens to add that it is not always so. One of her male correspondents gave up his tenure-track job, slipping down to adjunct status, so that his more ambitious wife could follow her scientific bent. Other men have raised children, kept alive long-distance romances, and (without asking for it) gotten much more praise for being "sensitive men." One father cited in Constance Coiner and Diana Hume George's book, *The Family Track*, notes that he cannot go to the laundry room with his young son without attracting oohs, ahs, and romantic overtures.

Still, the two-body problem—unlike the blackboard-erasing one—is mostly unsolvable, and it is mostly regarded as the woman's problem. Having children, in fact, enhances a man's academic career, according to recent research by Mary Ann Mason, but subtracts from a woman's. And women in same-sex relationships often suffer in silence.

If readers feel better by venting to Ms. Mentor, they're welcome to do so—and the rest of this book will include many a vent, rant, and animadversion, as well as clever, poignant, and brilliant epistles.

But perhaps the most memorable comment about Isabelle and Peter's marriage came from an economist: "Yes, it's true that 50 percent of marriages end in divorce. But you neglected to mention that the other half end in death."

Stewing in Graduate School

Many are the woes and afflictions piled upon graduate students while they learn their trade—and so it can be extremely satisfying to moan, obsess, and whimper about the quirks of faculty members and bureaucracies. Maybe the professors used to be just like you, but they are so much older now. The bureaucracies, Ms. Mentor can guarantee, will outlive all of us.

The Look

Q: Whenever we pass in the hall, one of the old profs on my committee frowns, looks sickly, and squints. I think he hates me. But my roommate says that I shouldn't "personalize," and that "Dr. Sour's" behavior has nothing to do with me. He probably just has gout or heartburn, or needs a root canal. What do you think?

A: Root canal.

Am I Too Old for Graduate School?

Q: I want to go to grad school in history, after twenty-plus years in the business world, because history is my passion. I'll be forty-seven, or maybe even fifty, when I finish grad school. Will I be too old?

A: Ms. Mentor gets many a plaintive epistle like yours. "Am I too old for a career in . . . ?" "If I go back to grad school, I'll be fifty-five, or eighty, or a hundred and twelve when I finish my degree. Dare I do it?"

Ms. Mentor always favors daring, for you will still be fifty-five or eighty or a hundred and twelve eventually. Do you want them to write "He was always cautious" on your tombstone?

Life and art are full of runaways and castaways and escapees. Ms. Mentor knows a chemist in North Dakota who yearns to be a Las Vegas blackjack dealer, and a journalist in New Orleans who fantasizes about being a stripper. There are readers who envy Gregor Samsa, the beaten-down clerk in Kafka's *Metamorphosis*, who wakes up one day, transformed into a giant cockroach. At least he doesn't have to go to that awful office anymore.

Of course, you will never again be twenty-two ("the right age")—which means that you're unlikely to be a trumpet player, a mathematical wizard, or a ballet dancer. But former Louisiana Gov. Mike Foster enrolled in law school at the age of seventy, and Ms. Mentor knows a fifty-six-year-old photographer getting a bachelor's degree in music, a sixty-year-old physician getting his in women's studies, and an eighty-year-old who just received her Ph.D. in urban studies.

Ms. Mentor's files also include the late-in-life painters Clementine Hunter and Grandma Moses, and the novelists Sara Ruffner and Helen Hooven Santmyer, whose first books came out when the authors were in their eighties. Lillian Carter, former President Jimmy's mother, joined the Peace Corps in her sixties. Col. Harland Sanders discovered the profitability of Kentucky Fried Chicken when he was already retired, and Col. Tom Parker was no spring chicken when he took on managing a raw young rooster named Elvis Presley. Mother Mary Jones turned union organizer at fifty and pummeled "the Rockefeller gang of thieves" until she was a hundred years old.

All these people were building on what they'd already done all their lives, and finally getting paid for what they'd done intuitively: storytelling, strumming, selling, being a burr under the saddles of the powerful. Ms. Mentor was giving free and impeccable advice to benighted neighborhood tots by the time she was five. She now calls that an internship.

And now she asks: What do you bring to the study of history? Are you an obsessive reader of biographies and history books? Is your TV always set on The History Channel? Are you a Civil War buff or a reenactor? Do you enjoy writing well-researched, thoughtfully grumpy letters to the editor? Do you know foreign languages and love poking around libraries? Are you fascinated by human error? Do you salivate when there's intellectual controversy? Does history, for you, pass what Francis Crick, the codiscoverer of DNA, called "the gossip test": "What you are really interested in is what you gossip about"?

Graduate school is an intellectual exercise, an accumulation of grades and credits, and a genuine sacrifice. Earning a Ph.D. in the humanities and social sciences can easily consume eight years or more and cost well over $100,000 in tuition and lost income.

Grad school is also acculturation, boot camp, indoctrination. Students learn the jargon and mores of their field, and working-class students are pushed into middle-class norms ("Bella" was advised to get rid of her regional accent and hide her bowling trophies).

Adult would-be students should also take Ms. Mentor's tough little quiz: Are you willing to reinvent yourself to fit someone else's script, especially if it seems snotty and mean-spirited? Can you handle new roles and risks, or will you resent the lack of respect for your past achievements? Can you listen respectfully to airy pomposities from youngsters half your age without laughing or spitting? Are you resilient and resourceful enough to get something from everyone?

Suppose you are, and you've written a prize-winning dissertation, but now it's job-market time—which will probably include a sickening dose of age discrimination. You may omit the date of your B.A. on your vita—but any signs of aging may be used against you in job interviews. If you're asked (illegally) about your health, say you work out every day (even if you only hoist a glass). Never mention ailments or your beautiful grandchildren. Move quickly. Focus on your own intellect, color your graying hair, get an up-to-date haircut, and beware of dated slang and cultural references. Don't complain about hippies, and treasure friends who can joke with you about academe and snort at terms that patronize mature adults ("still manages to keep busy," "young at heart," "spry").

Ms. Mentor admires your passion, and she likes knowing that realistic, smart people of all ages are in graduate school. Mature adults synthesize knowledge faster, because they already know so much. They chuckle at the posturings of young turks and theory jocks, and they don't crawl into a hole at the thought of a B minus.

Most people reach a point in life where they can choose to wither or to bloom. Ms. Mentor always chooses to flower. "She followed her dream" does read much better on a tombstone.

—

Reader Response: Some of Ms. Mentor's female readers have run into self-appointed experts who say, "Why would you want to get a Ph.D. at your age? You'll never use it." Ms. Mentor wonders if men do not pursue degrees later in life (more's the pity). Or if they do, are they lauded instead of patronized? As education budgets shrink, Ms. Mentor also wonders why universities do not deliberately choose older people. A newly tenured sixty-year-old is not apt to hold a tenure line for thirty years and keep out "new blood"—although Ms. Mentor would like her to.

Is He the Right One to Direct My Dissertation?

Q (from "Nedra"): It's time for me to choose a dissertation director. I'm leaning toward "Professor Porter," noteworthy in his field and always helpful to me. But other students say he has a reputation as a sexist and that I won't get the help that male students do.

A: Ah, gossip, the opiate of the underdog. The mighty needn't gossip—they can conspire, call a press conference, deploy weapons of mass destruction. Their underlings have the more colorful and indirect tools of the powerless—eavesdropping, backbiting, lampooning, whining, and rumor-mongering—all the things that graduate students do so well.

Unless they're unionized, grad students are smart trout in a vast, underpaid pool. Especially in English, math, and introductory languages, they teach the same beginning-level courses, share the same bullpen offices, and handle the same slings and delights as fledgling instructors—the "great class," the "bad class," the spontaneously perfect moments, and the resentment that goes with feeling that "I taught them that, and they refused to learn it." It's trial by fire—as are the cutthroat graduate seminars in which students jostle to impress their profs.

Outside school, the younger singletons drink and party together. Some get embroiled in intricate romantic configurations. But at the dissertation stage, students must step out from their cozy-though-contentious cohort. If they've stayed in school all their lives, doing their homework dutifully and getting A's, they must now—for the first time—make a decision that will determine the shape of their careers and the direction of their lives.

The ideal director treats all of his or her charges equally—doling out research ideas and grant opportunities, warning against unreliable sources or immense projects that will take a lifetime. The director may have to cajole or bark about deadlines. The ideal director is neither The Great Man (who has no time for anything except his pursuit of the Nobel) nor The Great Mom (who has too many younglings to nurture and not enough time to challenge any of them). The director should be a well-known scholar who pays close attention to shepherding the flock, ewes and rams alike.

But is Professor Porter a sexist? Ms. Mentor reminds you that a piece of gossip rarely survives unless it is colorful or scurrilous. "Professor Generous is so wise and kind" will not travel far in the rumor mill. It isn't entertaining, nor is it a warning. "Professor Venom hates Professor Generous and has always humiliated and flunked Prof. G's students" is a rumor that will survive for generations, even if there was no truth to it in the first place.

Thinking in us-versus-them terms, grad students place great faith in student folklore. One of the functions of grad school, after all, is to make you question your own intuitions so you'll feel ignorant and small. But you're also learning to use research tools, and it's time to turn them on Professor Porter.

Everyone has a track record. Check his past students' dissertations in the library and read the acknowledgments. Notice whether he's directed students of both sexes and how much time they've taken to finish their Ph.D.'s. Did the students' committees consist of both genders? (If he's an arrant sexist, female faculty members may not want to work with him.)

You can also check his publications. Does he collaborate with women and acknowledge women's contributions?

Watch Professor Porter's behavior with colleagues and students. Does he listen to women as well as to men? If he's middle-aged, does he seem to have trouble with women's voices? (Many well-meaning men do lose the ability to hear high-pitched sounds, and the wise woman will learn to speak lower and louder.) Observe his wife at department parties.

Meanwhile, since you've been told that Professor Porter is a sexist, ask for proof. Ask for stories. Casually ask his former students, "What was the best thing about working with him?" If they're publicly loyal, but they hem and haw, you'll know something's lurking. Do not blurt: "Is he a sexist bastard?" That just puts them on the defensive.

Some tenured academics, like the Greek gods, do indulge in mild flirtations and convoluted power plays. Ms. Mentor hopes that Professor Porter is not in the thick of those battles, but occupied in his lab, in his books, at his computer, pushing forward the frontiers of knowledge—and being deeply honored when you ask him to be your director.

There is no better title than "Mentor."

Am I Destined to Be a Serf?

Q (from "Wanda"): As a grad student at Super U., I'll have to do my dissertation with the only professor in my field, a recent widow who's terribly dependent on her students for company, emotional support, and household chores (taking pets to the kennel, painting the garage, even killing mice). One student before me lost his partner of five years because they never saw each other, thanks to "Dr. Widow's" time demands. She's very kind, melancholy, and needy, and I feel terribly sorry for her. And for myself.

A: Ms. Mentor, who carries the wisdom of centuries with her, sympathizes with the young who feel trapped. Her own adviser, the famous Euclid, long ago taught her that mathematical and social problems can be solved only if you know what the givens are, the fixed conditions that cannot be changed. You cannot make a stadium from a sow's ear. And so Ms. Mentor wonders: What are the limits in your circle?

Must you work in Dr. Widow's sphere? Must you be at her university? Must you be at her beck and call?

Ms. Mentor despises the notion that graduate students are the indentured servants of faculty members. Female graduate students often rightly complain that their male professors "look at me, and they're thinking only one thing. Baby sitter!" Burly male students are often treated as in-house furniture movers: "Earl" threw his back out permanently while moving "Dr. Great Man's" fridge, and there was no worker's compensation.

Graduate students are not their professors' sexual toys, nor should they be coerced into activities that are painful or bizarre—such as gathering tiger dung to fertilize a professor's marigolds, or drinking noxious liquids, or taking unusual drugs "in the interests of science." Grad students are, after all, human subjects.

And now Ms. Mentor, having completed her rant, returns to patient Wanda who—if she blindly follows the map she has been given—may wind up as Dr. Widow's servant-companion, not just her apprentice.

Ms. Mentor believes that we should all show compassion and generosity toward our fellow creatures, but Wanda cannot easily set up boundaries ("only Wednesdays and no mice"). Wanda may find good advice in *Difficult Conversations: How to Discuss What Matters Most* by Douglas Stone, Bruce Patton, and Sheila Heen—but it should not be the bible governing her graduate work.

Wanda's job is to do independent research, not to walk on eggshells for fear of offending or disappointing the person who will most influence the start of her career.

Ms. Mentor wonders why Wanda would sign up for such an ordeal.

Which brings Ms. Mentor back to the givens, especially the common belief among the young and the new that the world of adults is immutable, and that newbies have to suck up what's served.

Nay, says Ms. Mentor, who asks:

Is Dr. Widow truly the only one in Wanda's field? Ms. Mentor urges Wanda to seek related project ideas from other professors in her department. They will be flattered, and she will be able to gauge their enthusiasm for her and her work (without mentioning any doubts about Dr. Widow). Unless Dr. Widow has done something utterly unprecedented—such as discovering a new element, widorium—there should be someone else who can shepherd Wanda's work.

If there truly isn't, then Ms. Mentor urges Wanda to apply to other graduate schools—and interview potential directors before she enrolls. Yes, yes, Ms. Mentor knows that Wanda has a Super U. fellowship or assistantship, and she'll lose money and she'll appear flaky and she'll have to leave her friends and the apartment she loves. . . . Yes, but life is long, and graduate years are short, and losing a little money and time is nothing compared with leaving graduate school exhausted, depressed, and resentful, and asking yourself bitterly (as so many students do anyway): Do I really want to be an academic?

Wanda should be cordial toward Dr. Widow but must not be diverted from her own straightforward path toward the training, the degree, the teaching, and the learning. Wanda must keep her eyes on the prize.

Or, as Euclid long ago told Ms. Mentor as they strolled past his office in the library at Alexandria, one of the marvels of the ancient world: "You know, the shortest distance between two points is a straight line."

My Dissertation Director Is Godlike, and Doesn't Favor Me

Q: My dissertation director, "Zeus," has godlike white hair, a thunderous voice, and a circle of toady favorites. Students in the in-group get to give papers with Zeus at conferences in "Athens" and "Rome." The outies stay home doing boring Net and library searches, which Zeus collects, harrumphs at, and makes us do over for trivial mistakes. I'm an outie. Am I dead?

A: Not quite, for you're wise enough to consult Ms. Mentor, who has whole dossiers from distressed dissertationeers.

"Eden's" director, for instance, took four years to read her first chapter. "Cruz's" took seven years to write up their group's research—by which time Cruz had been denied tenure for lack of publication and was working part-time as a masseur. "Gina" was dropped by her director, who declared, "You're just screwing around; you'll never finish," while "Justin's" director, most devastating of all, wrote a hostile report for Justin's dossier, had a stroke, and died.

These tales are not comforting, but Ms. Mentor derives a major moral from them: The only work that students control is their own.

Eden could have asked her director, politely, "Would you prefer that I work with someone else?" Cruz might have offered to write up the lab results himself. Gina should have worked more quickly—but since she did finally finish and is now writing her memoirs, she can show the world how graciously she rises above adversity. And even poor Justin can recover, if he learns to schmooze and self-promote. He can find the new mentor to write that glowing letter his dossier needs.

Ms. Mentor, in short, refuses to see graduate students as helpless gobs of jelly. They need to be oaks, not reeds, and they need to plant themselves early.

When "Genevieve" was accepted by four Ivy League graduate schools, for instance, she visited all of them (at her own expense), lunched with current students, and interviewed potential dissertation directors. But "Oliver," who enrolled at Midlevel Grad School because of its football team, chose for his director a military historian—the one professor who happened to be in the office late one snowy Thursday afternoon. And so Oliver wrote his dissertation on Pickett's Charge, about which he cared not a whit.

As sage readers might predict, Genevieve finished her dissertation with distinction, and landed a tenure-track job at a Big Ten school. Oliver also finished but, always distractable, fell madly in love with another professor on his committee (always a mistake, decrees Ms. Mentor). Then he followed his Love Object to "Dr. Object's" new post in a small mining town in the Far West—where they had a falling out, and Oliver wound up as a substitute math teacher and wrestling coach in a decrepit nearby village.

"But what about me and Zeus?" you're champing. Ms. Mentor hopes that Zeus is the best director for your field. Ms. Mentor trusts that you are self-motivated. "I don't know what you want me to do. Help me, help me!" is not a professional stance. She hopes you've defined your own project and that you're able to set goals, meet deadlines, and read and think and compute productively and independently.

Directors do favor workers over whiners, and opportunities do flow to dedicated, creative students who'll reflect glory on their mentors. Zeus, like all of us, wants to be lauded for the satellites he's launched. Lesser lights, as you've seen, get dim-bulb tasks—and sometimes even flame out on those.

So what can outies do to change a director's opinion? They can rant and moan that all the professors hate them (rarely true: most profs are too busy with their own careers and digestions to be malicious or devious with students they barely know). Outies can switch directors, seeking professors who are more compatible or appreciative.

Some outies, wisely taking the long view, choose not to be academics and quit—for there are few tenure-track jobs and most go to the most motivated and most mentored. Or outies like you can decide to impress "Zeus" by working obsessively, producing better writing and research than anyone else, and making sure that Zeus sees the New Professional You: tough, talented, and terrific.

After all, a true outie would never have the good sense to write to Ms. Mentor. She wonders if you might be, secretly, an innie.

A Time to Speak, a Time to Remain Silent

Q (from "Bonnie"): At academic conferences, I have a social problem. If you don't know anyone well enough to chat with, what do you do in breaks between talks? I typically read, but people give me strange looks. I don't feel comfortable introducing myself to any professors, because I'm only a grad student.

Q (from "Troy"): I've spent three grueling years in a master's program where every tenured professor believes that a letter of recommendation is some sort of letter from the gods, allowing only the hand-picked few to enter the afterworld where deities rule. I've maintained a 3.5 grade-point average and performed (arts) nationally more than any other grad student. But for some reason, I have not been able to find anyone on the faculty who'll write me a letter of recommendation. Are there ways to circumnavigate the need for letters due to personal conflicts?

A: Oh, the perils of opening one's mouth. Ms. Mentor is reminded of "Renwick," a bright young historian with a top-notch degree and stellar references who landed a plum job at "Rocky Mountain State University."

Three years later, he was fired.

Renwick's publishing record was very good, his teaching was passable, and he was a vocal department citizen.

What went wrong?

It started with his first fall faculty meeting. Renwick arrived late, wearing tattered shorts and a dirty T-shirt, and noisily clambered over a senior professor to get a front-row seat for the department chair's welcoming speech—after which Renwick bellowed, "Why are our salaries so low? Can't you do more to get us a living wage?"

Later that week, Renwick barged into a meeting scheduled for tenured faculty members only and was miffed when told he would have to leave. ("Why should I?") Within weeks staffers were fleeing from his withering critiques, and by mid-semester, Renwick was the scourge of faculty meetings. He never caught on to "departmentese," that subtle language with which academics dance around a topic. Nor did he notice the eye-rolling, coughing, and suddenly remembered medical appointments that greeted his pronouncements.

By the time Renwick's contract came up for renewal, the decision took just four minutes.

Ms. Mentor advises readers that once you have a Ph.D., you are a certified expert in your field—whereupon the grading standards suddenly change. What separates the goats from the iguanas are the people skills you've already acquired. Any unit can hire a competent teacher-scholar, but they also want a colleague who is pleasant to be around, shares the work cheerfully, and enhances their work days.

They can't use a bully, a pompous ass—or a mouse.

Which brings Ms. Mentor to Bonnie, waiting shyly, and Troy, chewing the rug. Bonnie already has good social radar ("political instincts"), for she knows it's peculiar to read when you should be talking, and it's good to be approachable. Her next step is to improve her SQ (Schmooze Quotient), her ability to create small talk by commenting on a speech, an idea, or a current event. Bonnie can watch TV discussions, read advice about conversations, and imitate the infectious enthusiasm of Southerners. She should attend conference cash bars, field trips, and caucuses, and resolve to ask at least five people about a speaker's point, or about local restaurants or hotel amenities.

But if she accosts Big Names, will they think she's a groupie or a stalker?

Most likely they'll be afraid she's another fawning bore—and they'll be extraordinarily grateful that she's not. Like other human beings, Big Names prefer the new, the different, the humorous. They're not above discussing what they think about the crab dip or about the latest drunken celebrities. They enjoy the anonymity, when they can talk with ordinary folks about ordinary things.

Ms. Mentor once listened, entranced, as a Pulitzer Prize winner ranted about his sadistic dentist.

"But what if I say something dumb?" Bonnie may wonder, to which Ms. Mentor responds: "So what? You're not being graded."

Bonnie can admit she's a graduate student, finding her way—but she should also have business cards. She wants to be remembered.

And Troy? By now he's really steaming, waiting for Ms. Mentor's attention. His letter sounds angry, bitter, and self-absorbed, and he has evidently annoyed his professors so much that no one will write him a letter of recommendation. That is an exceptional feat. Ms. Mentor does not know what he has done—what are his "personal conflicts"?—but without references, he will not be able to get an academic post. His professors seem to be protecting their reputations, or the world of academe, or both.

Many Troys and Renwicks never recognize that they have behaved badly. "I'm better than they are, and they were jealous" is a common refrain. But rare are the saints, in or out of academe, who enjoy being railed at. If Troy is an insistent critic who alienates everyone, he need not lower his standards—but he can certainly lower his voice.

Shy, eager-to-please individuals like Bonnie will be valued for their efforts, and anyone can learn a modicum of charm. Smiling is always welcome, and the most valued conversationalists, like the best scholars, are often the best listeners—those who hear, remember, and build on what others know. For being truly smart means being truly attuned to the words and needs of others. That, Ms. Mentor knows, is where perfect wisdom resides.

Is My Prof Stealing My Research?

Q: "Professor Hectare," my dissertation director, has invited me and two other grad students to work on a special project next winter: a book that he'll publish under his name. We'll be listed in the acknowledgments ("with help from . . ."). Dr. Hectare calls this the professional opportunity of a lifetime. We'll meet the most prominent people in the field, travel to professional meetings, and be paid to do research in important libraries. It sounds great, but . . .

I worked as a research assistant for four years between my B.A. and grad school. My research work is very professional and was well-paid, and I often got byline credit ("This story is based on research by . . ."). The idea of doing my professor's research and *paying* tuition for the privilege *and* not having my work acknowledged except as one of a group who "helped" in an undefined way seems like a gross rip-off.

A: Ah, yes, everyone wants to be like Ms. Mentor—with an ivory tower of her own, dispensing her perfect wisdom only when she chooses, and getting paid for it.

All others must go through a rigorous and puerile apprenticeship before they can call their work their own. Ms. Mentor believes that your work should be treated and celebrated as your own intellectual property, but academe does have a sordid history of credit delayed and justice denied.

Before the rebirth of the women's movement in the 1970s, faculty wives routinely served as unpaid "research assistants." Often their words turned up in the great man's publications under his name alone. (For tales of horrific spongers, Ms. Mentor recommends Dale Spender's book *Women of Ideas and What Men Have Done to Them.*)

Nowadays, there are some traditions and rules. In science, the P.I. (principal investigator) is usually listed as senior (first) author on an article, with other contributors listed as coauthors. Among engineers, the writer of the article is traditionally listed as first author. While there have been controversies about the order of names and how many should be included (one notorious paper listed more than nine hundred "coauthors"), engineers and scientists routinely expect author credit.

But things can get ugly. Heidi Weissmann, a New York medical researcher, discovered that her department chief republished her work under his own name. Carolyn Phinney, a University of Michigan researcher, was awarded more than $1 million by a jury that found that her supervisor had stolen her ideas and used them to secure a grant. Yet when Antonia Demas, a Cornell grad student, discovered that a senior professor was claiming her work as his, the university dismissed her case.

In the humanities, Ms. Mentor regrets to say, things are murky from the start. As underlings in the academic hierarchy, graduate students are supposed to be humbly grateful for all the training they can imbibe. Sometimes they're paid, but often they receive only an inside-the-book acknowledgment.

Far be it from Ms. Mentor to pass on gossip. But one huge series of literary criticism, all published under one famous professor's name, is rumored to be the work of grad-student hirelings (some of whom make egregious errors).

Sometimes humanities professors do reward graduate-student collaborators with money or name credit. Cheyenne Bonnell, whose diary transcriptions make up a quarter of *Kate Chopin's Private Papers*, is listed as associate editor after the principal editors Emily Toth and Per Seyersted.

Generous mentors can create once-in-a-lifetime opportunities. The late Stephen Ambrose's history students, for instance, spent summers retracing the steps of Lewis and Clark with their professor—sharing discoveries over campfires first, and later in books and articles. Theirs was a genuine community of scholars.

Ms. Mentor thinks it may not be too late to create that kind of community for yourself. Tactfully ask the other grad students if they're "comfortable with" the acknowledgment deal. Tell them that bigger credit will be an immense help on the job market (always the strongest argument). If they're willing, you can all ask your professor, politely, about spinning off your own articles, using the research for your own pursuits. If you must, offer to wait until after his book has appeared ("priority of discovery" ranks highly with traditional academics, along with "whose is bigger").

Even if you must go it alone, tell Dr. Hectare that you have four years of research experience—he may not know that. Tell him you're eager to begin developing a publication list. Show yourself to be bright, eager, experienced, and ambitious.

And shrewd: Never say "rip-off." At least when you're in public, always say "collaboration."

Do I Have to Sleep with Strange Men?

Q: I'm one of four chosen grad students in "Professor Deuce's" research group. When we travel to research sites and meetings this winter, his grant will pay for two double rooms for us students, two to a room. But I'm the only woman in the group. Eeeeeek! I don't want to share a room with a strange man—even a fellow researcher.

A: "Well, we can all bunk together" might seem to be the modern way—though to Ms. Mentor it still sounds, well, indelicate. In her long-ago youth, before the Sexual Revolution, there were only two acknowledged sexes (genders had not yet been invented). Those two sexes were to be kept apart until united in matrimony. Young people attended school primarily with persons of their own sex, and only one sex (and one race) was groomed for academic leadership and success.

That situation stank. Ms. Mentor is much happier to have today's muddles—for they are signs of progress and possibility. But awkward sleeping situations do occur where women are most rare: in STEM (science, technology, engineering, and math) disciplines. Some STEM professors have been notoriously clueless—"truly afraid of interpersonal conflict and even emotion," writes one of Ms. Mentor's correspondents. "That explains why they devote their careers to, for instance, the life cycle of cockroaches."

Yet some profs do manage. One reader who shared a hotel room with her male adviser says, "I have to admit I was a bit anxious about it, but I trusted him and that makes a big difference." Another feels room sharing would be fine if she and a male student had a "genderless" relationship, but not otherwise.

For gossip on the subject, Ms. Mentor is especially grateful to "Ms. A," a correspondent who recently "graduated, woohoo!" from "Holy U.," a religiously affiliated school where it's "forbidden" for opposite-sex groups to share rooms. Nevertheless, at one memorable conference, Ms. A and her companions did it.

Ms. A and Ms. B (another student) shared one bed. Mr. C and Male Prof. D shared the other. And everyone was sworn to secrecy, lest Prof. D be fired for sharing a bed with another man. Holy U., it turns out, also expels people for anything that looks like homosexuality.

Ms. Mentor is proud of Ms. A and her friends for subverting the system. In a bigoted university, surrounded by prejudices, one should seize all such opportunities to defy authority.

But their adventures also make Ms. Mentor glad that she lives in an ivory tower. She never has to wake up next to a stranger of any sex and wonder Who Knows.

Nor, of course, does she have to deal with other messy questions, such as: Who gets to bunk with the oddball (the woman)? Who'll have to explain things to suspicious partners or spouses? Who has the most fervent or eccentric rituals, including snorings and snuffings?

And now that she is truly uncomfortable, Ms. Mentor exhorts her original correspondent to think first of her own comfort. If there is no one in the group whom you would be comfortable bunking with ("genderlessly,"

Ms. Mentor presumes), then you should not do so. Go to your professor and say, "We have an awkward situation here: I'm the only woman. How can we handle the accommodations on our trip to Aruba?"

The "we" engages the professor in the solution; "you" sounds accusatory. Some may think you're engaging in troublemaking, princess behavior—but in fact you're asking for equal educational opportunity. You're protecting your professor from gossip as well as grievances ("hostile environment"), and cranky, anxious, sleep-deprived assistants.

Moreover, many a male prof wants to be sensitive and egalitarian—a good guy. You can show him how. You can offer to share with a female roommate, if he'll contact the meeting organizers or colleagues and find you one, or help you to do so. You can ask for the names of women in the field and contact them yourself. What better way to network?

Or Professor Deuce can suddenly find "floating" money in his grant to cover another room for you. Or he can tell the three male grad students that they must share a room. He can also spring for a cot or rollaway bed if they start kvetching about sharing a double bed. Best of all is to find a female professor to room with you. Not only will she almost certainly take pity on you and pay the whole bill, but she'll also have the knowledge you need: how to cope as a woman in your field. She may be eager, in fact, to spill what she knows to willing ears.

In short, you'll be in a position to be mentored. And Ms. Mentor knows there is no better way to sleep well.

But Will I Have to Publish?

Q: I went to grad school because I love literature. I've been force-fed a diet of dullness (heavy theory), but I still enjoy reading and talking about novels. I'm writing my dissertation slowly, not enjoying it, and I don't think I ever want to write academic prose again. But I do want to teach. Will I have to continue writing and publishing these turgid things?

A: Ms. Mentor often hears your query from her spies at academic meetings, and she imagines a car full of wriggling, hot, and dusty tots wailing, "Do I really hafta publish?"

You know you will have to teach, and that's scary, but it's a known beast.

You stand in front of fidgeting adolescents who glare at you, daring you to teach them composition. They click their pens. They try to hide their grubby little text-messaging fingers. A few are attentive; most are there because they have to be.

But you figure that it's a training ground. Eventually you'll teach undergraduate majors, or teach novels, or at least get much better at the modes of rhetoric, or however your college expects writing to be taught. You'll feel more confident and engaging. Students may even catch your puns.

And yet, unless you publish something, you're unlikely—ever—to get that full-time teaching job that will give you the more academically engaged students and the opportunity to teach your "'specialty'": Jane Austen, the white whale, the heart of darkness. You won't get to talk about postcolonialism or queer theory or those other semiesoteric things that get your juices going.

The job "market" is an apt term. You have to join the crowd of jostling Ph.D.'s and sell yourself. Everyone is smart, has stellar grades, has a brilliant dissertation, and at least one recommender who says so. Nowadays, nearly everyone has won a teaching award.

So why should Anywhere U. hire you? *That's* your career motivation to publish—to rise above the madding crowd.

Ms. Mentor admits that other things can push you toward the top of the hiring list: an Ivy League degree, for research universities; a religious background, for evangelical colleges where a "Statement of Faith" is part of the packet. Midwestern roots are a bonus if you apply to teach in rural Iowa or North Dakota. (Everyone's been burned by East Coast sophisticates who "cannot bear to live in a place where there is no first-class symphony"—a snobbery that makes Ms. Mentor shudder.)

It's also possible that someone on the hiring committee will fancy your Welsh name, your history as an embalmer, or your interest in obscure Canadian trendsetters. You can't control that, although Ms. Mentor knows you'll obsess about it anyway. If there were jobs reserved for southpaws, thousands of academics would suddenly claim to be lifelong lefties.

For among those who want permanent careers in the humanities, desperation does rule. Fewer than half of the Ph.D.'s in English will ever get tenure-track jobs, and there's no "real world" to absorb them instantly, as there is for chemists or economists. Some imaginative Ph.D.'s in philosophy once set up shop as listeners, getting paid to hear people spill their problems by the hour—and literature Ph.D.'s would be even better for Confidantes R Us. They like melodramatic stories, and they know the penetrating questions to ask: What was she wearing? What did he say? What was the hegemonic discursive context for the articulated significations?

But Ms. Mentor digresses. Your story will be much improved—and your job prospects immeasurably enhanced—if you have publications. That is your unique niche, the feather in your coffee, the cream in your cap. Without it, your Mom will still think you're special, but she isn't hiring today, more's the pity.

How to begin? You have, in fact, been working all your life toward publication. Ms. Mentor presumes that you enjoy writing; if not, you have perhaps misspent your youth. You've undergone a very long apprenticeship in grammar, punctuation, spelling, and diction. You know how to support a main point with specific examples. You may not write with much flair (that's frowned upon in academic circles), but you know how to manipulate the jargon.

You may also have some very original things to say. Ms. Mentor hopes you do, for a dissertation is supposed to be an original contribution to knowledge, or at least to your knowledge. If it doesn't fascinate you, there's truly no reason to do it. The late literary critic Leslie Fiedler used to claim that academics have a great tolerance for boredom, and Ms. Mentor wishes we were not so generous.

Ideally, you've had seminars in which you've learned what makes a publishable article. If not, you (or your graduate student organization, if you have one) need to organize a series of workshops on publishing, with star faculty members telling you how they did it and what you can do, especially with journal articles. Your department Web site and graduate-student handbook should list faculty publications and interests. Choose the most-published and the biggest names, plus a couple of newly hired hotshots. Invite them to speak at the workshops and flatter them sincerely, and ask them to name the best journals in your subfield. Have them tell you how to target your writing to a journal's needs and audience, and how to approach editors. Make sure your classmates attend the workshops enthusiastically. You're sharing the keys to the kingdom.

You can also, in the privacy of your own study, read William Germano's two essential texts, *From Dissertation to Book* and *Getting It Published:*

A Guide for Scholars and Anyone Else Serious About Serious Books. They are your bibles for book writing.

"But I just want to teach!" you wail. Without a publication or two, or some unique talent, you're apt to languish in the adjunct pool (making about $2,000 a course with no job security) for as long as you're committed to academe. Publishing, whether in obscure journals or popular magazines, will give you a name, a face, and a distinction. If you want to teach in a community college, your commitment to students first will be cherished. But if you want to move to a liberal arts college or a research university, publication is the only path.

Finally, Ms. Mentor advises you to write every day and keep your writing muscles moving. Keep a pseudonymous blog if it frees your creativity, but not if it's a substitute for your dissertation or for writing that'll get a separate line on your vita.

For writers, anonymity doesn't pay off in publication. For readers, it's a fiendish time sink ("If I spend an hour or two poking through your blog for clues to your identity, I won't have to work on my dissertation"). Many academics claim that they've figured out who's written the letters that Ms. Mentor answers. Certainly, scads could have written—and maybe did write—this column's query. Ms. Mentor encourages everyone to claim it and to enjoy the notoriety.

Ms. Mentor knows that it is never gauche to brag about your writing and how it's improved, amused, and consoled the world.

—

Reader Response: Many readers urged Ms. Mentor to do more to celebrate community colleges. They require less publication, and some require none. They teach many more students, reaching out to the community and to many students who wouldn't otherwise be able to go beyond high school. Community colleges pay their faculty better than universities do, and their parental leave and medical benefits are better. They represent America's most democratic ideals, and they are among the gems of academe.

Should I Hide My Weak Spots?

Q (from "Darla"): My classmate "Lucifer" and I are both on the job market this year. He's always been self-centered and treacherous. How can I keep him from backstabbing me if we both wind up at the same interviews?

Q (from "Sean"): Because of panic attacks, I haven't worked on my dissertation since June. My friends say not to tell my adviser about the attacks, because he might use them against me. But "Dr. Worldly" is so sophisticated. I'm sure he'll understand.

A: Sometimes Ms. Mentor has to burst hopes, shred bubbles, and be the Grinch. While it is true that scholarly types can be generous, open-minded souls who'll share software, footnotes, and recipes for cat treats—they can also backstab, withhold, and compete to leave you penniless, naked, and shivering in the cold (metaphorically speaking).

In short, they cannot always be trusted to make nice.

Ms. Mentor's ruminations here are also inspired by a question from another correspondent ("Grace"), a job seeker whose best friend is on the market this year, in the same field. "How can we keep from badmouthing each other?" Grace and her friend wonder. That inspired Ms. Mentor to start a tip sheet on "How Not to Backstab" . . . until she noted that the same list of tips, slightly reworked, could so easily become a demonic manual on how to backstab.

Ms. Mentor does not advocate any of the following tips on backstabbing but wishes her flock to be forewarned:

How to Backstab

- Seize credit for everyone's work. Insinuate yourself with your major professor and brag about your unique contributions to your group's research. Get your boss to list you as coauthor of everything. ("He wouldn't have gotten those results without my help.") Describe all group findings as if they're yours ("my data"). If you must mention any classmate competitors, always sigh and look wounded. If you're an unscrupulous principal investigator, steal your students' work.

- Hint that your classmates and underlings are slothful. "I was here at 7 sharp, but Jody didn't waltz in until 9:30. By then we were already on our second rat gavotte."
- Be slavishly charming to those above you. "I'm so glad to work for you, Dr. Vibration. The others don't know just how eminent you are and how your research on insipidity has changed the entire field of psychology."
- Drop names. "My mentor, Dr. Almost Nobel Prizewinner, highly recommended this project. I know you're able to appreciate just how innovative my work is." (Oozy smile.)
- Self-promote. "I discovered the main text," or "Mine is the biggest," or "I'm the first Centervillian ever invited to give the keynote address at Marigold. Of course, most of the field work is puerile, hopelessly jejune. But mine is totally cutting edge."

If less-discerning members of the professoriate are making the decisions, a pushy, flashy Lucifer who's followed those rules may get the coveted interviews instead of honest, plodding Darla. If he's truly dastardly, he might also steer the search committee to his unwitting competitors' MySpace or Facebook entries. Those pages have colorful social information and revealing pictures that a hiring committee ought not to know about.

What can Darla do? She should have her own Web page. She should keep up a constant dialogue with her adviser, documenting which work is hers. She may need to find the smallest publishable unit and get it out—fast. If she's in science, where grant money goes to the first discoverers, she has to plant her research pickax first, just as the big boys do, and not be dissuaded by murmurings about teamwork. ("Why such a hurry? We're all just comrades here.") She needs to make herself known to peer reviewers and grant panelists. Wherever there are academicians, she needs to schmooze, and she needs to present herself as smart, confident, and independent.

As does poor Sean, currently crippled by panic attacks. He, too, needs to practice the art of self-preservation.

The young often find it comforting, even seductive, to think of their advisers as all-knowing: not only world-class experts in literature or biochemistry, but also infinitely wise in matters of the heart and soul. Surely, you think, Dr. Worldly is genial and forgiving, and he wants nothing but the personal happiness and professional successes of his charges.

But you could be wrong.

Dr. Worldly may be sympathetic, at first, if you tell him about your panic attacks, but he will also start watching and wondering if you'll produce. A single crisis, such as a family death, can be handled—but a chronic illness will make him wary. He may stop delegating responsibilities or funneling courses to you. ("Sean may not be able to handle teaching alone.") He may hesitate to nominate you for grants and awards. He may hedge in recommendation letters, as in "Sean has had to overcome some challenges, but . . ."—words that will kill your chances in overcrowded fields.

Too much candor can mean too much vulnerability, and Dr. Worldly is not your mother, your counselor, or your life partner. Men often find it especially difficult to hear about other men's feelings—and ultimately, Dr. Worldly is your boss. His job is to make sure you finish an original piece of research or writing.

If you're in the sciences, he may have a grant that will be renewed only if all the pieces (including your part) are done by a certain date. If a grant isn't renewed, half a dozen people may lose their jobs.

"Ms. Mentor, you have no milk of human kindness," she hears her readers say—but Ms. Mentor knows that a grad student's life is lonely, stressed, and sad. She prescribes writing and support groups, online discussions under pseudonyms, role playing before job interviews, and places to vent outside the school.

But do not cry in your office.

Ms. Mentor wants Sean and Darla to be dry-eyed and self-protective. Lucifer already is.

How Can I Find the Time?

Q (from "Alvin"): How do I finance my last dissertation year if I'm not a TA?

Q (from "Beulah"): They've got me teaching five classes of freshman writing. How can I possibly find time to write and publish?

Q (from "Cheryl"): What next? Now that I've gotten the right drugs and good therapy, my neuroses no longer have a death grip on my life—but they cost me nearly two years of dissertation time, along with my teaching assistantship. I'm now an office temp by day, a dissertation writer by night, and an occasional e-mail correspondent with my dissertation director. How will I explain the lost time when I'm on the job market—or will everyone just dismiss me as a loony?

A: Ms. Mentor is reminded of the bird fancier and the tiny bird he thought was a dove, but he wasn't sure. And so the fancier cajoled the little bird into opening its beak, and sprinkled its mouth with a pungent green herb.

Why?

Because only true dove can stand the taste of thyme.

Oh, all right—Ms. Mentor's story has nothing to do with the matter at hand. It's just her wicked little trick to seduce readers into wasting a few seconds. Do you feel guilty?

If you do, you are an angst-ridden, time-tortured academic.

Thyme is cheap, but time is precious. It is the thing we yearn for, the thing we fear losing, the one thing that cannot be regained. To Alvin and Beulah, Ms. Mentor's answer is simple.

Get time and money any way you can, so you can finish your Ph.D.'s and resume your lives.

Unless you win the lottery, have a working partner, or were born into a very wealthy family, you'll have to finance your last year with a job. If there's nothing research related (a lab, a political campaign), look for something that adds to your skills. Office temping, for instance, can teach you about business and technical writing—hot fields where there are tenure-track jobs. Susan Basalla and Maggie Debelius's book, *"So What Are You Going to Do with That?" Finding Careers Outside Academia*, brims with tips.

But do not assume that a few sections of freshman comp will propel you through the dissertation. Comp is usually underpaid, and it also draws from the same creative part of the brain needed for writing. If you're hunched over, grading hundreds of papers, you're depleting your store of words, emptying your house of ideas.

Ms. Mentor exhorts you not to be a martyr. If you teach comp, choose a few key things to grade (such as thesis sentences, transitions, comma usage) and pass over the rest. If students' pages are bleeding with red ink, the most conscientious will be devastated. The others will be bored and annoyed. You will be brain-dead.

English Ph.D.'s take longer than any others to get their degrees. From the time they start grad school, biochemists, electrical engineers, mathematicians, and computer scientists take six or seven years. Political scientists take nearly nine; English professionals take close to ten. And so Eager Ernestine, a literature lover starting grad school in 2008, will most likely collect her Ph.D. sometime around 2018—or three presidential elections later.

Ms. Mentor urges students to move faster into academic adulthood by being ruthless. Beulah, for instance, must make her freshest hours of the day her Writing Time, with a reasonable goal: "one lousy page a day." She must become best buddies with her Creative Angel, who lets her dream, free-write, mull, and flow. She must squelch the other side of her brain, the Demon Editor/Internal Critic, who's always muttering, "It stinks . . . you're an elitist, pathological nogoodnik . . . do something useful and wash the floor."

One lousy page a day means 365 lousy pages by the end of the year. And most of them won't be lousy at all.

Harken, too, to Ms. Mentor's Mighty Maxims for Time Management:

- Each night, make your Must Do list for the next day. List your daily Writing Time as an appointment.
- Rank your Must Do's in order of importance.
- Write a Should Do list of things you might do if you had time, such as "wash the floor" or "shop for good china" or "worry about what other people think."
- Burn the Should Do list.

When you're on the road, the Must Do list belongs in your datebook or handheld computer, which travels with you to all professional occasions. Don't waste others' time with "I'll call you when I check my schedule." Keep your datebook current and write down all appointments.

Save your memory—your creative space—for writing. Do not clutter it with trivia.

If your home and office are too busy, find an out-of-the-way coffee-house where you're not apt to meet anyone you know. During your sacred Writing Time, do not talk to anyone. Answer no phones. Surf not the Net.

Snack if you must, but Ms. Mentor particularly favors a large double caffeine jolt. Think of Balzac, the prolific French novelist, who consumed fourteen to twenty-four cups of espresso a day.

"But, Ms. Mentor, what if I follow all your rules and fall behind anyway, like Cheryl?"

What if job interviewers ask Cheryl, "How come you took so long? Lazy?" or, "If we hire you, will we have to worry that you'll crack up or go postal?"

Such questions are both boorish and illegal, and they'll only be asked if your vita has unexplained gaps. If you simply list the years you were a grad student ("1997–2006"), no one need know about lost time or missed chances.

As long as you're chugging along, your troubles are under control, and your director's pleased, your career prospects are as good as anyone's.

Brighter, in fact—because you were wise enough to query Ms. Mentor. That is an excellent use of your time.

What's My Best Ritual for Writing?

Q: To combat writer's block, should I emulate D. H. Lawrence, who prepped for writing by throwing off his clothes and climbing mulberry trees in a frenzy, or Dame Edith Sitwell, who stretched out in an open coffin every day before she wrote—or should I find my own best practices?

A: Yes.

Rumblings of a Dissertation Writer

Q: Writing dissertation. Must be last person on earth, never see anyone anymore unless teaching. Does that count as seeing people? Think not. Need a laugh. Pray each night to write damn thing and finally finish Ph.D.

without turning into bloviator. However, noticing that friends and family glaze over quite soon after asking about research. Hate to bloviate. Thus, no pronouns. Plan to eliminate other parts of speech as needed, maybe take vow of silence. Good?

A: Maybe. Maybe not.

Ms. Mentor obviously captivated by your writing style. Impressed by your efforts at minimalism. Thinks it's catching, but will try to extricate self and talk more ordinarily. (What is normal among academics? Ponder.)

Everyone knows dissertation stress. What you're doing will never be finished, or it will be laughable and absurd. In a just world, you would be hanged as an academic fraud and your remains fed to feral dogs (they'd call it recycling). Your B.A. would be yanked and your records deleted. Your weaselly, smiling graduate photo would be posted on your high school's Wall of Shame.

Or you could ignore all those febrile fantasies, decide to do a good-enough dissertation, and finish it—or not.

Half of ABD's (All But Dissertationeers) never finish, but they are not failures. They've chosen other things—such as a social life, or children, or a career that doesn't require years of poverty (and maybe chastity) before a tenure-track job perhaps materializes in a Remote Village.

But suppose—against all odds, and despite the clamoring of un-schooled relatives ("You're writing about 'theory'? Will that get you on the bestseller list or something? Will they make a movie of it with Sandra Bullock?")—you still want to "do the diss."

Finishing is character building, you say.

And your discoveries will revolutionize the field.

And, besides, you love the work—now, finally, you've gotten to where Ms. Mentor's perfect wisdom might be of use. As Emerson famously said: Nothing great is ever achieved without passion.

You have to be driven to do it, external rewards or not. If you're not passionate about your subject, why bother? But assuming that you are passionate, Ms. Mentor will now suggest ways to get yourself to finish the diss.

Writer's block is fear—fear of getting something wrong, not getting an A, being unmasked as an impostor at last. Every writer except the most doltish of hacks approaches a blank page or screen with trepidation, and the hardest word to write is the first.

Ms. Mentor assumes you've already broken your dissertation into manageable parts and set up a timetable: one month for Chapter 1, one for Chapter 2, for instance. (Your director and your committee can help with planning, as can such books as Joan Bolker's *Writing Your Dissertation in Fifteen Minutes a Day.*)

You also need to set weekly and daily goals: three pages a day, or two hours, or another unbreakable quota, preferably at the same time each day. If you have rambunctious children, try early morning or very late hours, when the world is quiet and no one is moving except a few randy ne'er-do-wells, logged on to their computers from strange time zones.

Do not get on the Internet.

Turn off all phones and tuck your cell phone into a little padded pouch, wish it good night, and hide it where you cannot see it light up, vibrate, and dance.

Write by hand—as Ms. Mentor writes her first drafts—so as to sneak up on the work. Tell yourself, as Anne Lamott recommends in *Bird by Bird*, that you're about to write a "shitty first draft."

Then do it.

Editing a mess is much easier than grunting out the first draft. Anything is easier than the first draft (except, of course, root canals without anesthesia, or being devoured by wolves; those really hurt, or so Ms. Mentor has been told).

If you can isolate yourself totally from anyone who speaks, do it for the first draft. Lock yourself in your carrel. Hide out in mountain caves. Let beauty-school students practice pedicures on you while you scribble.

Encourage roommates to surprise you with treats, but only on Fridays after 5 P.M. Ignore their grumbling. Put your fingers in your ears and chant, "La la la la la." True friends will understand.

Of course, many people won't, and the Dissertation Era may mean giving up on those people who, well, aren't into your future plans.

Except for family members whose caprices are inescapable, you do not need narcissists who tell you their love problems incessantly (unless their stories are vivid, lurid, and ever-changing, and you can use them in your chapters about neurotic behavior). You do not need broken-winged people, addicts, or complainers who have to sleep on your couch for a few days to "get my head together." You do not need people who "will be great" once they get over their bigotries or their resentments of you. ("Why are you always writing? Let's go get a beer and forget your silly homework.")

Anyone whose moods get you down, or who picks a fight when you're trying to finish a chapter, or who disparages your work, does not belong in your life.

Find a writing critique group, if you have a strong ego. If you're not sure, convene a group of friends in which all of you make deadlines for one another and meet once a week to celebrate what everyone has written, taught, sold, or cooked. Have lots of chocolate.

Yes, give up useless parts of speech, especially adverbs. They are the softeners, the wimps of the grammatical world. You need to be ruthless, self-protective, fierce, whatever your mode.

Some writers are gushers, bloviators who spew everything in their first drafts and then pick out the best chunks. But you may be a bleeder, a one-word-at-a-time agonizer (as Red Smith said, you sit at your desk "and open a vein"). Or you may be a Beavisite, converting all long jargonized theoretical explications into the simplest of language: "Cool" or "It sucks."

Now all you have to do is explain yourself to the world.

Good.

Should She Hire a Ghostwriter?

Q (from "Honest John"): I'm a troubled member of a dissertation committee at Private U., where I'm not a regular faculty member (although I have a doctorate). "Bertha" is a "mature" student in chronological terms only. The scope of her dissertation research is ambiguous, and the quality of her proposal is substandard. The committee chair just told me that Bertha is hiring an editor to "assist" her in writing her dissertation. I'm outraged. I've complained to the chair and the director of graduate studies, but if Bertha is allowed to continue having an "editor" to do her dissertation, shouldn't I report the university to an accreditation agency? This is too big a violation of integrity for me to walk away.

A: Ms. Mentor shares your outrage—but first, on behalf of Bertha, who has been betrayed by her advisers.

In past generations, the model of a modern academician was a whiz-kid nerd, who zoomed through classes and degrees, never left school, and scored his Ph.D. at twenty-eight or so. (Nietzsche was a full professor at twenty-four.) Bertha is more typical today. She's had another life first.

Most likely she's been a mom and perhaps a blue-collar worker—so she knows about economics, time management, and child development. Maybe she's been a musician, a technician, or a mogul—and now wants to mentor others, pass on what she's known. Ms. Mentor hears from many Berthas.

Returning adult students are brave. "Phil" found that young students called him "the old dude" and snorted when he spoke in class. "Barbara" spent a semester feuding with three frat boys after she told them to "stop clowning around. I'm paying good money for this course." And "Margie's" sister couldn't understand her thirst for knowledge: "Isn't your husband rich enough so you can just stay home and enjoy yourself?"

Some tasks, Ms. Mentor admits, are easier for the young—pole-vaulting, for instance, and pregnancy. Writing a memoir is easier when one is old. And no one under thirty-five, she has come to believe, should give anyone advice about anything. But Bertha's problem is more about academic skills than age.

Her dissertation plan may be too ambitious, and her writing may be rusty—but it's her committee's job to help her. All dissertation writers have to learn to narrow and clarify their topics and pace themselves. That is part of the intellectual discipline. Dissertation writers learn that theirs needn't be the definitive word, just the completed one, for a Ph.D. is the equivalent of a union card—an entree to the profession.

But instead of teaching Bertha what she needs to know, her committee (except for Honest John) seems willing to let her hire a ghostwriter.

Ms. Mentor wonders why. Do they see themselves as judges and credential-granters, but not as teachers? Ms. Mentor will concede that not everyone is a writing genius: Academic jargon and clunky sentences do give her twitching fits. But while not everyone has a flair, every academic must write correct, clear, serviceable prose for memos, syllabi, e-mail messages, reports, grant proposals, articles, and books.

Being an academic means learning to be an academic writer—but Bertha's committee is unloading her onto a hired editor at her own expense. Instead of birthing her own dissertation, she's getting a surrogate. Ms. Mentor feels the whole process is fraudulent and shameful.

What to do?

Ms. Mentor suggests that Honest John talk with Bertha about what a dissertation truly involves. No one seems to have told Bertha that it is an individual's search for a small corner of truth and that it should teach her how to organize and write up her findings.

Moreover, Bertha may not know the facts of the job market in her field. If she aims to be a professor but is a mediocre writer, her chances of being hired and tenured—especially if there's age discrimination—may be practically nil. There are better investments.

But if Bertha insists on keeping her editor, and her committee and the director of graduate studies all collude in allowing this academic fraud to take place, what should Honest John do?

He should resign from the committee, Ms. Mentor believes: Why spend his energies with dishonest people? He will have exhausted "internal remedies"—ways to complain within the university—and it is a melancholy truth that most bureaucracies prefer cover-ups to confrontations. If there are no channels to go through, Honest John can create his own—by contacting the accrediting agencies, professional organizations in the field, and anyone else who might be interested.

If there is media attention, though, Bertha may be portrayed as a villainess instead of a victim, and Honest John will be hated by everyone associated with Private U. As in every battle over integrity, the air will be charged with rancor, and inflamed e-mails will fly about and be secretly forwarded. Some heads may roll.

And yet—there is no reason to attend graduate school, or to write a dissertation, unless one wants to be educated. Every student deserves to be taught, and any faculty member who will not be a real mentor needs to go into another line of work.

Ms. Mentor wants a clean, honest universe, and she wants it now.

—

Reader Response: Many thoughtful readers commented on whether a graduate student should hire a dissertation editor. Ms. Mentor's correspondents agree on the ethics of hiring a proofreader (acceptable) or using a ghostwriter (vile and fraudulent). Editors may shape, question, and teach, but should not be creating an argument or calling for more research—yet some editors confessed that they had done exactly that. A few correspondents claimed that hiring an editor for one's dissertation, and paying the editor out of one's own pocket, was the accepted thing at their institutions.

Ms. Mentor sighs and wonders what Ph.D.-producing professors are doing to earn their salaries.

Lend Me Your Ears

Q: One of our younger female graduate students has been wearing "squirrel ears" [species changed to protect identity] while in the department this summer. She wears the ears at all times, even when meeting with faculty members. Since our department is rather large, I do not know her personally. What should I do?

A: It seems to Ms. Mentor that you are not called upon to do anything. As the late, great Ann Landers used to say, "MYOB" (mind your own business). And yet . . .

Of course you want to know (and so does Ms. Mentor): Why is "Earie" wearing the squirrel ears? One supposes it could be a matter of religion or disability, but let us assume that it is an eccentric fashion statement—in which case Ms. Mentor will take it upon herself to discuss academic fashion. That is a subject that, whenever mentioned, evokes snorts and derisive comments, such as, "Fashion in academe? Oxymoron!"

Nevertheless, there are ways to dress in academe, just as there are ways to comport oneself, and every choice does send a message. Earie may feel that she's simply a free spirit expressing a larky individuality. She may not realize that she is being watched, as we all are. People are always observing one another, making judgments, and groaning or chortling.

Certainly there is a public image of fashion for academics. For men it is the tweed jacket with elbow patches—a style that Ms. Mentor has not seen for several generations, but the memory lingers. For women it is the frumpy Marian-the-Librarian look—thoroughly unlike Julia Roberts's professorial character in *Mona Lisa Smile* and even less like the Amazonian Shannon Tweed, the women's-studies professor in one of

Ms. Mentor's all-time favorite movies, the underrated gem called *Cannibal Women in the Avocado Jungle of Death*. (Ms. Mentor has never met another living soul who's seen it.)

Recent real-life scholars have moved closer to mainstream fashion norms. For job interviews, almost everyone wears black, beige, brown, or blue. Women usually wear pantsuits, or dresses with jackets; men usually wear jackets and ties (and pants). But away from the job market, fashion eccentricities tumble out: piercings, tattoos, depraved haircuts, voluminous or tiny clothes, and squirrel ears.

Yet eyebrow, lip, or tongue piercings always evoke some "Ewwww's," and not just from Ms. Mentor's fuddy-duddy generation. Tattoos may be gorgeous art, but large, snakelike ones elicit stares from small children and finicky grownups. Many medical schools forbid students' wearing nose rings, lest they scare patients just coming out of anesthesia.

"But I think it's beautiful art, and so do all my friends, and anyway, while I'm a student, I should be able to do, or wear, or look any way I like, shouldn't I?" Ms. Mentor always pauses at the use of the word "should." Her mission is to explain what is, not what should be.

Body art and nonmainstream fashions will make you seem less professional, less serious. You may, in fact, be much smarter and more creative than the nonpunks and non-Goths around you. But you'll also be a misunderstood and underrated genius. And that has consequences.

Earie may look cute in squirrel ears. Ms. Mentor hopes so, and that she doesn't look verminous or ratlike. Ms. Mentor wonders if the ears are squirrel-red, or even a bright purple or vivid green. For Halloween or Mardi Gras, Earie's look is uniquely chic.

But in the classroom, and at department meetings, and in the halls of Everyday U., Earie will look quite weird. She may have trouble controlling rambunctious undergraduates or gaining their respect.

Meanwhile, her professors, those who will be writing reference letters or recommending her for assistantships, will see her as someone who's unwilling to fit a professional mold. They'll view her as less than serious, or downright strange. Odd ducks are treasured as "crazy, but I love her" types, and they may be gossiped about with affection—but they're much less apt to get the scarce goodies.

From a conventional point of view—and academics are conventional people—a student with a standout appearance will not seem to represent her university well. Earie's not apt to be trotted out to meet dignified visiting scholars, donors, or pooh-bahs in her field. She'll miss those invaluable moments for networking, for meeting and sniffing about with the big cheeses.

There are others who miss out: students who display too much cleavage, or who wear short, overly tight, or very casual at-the-beach clothes. If your undergraduates are not looking at your face, or if randy graduate students or visiting poets are trying to brush against you, you are communicating a message that is not, well, intellectual.

Ms. Mentor knows that she will get letters blasting her for being old-fashioned and hopelessly petty and bourgeois. She'll be told about famous Goths who have won endowed chairs, and punks who have world-class portfolios. (She'll also be reminded that art school is different, and she agrees.)

But we are not all artsy geniuses whose charisma is so extraordinary that the world won't notice that we look funny. Most of us are A-minuses. We do best with a little help from our friends. But Ms. Mentor's correspondent is not even one of Earie's friends.

Ms. Mentor is left with an exquisite etiquette problem, should her correspondent wish to do some freelance mentoring. How does one say to a total stranger, "What's with the squirrel ears?" and "Wanna commit professional suicide?" How does a stranger resist the temptation to whisper, in a rodentlike way, "Psst! Do they call you Rocky or Ratatouille?"

Maybe the best way to be tactful is to be a little sly. One could just leave this column, anonymously, in someone's mailbox. Squirreled away, of course.

—

Reader Response: (1) Ears: An alert correspondent thought she might be the "Earie" in this column. She was wearing costume animal ears, she writes, because she had lost a friend and wanted to cheer herself up. Observers who might be curious about her motives for wearing animal ears should just speak up and ask her, she believes. Another reader informs Ms. Mentor that ear wearers may be "furries," a growing set of "cosplay" (costumed role-playing) students who dress as furred creatures for fun and fetishism. Ms. Mentor would still recommend discreet and silent gawking, rather than asking a stranger, "Are you grieving or do you have a fetish?"

(2) *Cannibal Women in the Avocado Jungle of Death*: Some three dozen letter writers outed themselves and their friends as fans of *Cannibal Women in the Avocado Jungle of Death*, that wild, magnificent comedy about a women's-studies professor who finds feminists and barbarians alike in a strange green world. Ms. Mentor had thought it was her own little fetish. Instead, she's gotten boasts from locals ("the jungle is on campus at UC-Riverside, and I watched them film it!"), and she's heard from "I-laughed-my-head-off" devotees in a dozen other states, including an eighty-five-year-old man who says it's his reason for living.

When Do I Become "Doctor"?

Ms. Mentor's correspondents torment themselves over titles. When do they become "Doctor"? Do they have to wait until they walk onstage in their rented robes? And what is the male spouse of a female doctor called?

Ms. Mentor, in her perfect wisdom, rules that you are a doctor once you receive the diploma that says you are one. If you are Dr. Selena Cross, your husband is Mr. Red Cross. Or, better yet, Mr. Red Shoes, for Ms. Mentor thinks it inordinately silly for anyone to change names upon marriage.

Soon enough, someone will ask if you're a "real doctor" or "just a Ph.D." And you will whimper.

Foraging for an Academic Job

"You wouldn't by any chance have a system by which every seventh person who e-mails you gets a tenure-track job, would you?" one reader wrote.

Ms. Mentor wishes she did, although she does not know how she would hide it from the other six who did not get the job. The job market for new professors is capricious and cruel, and other writers to Ms. Mentor thinks she holds the magic key.

She doesn't.

If you have an advanced degree in nursing or accounting, you can get a professorial job almost anywhere. If you're in literature or American history, your chances diminish every year. Fewer than half the Ph.D.'s in most humanities fields will ever get the tenure-track jobs for which they're trained. Often the job search is the first time these stellar students have ever encountered failure.

The average job opening in English, for instance, will attract more than one hundred, or even several hundred, applicants. There will be a first weeding, screening out those who are totally unsuitable (they're in the wrong field or haven't finished the dissertation); those who make wildly inaccurate assumptions (they want to teach queer theory at a small Bible college); and those who seem unprofessional or crazed (haikus, scented pink paper, cash bribes).

At least twenty or thirty of the remaining applicants will seem fine on paper, but the search committee must whittle the group down to fifteen or so for phone and then in-person interviews. Sometimes it's luck, good or bad; sometimes there's a flair factor that catches a committee's attention (maybe the applicant writes on sports literature and used to be an Olympic archer).

The next step, for those in English, is an interview at the Modern Language Association meeting, held in stuffy, dreary hotels in the dead of winter, with an air of depression and tragedy over everything. Then two or three candidates may be invited for an on-campus visit.

And finally one, just one, gets a job offer.

The system is brutal, and search committees try to be kind. But they are overworked, handling their hiring while they also teach, serve on committees, and try to do research. They may slip up on clerical work and treat candidates shabbily. But applicants should not wallow in anger, obsession, or self-loathing. Better to think about alternatives. Susan Basalla and Maggie Debelius's book, *"So What Are You Going to Do With That?"* *Finding Careers Outside Academia*, is an antidote to despair, with specific things grad students can do to prepare themselves "in case it doesn't work out." The nonacademic job may be a better fit and may be what you wanted all along: new projects, free weekends for pleasure reading, no stage fright, the freedom to live where you want to.

Ms. Mentor exhorts academic job applicants to concentrate on what they can control: their self-presentation through vitas, cover letters, e-mail messages, Web sites, phone calls, interviews, and follow-up letters. Never apologize, never misspell, and keep up a charming, cheerful façade. Do your homework. Ms. Mentor recommends "Career Talk" and the other columns and forums on the *Chronicle of Higher Education*'s Career Network site (http://www.chronicle.com/jobs), and these books: Mary Morris Heiberger, Julia Miller Vick, and Jennifer S. Furlong, *The Academic Job Search Handbook*; A. Leigh DeNeef and Craufurd D. Goodwin, *The Academic's Handbook*; Kathryn Hume, *Surviving Your Academic Job Hunt*; Christina Boufis and Victoria C. Olsen, *On the Market*; and Emily Toth, *Ms. Mentor's Impeccable Advice for Women in Academia*.

Finally, those prone to melancholy should not read the letters in this chapter. They are culled from many, many more, and they are mostly about disappointments and disasters. Those with tenure may read them. Others have been warned.

How Grand Is My Vita

Q: I swell with pride when I contemplate my twenty-three-page curriculum vitae listing all my presentations great and small, publications, teaching, service to all and sundry. But will potential employers think CV in my case means "completely verbose"? Must I amputate some of my dearest items to conform to the limited attention spans of those unworthy people who nevertheless have the power to hire?

A: Yes.

I Erred

Q: After gulping down half a bottle of vodka, I wrote my first job letter, and royally screwed up the guy's name and address. Instead of "Dr. George Boss," I wrote to "Dr. Pennypacker Hall," and called him "Dear Dr. Hall." They must think I'm insane or dyslexic. I know application letters shouldn't admit weaknesses ("I'm a recovering alcoholic"), or vices ("I lust for long-legged cheerleaders"). But should I apologize and try again with Dr. Boss? And now that I'm sober, how do I write a letter that'll make me sound like a sociable fellow, but not a worm or a wimp?

A: Ms. Mentor advises you not to make yourself any more memorable by groveling. But tape a copy of that fatal epistle near your computer, and another where you once stashed the liquid courage that you've now thrown out. Reminders of past follies are a powerful kick.

You needn't present yourself as a "sociable fellow" on paper. You are not asking a university to party with you. Rather, your letter should be a well-written, perfectly proofread, clearly printed professional document so compelling that it will win you a first interview, by phone or at a conference. Once you star at that, you'll get the on-campus interview where you can be witty and charming—but not crassly frank, as in these statements by candidates: "While I have no liking for the racism that I know pervades the South, your school would perhaps be suitable for me for a few years." "I want to be in a warm climate, so I'll have a good place to retire after I put in my time." "I detest teaching introductory courses, and know that a department of your distinction would not require that of me."

The first item shows rude regional bigotry; the second sounds lazy and uncommitted; the third demonstrates a pomposity out of touch with reality. Virtually all new "hires" teach introductory courses in every climate, in every region, and they have to be ready to move.

Ms. Mentor wants you to go into academia only if you have a deep, abiding passion for the work, for the intellectual substance. Nothing else will sustain you if you do not love what you teach.

My Alma Mater Dumped on Me

Q: I applied for a job in the honors college of my alma mater ("Juneville State"). It's the program where I came of academic age. I founded the literary journal, got all my degrees there, won all the honors. I've been teaching at another college for ten years, but when I saw that Juneville had an opening . . . Well, I expected at least a courtesy interview, but instead got a form e-mail to "Dear Applicant," thanking me for applying and regretting that I was not selected. Is this the height of rudeness, or what?

A: At least "Or what." You know the personalities, but Ms. Mentor, in her perfect wisdom, knows how academic units work. You may be the victim of bad practices that proliferate in our troubled times.

It may be bureaucracy. A human-resources office may now be in charge of hiring at Juneville State, and it may be treating all job applicants with an equal and abysmal lack of tact.

Or Juneville may be choosing not to hire its own graduates, and there's an entire mythology about that:

- The Grass Is Greener. "If she's already here—or been here— someone else from somewhere else must be better." That suggests that many academics do not think highly of themselves. They believe that somewhere, over the hedge, is the savior who'll ride into town and lead them into the promised land of huge raises, waves of acclaim, and joy without end. That can't be someone they've known since she was a teenager. Besides, she might notice that . . .

- The Bodies Aren't Buried. Your professors may have trouble envisioning you as an adult, as a peer. Like parents, they saw you when you were baby-faced, and they can't see you as a fully functioning, self-diapering scholar and teacher. They may also fear what you remember about them—about bad teaching, or scandalous behavior. Since you left a decade ago, maybe they've changed spouses; changed sexual orientations; changed religions; or their kids have humiliated them in exotic, soul-searing ways. You're a living witness, and that makes people nervous. And finally . . .
- Inbreeding's Not Allowed. Many universities have policies against "inbreeding." That clumsy agricultural term, which reminds Ms. Mentor of udders and snouts, means "Thou shalt not hire thine own graduates." Except for Ivy League schools and very religious denominations, most schools seek to hire outside, diversifying their gene pools.

Ms. Mentor wonders why your former faculty didn't just tell you that, and she agrees this is worth a snit. The next time Juneville invites you to donate money, you might consider writing a soul-satisfying, scorching letter beginning with, "Why should I donate to an institution that does not respect its alums?" A colorfully worded, clever, and ruthlessly belligerent letter can be a thrilling revenge. You can imagine the recipient curdled in shame, weeping, writhing in guilt and self-loathing.

They are not worthy of you.

Fearing the Reaper

Q: I'm a recent Ph.D. whose major professor is not in good health, and I'm afraid he may pass away before I get a stable position. If I ask him to write a reference for my dossier now, am I being foolish, ghoulish, or wise?

A: Wise.

Can I Dazzle Them with My Energy?

Q (from "Linda"): I've noticed a seemingly innocent word in job postings: "energetic." It appears to be a buzzword for "young"—an attempt to insert age discrimination into hiring. After all, an older applicant like me (fiftyish) might well be deemed not energetic. How does a committee define "energetic," and how would job candidates know they lacked it? Can I build up my energy, and reflect that on my CV?

A: At least the ads don't demand "sizzling" or "nubile."

Ms. Mentor agrees that "energetic," like its cousin "dynamic," can be a code word for "young." It can also imply a preference for certain regional styles—the fast-talking repartee of New Yorkers, for instance, over the measured conversation of North Dakotans. It may cloak a preference for Italians over Norwegians, or frenetic skinny people over stolid fat ones. It also seems to discriminate against people with disabilities.

Most devisers of job ads would probably deny it and say, "We want only the best" or "We're a new community college, and we need people to run the extra kilometer" or "You're just paranoid." Nevertheless, Ms. Mentor's files show that hirers often do prefer, well, particular kinds of people.

Once upon a time at Far West Big U., for instance, a search-committee member wondered aloud: "Can job candidate Venerable, who seems to have big-time arthritis, get around this campus fast enough? Maybe we need his medical reports." Once told that asking for medical reports was illegal and that Dr. Venerable was the same age as Mick Jagger, the member retreated, harrumphing. (A decade later, Dr. Venerable was still hiking and cross-country skiing, Mick Jagger had had a hip replacement, and the committee member was dead.)

More recently, at North Medium U., a search-committee chair lobbied furiously for hiring Dr. Ingenue over Dr. Matron, although Dr. Matron had more publications and much more teaching experience, because "Dr. Ingenue is livelier." "You just like them perky and malleable," retorted his enemy.

Ms. Mentor likes all professors to be eager and curious—but the young, the able-bodied, and the foxy are not the only "energetic" faculty. Many courageous professors with disabilities have made themselves as dynamic as the nondisabled—through dramatic gestures and well-trained voices, as well as PowerPoint and its cousins. Professors have hired students to be their ears and eyes—and thereby taught all students that being deaf or blind does not affect the brain. Teachers with "invisible disabilities" have endured chronic pain without publicly wincing and have concealed artificial limbs. Many have been considered "antisocial" for going home early and needing to rest to stay out of the hospital.

James M. Lang, who wrote his first book about his own disability (*Learning Sickness: A Year with Crohn's Disease*) is a rare tenured success story for someone who did not "pass." Ms. Mentor knows one professor who heroically, and secretly, performed kidney dialysis for herself in her office, lights off and door locked, during lunch hours. Her students, who loved her wry sense of humor, never knew until she got tenure and "came out."

Her CV, like Linda's, portrayed someone full of energy: teaching, publishing, organizing, committee-ing. Linda's CV could also include other dynamic work: serving on school or hospital boards, helping in battered women's programs, consulting, tutoring, service learning. Whatever she did in her earlier years, Linda was not a homebound eater of bonbons. She's been a self-starter all her life.

At interviews, Linda should talk quickly and clearly, sit up straight, move briskly, respond vivaciously. Among academics who live to pontificate, "active listening" will be irresistibly charming. "Mature" candidates can be more flexible, tolerant, and self-confident. They've failed at some things before, and moved on. There's not much they won't try.

Ms. Mentor has just one warning for the mature and energetic: Do not tell the young people how to run things, even if you know better. Let them see you as a colleague, even though their lives would be ever so much better if they would just follow your advice.

It hurts to bite your tongue. Yes, Ms. Mentor knows.

A Home for the Fleas in My Hair

Q: I have a striking, unusual hair style that I think is very original, but I've been told that it may put off future employers and cause them not to hire me. What should I do?

A: Snip.

Ignore the Rules and Make Your Own Problems

Q (from "Gilbert"): I'm an ex-scholar who'd like to return and teach English, but all the institutions want three letters of reference, besides a cover letter and a CV. Being a businessman for many years, I do the math. For a hundred job applicants, that's three hundred people writing letters. What a colossal waste.

Does academe hold people's time in such low regard that they can make this demand? I either apply, adding a snide, "I cannot in good conscience ask references to take time out from their busy days to write letters on my behalf," or I do not bother to apply for those positions. Am I missing something?

Q (from "Norbert"): For two years, I've sought employment in English at any college besides the one where I'm an adjunct. Most universities want those who are "published." But with finishing course work and teaching, how am I expected to find the time to publish? Can't I get a job without having to do that, too?

A: Ms. Mentor can see it all now. You arrive for your job interview at the most posh hotel in town, where you're met by the local chapter of Plutocrats R Us—millionaire alumni, billionaire builders, all dropping by on their private jets to meet you. Their female companions, dripping diamonds, whisk your wife off to fashionista spas, while you are wined and dined and begged to consider a job paying a measly $3 million. Plus, of course, the summer house, private schools for the youngsters, and Jaguars for all.

And you didn't have to submit references. And you didn't have to publish a thing.

Because you're a top-of-the-line football coach.

Such wooing and swooning won't happen to Gilbert or Norbert. As full-time instructors, they may start at $30,000, or 1 percent of a top football coach's salary. Universities will do anything for bowl games and ecstatic moments, but no one expects the young to be thrilled by tales of "my interpretive breakthrough with Foucault." ("I was polishing the ceramic swan when I had a flash of blinding insight. . . .")

And so, when you apply for a job in academe, and you're not the football coach, you have to follow the rules, or be sent to the showers early. Gilbert, with his snide little note, may be a high-minded, independent thinker—but he'll come across as an arrogant know-it-all. (Academics do have their pride.) Sending reference letters is a prerequisite, like showing up for work fully clothed. Without the minimum, you're thrown naked into the cold.

The winners who do get interviews are the ones with an extra flair factor. Awards help, but except for the lovely teaching-oriented world of community colleges, nothing trumps publication. Even a small book review shows that you've joined the intellectual conversation that is part of your profession. Publication is the way you stick your head up over the savannah and shout, "Academic World, look at me!"

That world isn't apt to look at Norbert, buried under paperwork and offering nothing special—for every Ph.D. in the pack is smart and has a degree. Norbert needs to prioritize. If he's spending ten hours grading a set of papers, he's being too picky and needs timesavers: student group work, peer mentoring, grading for just two or three things. He needs to routinize: errands all in one afternoon; children who pitch in, or at least keep their bedroom doors closed; housemates who'll lower their standards for neatness and cleanliness. Writing groups and blogs help, but Norbert must also set aside one day a week, or one afternoon a week, or 5 to 6 A.M. every day, for professional writing.

Even if he produces only a paragraph of bad off-the-top-of-his-head prose every day, he'll have an article-length draft in a month. Then he can edit and shape it, and get it out to journals in another month or two. It needn't be perfect, but it needs to be out—or Norbert will drown in the adjunct pool.

Unlike football players, academic standouts can be paid for their skills throughout their lives—but first they've got to suit up for the game. When candidates like Gilbert and Norbert deliberately sabotage themselves, Ms. Mentor cannot sit quietly on the sidelines. She grumbles, twitches, and fumes.

I Have a Tough Secret

Q (from "Lester"): What's too much information about food sensitivities in job interviews? I won't pass out or have a disfiguring rash, and I don't carry a hypodermic, but I can wind up dashing to the loo every fifteen minutes for days. How does one convince new colleagues-to-be that he absolutely cannot eat unknown food—even if it doesn't seem to contain the bad ingredient (gluten)—without seeming like a total hypochondriac, insulting them, or giving a lurid blow-by-blow description of what might ensue? "I cannot eat flour or processed food" or "I have celiac disease" do not work for those without personal experience. Their local deli will survive without my business, but my digestion is more fragile. Should I just say so?

Q (from "Lena"): I have a hidden disability that can flare up unexpectedly and make me dizzy or send me streaking for the bathroom. It's mostly controllable by medication, which I use for on-campus job interviews. Do I have to tell possible employers about it? I would like to be honest and brag that I've still managed to get a Ph.D., publications, and a teaching award, despite my disability. But I also know about prejudices. Should I try to pass as "nondisabled"?

A: Ms. Mentor has a dream—that one day all campuses will have a rainbow of people moving easily through wide hallways for wheelchairs, finding sensor-equipped bathroom fixtures, using computers adapted for voices as well as fingers, eating in cafeterias that cater to and explain everyone's dietary needs and quirks, and sharing a community attitude that everyone is welcome.

But such a utopia is far away. The Americans with Disabilities Act, passed in 1990, has helped get parking spaces, better bathrooms, ramps, and many other "reasonable accommodations" for disabled people and yet . . .

The bitter truth is that it will be easier for Lester and Lena to get hired if they hide their disabilities—even though people with disabilities are the largest minority group in the United States. According to the U.S. Census, a fifth of Americans belong, and anyone can join in a minute. All it takes is a bad fall in the shower, or one drunk driver, and you're a lifetime member.

There are many myths about disabled workers, especially that they're "too costly." But most accommodations are cheap and simple: phone headsets, easy-to-use software, desk rearrangements. Academe, with its movable schedules and student helpers and online courses, is ideal for deaf or blind people to keep sharing what they know.

The biggest barrier, a Cornell study shows, is attitude—fear and loathing. Only people who really care will do the right thing, like the very poor rural African Americans, a century ago, who began training their blind children in music. Their success stories include Clarence Carter, the Blind Boys of Alabama, and Ray Charles. "Too costly" is really about a rigid and stingy perception of who is worthy and who is not.

Ms. Mentor calls it a very Puritan belief—the idea that if you're not perfectly able, it is somehow your fault, and you deserve to be punished. (You didn't wear your seatbelt, or you devoured a Whopper and enjoyed it.) In various pockets of righteousness around the United States, Ms. Mentor's loyal readers have been scolded by strangers for enjoying a beer or eating meat. Those with visible disabilities, what Rosemarie Garland Thomson calls "extraordinary bodies," know about being stared at, stigmatized, patronized, and denied insurance. But even the most virtuous, careful, and luckily insured Americans may have secret disabilities, such as food allergies or asthma or epilepsy. For job interviews, the Lesters and the Lenas will pack their inhalers, pills, canes, and sun hats—and hope they won't have to use them in public and be outed and faced with ignorance and prejudice. Unfortunately, as disabilities scholar Lennard Davis points out, "We live in a world of norms"—and when you're a job candidate, it's not up to you to educate the world.

Lester, for instance, shouldn't feel called upon to give potential colleagues a long lecture on gluten intolerance (which includes wheat products, beer, soy sauce, and mustard). If faculty children happen to be around and ask, "How long before you have to poop?" he need not excite them (and disgust his hosts) with detailed answers. Talking about ailments is never charming, and charm wins jobs.

Ms. Mentor advises Lester to tell his hosts, calmly, that he has a "wheat allergy" (sounds less hostile than "gluten intolerance")—and so "I have to be careful about what I eat." And then he should follow whatever regimen works at home—including secretly bringing his own food, and never trusting restaurant protestations that "Our food will never make you sick."

Lester must make his disease sound like a nuisance, not a lifestyle—for employers, fretting about medical costs and crises, often won't hire a candidate with a chronic illness. And yes, that violates the Americans with Disabilities Act, but there is little that candidates can do. Right now, Lester must come across as a winning soul who shrugs off illness and cheerfully soldiers on.

Lena is also more likely to be hired if she "passes." Ms. Mentor knows that some outraged readers will say she's promoting dishonesty ("They should take Lena as she is"), but Ms. Mentor would rather have Lester and Lena in place, able to bore from within, asking pointed questions, making disability something to be talked about. If they languish, unemployed, students are deprived of many vital things that they need to know.

Ms. Mentor prefers teachers and students to be unique and extraordinary, to be leaders in a world where people can sashay, limp, or wheel themselves about—keeping pace with the slowest and helping them along. We will all be disabled eventually, if we do not die first. People with disabilities may have to conceal their vulnerabilities for now, but not when there are enough of them, and enough people with open hearts and minds. Ms. Mentor knows we could all use more of those.

The Caregiver

Q: I have been on the job market, more or less, for five years—the last three dramatically attenuated while I cared for my elderly and chronically ill mother. I taught faithfully as an adjunct, then cleaned her apartment, cooked her meals, helped her bathe, and ferried her to countless doctors. Last year she died, and now I'm in a wide-ranging job search.

I'm often asked what limited my search before—and what do I say? As a social scientist, I'm tempted to report that I was a participant-observer in the American experience of life-cycle squeezes, the health-care crisis, and aging parents. Sometimes I think this is the perfect answer—since it allows me to circle around to my own scholarly interests.

Yet even sympathetic interviewers obviously prefer a hard-driving, obsessive careerist. I've been one, single and childless, but I could have made no other choice about my mom.

Have I doomed myself by ensuring my mother's reasonably comfortable final years and meaningful death instead of jumping on the professional fast-track? Do I conceal what I was doing and just blame the terrible job market? I want to be honest but circumspect, humane but employed.

A: Your letter is one of the most wrenching Ms. Mentor has ever received, for it exposes the heartless side of academia. Far too many academics simply cannot see that life is more than the next paper, the bigger lab space, the longer vita, the national prizes. When search committees insist on having candidates with a "continuous work history," too often they lose well-rounded human beings.

The standard career narrative—the linear, upward-striving, no-swerving path—is possible only for those who are young, white, able, and lucky. They must either be monkishly single or possess a willing, I'll-handle-all-the-domestic-burdens-for-you partner (plus some kind of extra income).

Those doing the hiring are still, too often, powerful administrators who, when asked about children, the elderly, the sick, and the troubled, reply: "That's my wife's department." Hence, to Ms. Mentor's great sorrow, many campuses still lack day-care centers, even fewer have elder care, and only one that Ms. Mentor knows of (Michigan State) has a battered women's shelter.

Newer academics without traditional wives, and those blessed with people they care deeply about, will wind up making career sacrifices, until those in power—perhaps aggravated and humiliated by the likes of Ms. Mentor—wake up and notice real life. Devoted children make the most dedicated teachers.

Ms. Mentor also recommends Constance Coiner and Diana Hume George's *The Family Track*—an impassioned set of essays that should turn up, even anonymously, on the desks of all deans, department chairs, and hiring committees. (Anonymous givers may open their copies to the most relevant parts.)

As for job interviews, Ms. Mentor thinks your proposed answer is perfect: You are what you study—and you've never stopped doing your research. You've learned to craft it around the time available. Because you are resourceful and flexible, you have a continuous work history—and you will be, as the record shows, a compassionate colleague.

Your mother must have been proud of you. Ms. Mentor is, too.

———

Reader Response: Several years later, Ms. Mentor heard from the Caregiver that "sometimes your advice seekers have happy endings." That fall she was beginning a tenure-track job at a small liberal arts college. "My only regret is that my mom isn't here to see it, but I like to think she knows just the same."

Illegal Questions and Hostile Interviewers

Q: As a job seeker, I expect to be terrified—but right now, I'm outraged. At my on-campus interview with "Esteemed University," five different profs asked me illegal questions about my family. One laughed at my research ideas. One senior prof fell asleep during my job talk, but then raved later about how good it was. Everyone bitched about bad students, and the only humane faculty members I met are about to retire. Then finally, thanks to the chair's twenty-one-minute phone conversation while I sat in his office for our scheduled meeting, I almost missed my plane.

If they offer the job, I'll say no. But should I explain why?

A: Ms. Mentor wonders why you would want to tell off E.U. Many young people feel—naively, idealistically—that they can correct all the ills of the world by speaking out against injustice. But few people want to hear their faults described. Even fewer entrenched people will admit to having any failings at all.

The five who asked illegal questions may think they were just being friendly, caring about you "as a person." The one who laughed at your research ideas may be the department clown or eccentric. And the one who dozed off may be a "meeting sleeper," one who closes his eyes but purports to be awake and alert. Even the garrulous chair on the phone may have a plausible story.

Or they could all be exactly as you describe them: obnoxious, selfish, curmudgeonly, vicious flouters of all the civilized expectations of law and manners. But academia is a small world, full of infighting and gossip. If you hector E.U., you are the one who'll become known as a troublemaker and rude upstart who does not know your place. Once the academic grapevine pegs you as bad-tempered and mean-spirited, that could cost you the jobs that you really want.

And what if E.U. turns out to be your only job offer? Would you rather have no career at all? Ms. Mentor thinks it far cannier to take what looks like a bad job and mold it to a better one—or use it as a stepping-stone. Shouting, "You creeps!" always feels splendid. But it is best done quietly, in the privacy of one's home. Being known as an amiable visitor will do more to get you the job you want, and that is the best revenge.

Is It Research or Stalking?

Q (from "Kelly"): What kind of fool am I? I've always assumed it's a sign of respect to do your homework about people who will be interviewing you for a job. So I've researched the backgrounds of professors at departments where I have applied, planning to mention ways that my research might complement theirs. But when I rehearsed doing that in a mock interview in my department—I was mauled.

"You'll put them on the defensive," one prof warned, but my mentor was much worse: "If someone did that to me, I'd feel like the candidate was stalking me." She shuddered.

"But why?" I asked, and my profs snickered sourly. "Oh, faculty typically have low self-esteem," I was told. "Don't expose their vulnerabilities."

Is that fear real and pervasive? If I shouldn't talk about the hirers' specific strengths, how can I show enthusiasm and interest? Should I simply stifle the impulse altogether?

A: Ms. Mentor shares your bewilderment about academics who recoil when praised. She is always pleased when strangers laud her perfect wisdom. But our fallen world is, alas, full of people who lack sufficient savoir-faire, or bonhomie, or amour-propre. (They also find it annoying, rather than delightfully pretentious, when Ms. Mentor flaunts her French.)

Maybe the recoilers have had difficult childhoods. Maybe they were ostracized at an early age for being smart instead of sporty. Maybe they've been told that it's wrong to self-promote, or to discuss one's grades or salary. A few may simply be gnarly and secretive by nature.

In days of yore, before the Internet, it was not so easy to find out who was productive, who was moribund, and who had a secret identity (one of Ms. Mentor's teachers was rumored to be a frequent and potent contributor to a sensational magazine called *True Confessions*, though not under his real name). If a humanities scholar proclaimed that his work was "extraordinarily influential," there were few reliable citation indexes to prove him wrong. Even inquiries might be discouraged.

When "Verna" was hired jointly by two departments, for instance, she asked to see the vitas of her new colleagues, and the dean's assistant said, "Absolutely not. Those are confidential." Word of Verna's impertinence got around. Until she buckled down to ingratiating herself and taking people to lunch, she was shunned.

Worse was the case of "Endowed Professor Bart," author of a well-known textbook. Bart was hired at "Home on the Range University," where his lifelong friend "Dr. Iron Fist" chaired a bitterly divided department in which the Young Turks were demanding radical changes. They viewed Bart as a tool of the enemy.

No one now remembers exactly what they were fighting about. But since it was before e-mail existed, the weapons were battalions of paper memos. Today's youngsters will never know the thrill, the pulsating rush, of manually typing a vicious screed, then laboriously correcting any errors with Wite-Out, lest opponents deem you "illiterate" and put your memo on the bulletin board with a "C minus" scrawled in scarlet ink.

But in Bart's case, someone eventually committed an act that was considered heinous even at Home on the Range U., whose faculty members had long suffered from self-doubt ("Are we really a research university, or a cow college?"). Endowed Professor Bart had been hired as a renowned scholar to improve the "research profile." One day, without warning, copies of his vita suddenly appeared in department mailboxes, and Bart was unmasked.

He had published hardly anything at all except half a dozen slightly revised updates of his textbook.

Dr. Iron Fist attempted damage control, asking everyone to return Bart's vita, "as it was sent out in error." No one did, and copies proliferated. Job candidates got them, anonymously. Dr. Fist's wife saw half a dozen in her dentist's office. (Yes, it was a small provincial town, and cable TV had only just arrived.)

So what finally happened? Ms. Mentor's enthralled listeners are demanding to know.

Everyone lost face and the rumor mill hummed for years, but the practical result was the same as in most academic skirmishes: Nothing much.

The whole brouhaha taught Ms. Mentor—then a young duchess, just learning her craft—that it might not always be wise to circulate, or know, information about one's colleagues.

Then came the Net. Now most department Web sites for research universities list faculty publications. (Community colleges usually do not, since their faculties are more devoted to teaching.) Professors have their own Web sites, and some use Facebook and MySpace; RateMyProfessors.com trolls for faculty photos taken surreptitiously with students' cell phones.

In short, there is little secrecy for anyone, and Ms. Mentor agrees with Kelly that scholarly activity should be publicly known. That is what academic freedom means, including the competition to produce the most provocative title each year at the Modern Language Association convention ("Jane Austen and the Masturbating Girl" in 1994; "Is the Rectum a Text?" in 2006).

Kelly is wise to read up on her potential new colleagues. Her research on toads can lead to collaboration with Dr. Frog; her political theories may mesh nicely with those of Dr. Post-Marx. Her interest in Darwin's influence can lead to team teaching ("cross-fertilization").

So why do current faculty members, all Net-savvy, recoil at the thought of being Googled?

A few have muttered that "I have the same name as a notorious individual"—but surely you can explain that you're not *that* Snoop Dogg. There seems to be some peculiar notion of privacy afoot. But Kelly is not in a position to change it, and so Ms. Mentor will simply advise her to be strategic.

Do the research, but ask innocent, general questions: "What do you see as your program's greatest strengths now?" is flattering and encourages bragging. If someone does mention a publication, Kelly can say, "Yes, I'm eager to read that." "Tell me more" is always a winning response.

In short, a hiring interview can be a strange minuet in which the junior partner knows the steps but has to pretend not to. Ms. Mentor, of course, favors straightforwardness over pretense, and would much prefer Kelly as a colleague over the updated versions of deceptive Bart or his enforcer, Dr. Iron Fist.

But not everyone in academe is always wise, fair, or sensible. If they were, there would be no material for academic novels—and no need for Ms. Mentor.

Boxers and Bloomers and Thongs, O My

Q: As a very nervous public speaker about to give job-interview presentations, I've been advised to imagine my audience in their underwear. Should I?

A: Yes.

I'm Invited to Their Campus

Q: "McCoy University" has invited me for an on-campus interview, but the search is obviously rigged to hire somebody else. Instead of the department chair, some secretary called me to set up the visit. Should I cancel the whole charade, or go wearing old, grungy clothes and tell them exactly what I think?

A: Ms. Mentor grimaces at your rude language ("some secretary"). The working woman who called you was just doing her job. Wise chairs delegate chores to trusted employees.

Ms. Mentor also advises you to act as if McCoy's search is "real" and not a ritual ruse to get Algernon, a loyal instructor for twelve years, onto the tenure track at last. Some departments do conduct sham searches, but you must assume there is no Algernon, and do your best. Besides, Algernon could always retire, abscond, be fired for moral turpitude, or die—leaving a slot for you.

What to wear? Ms. Mentor recommends clean, reasonably fashionable, unmemorable clothes. Do not be super-chic, for it always makes the hirers feel inadequate. At one university, "the dude with the ascot" was talked about for years as the one who didn't get the job. Plunging cleavage and little-girl dresses are also career killers.

Wear a suit, whatever your gender: a jacket symbolizes self-confidence and authority. If you're a creative type, resist the temptation to waltz in with long scarves or strange body piercings. Departments rarely need free spirits; they need people who'll do boring committee work and not grumble too much.

No matter what happens: smile, be gracious, shake hands firmly, make eye contact, remember names, write a thank-you afterward. If the interview consists of canned, preprinted questions, and committee members merely write down your answers, assume that they're following an exceptionally rigid set of employment rules. Try to charm the committee as best you can (do not ask, "Are you robots?") and do not emulate other unfortunates Ms. Mentor finds in her files:

- "Arthur," wanting to seem spontaneous, did not practice his presentation, which ran forty-five minutes over the time limit. When he clicked on the lights after the last slide, half the audience had disappeared—and of the remainder, several were snoring happily in the warm darkness.
- "Belva," who carefully avoided joking about race, sex, religion, region, politics, or last names, thought it was safe to make a satiric comment about Hooters (which Ms. Mentor agrees is the tackiest restaurant concept in the universe). But the man who might've been Belva's boss turned out to have a soft spot for that establishment. He'd found his second and third trophy wives there.
- "Cilla" groaned about the poor physical condition of the campus and got frosty responses. Ms. Mentor reminds interviewees to seem upbeat, no matter the provocation. A candidate is a guest, not a critic.
- "Dempsey" had to excuse himself several times to smoke a cigarette, leaving the hiring committee twiddling and fuming.

Ms. Mentor also warns against hotel bars, which have been the ruin of many a poor candidate:

- "Alex," a two-fisted journalist seeking a career change to the calmer shoals of academia, got a big head start at the bar and forgot where he was—until he grabbed the dean's thigh and was firmly slapped.
- "Beatrice," a new Ph.D. in English, drove into town the night before her interview and slipped down to the hotel bar for a prim, solitary nightcap. A loud, boozy man offered her a hundred dollars for certain sexual acts. She refused, furiously. The next day, he turned out to be "Durwood," the chair of the department's hiring committee.
- "Calvin," offered his dream job at "Churchly College" while he was still on campus, roared into the hotel bar: "Drinks on the house for everyone!" and billed the bash to his room. When Churchly College got the bill, they canceled the job offer.

Alex and Calvin were history, but Beatrice salvaged the situation by pretending she did not recognize Durwood. He, in turn, seemed not to remember her. She got the job, and it was only long after tenure—and after Durwood's retirement—that she ever told anyone the story.

People are still laughing immoderately, but Beatrice's best revenge was her long years as a humane, compassionate department chair, especially admired for her hiring skills. Ms. Mentor doubts you will grow up to be Beatrice—but it would be good to try.

Not Abreast

Q: Other women seem to think it's all right to breastfeed during a job interview, but I think it's distracting (to say the least) to worry about hiding my nipple while discussing my research. Am I right?

A: Yes.

Well, She Looked Pregnant

Q: "Nervosa," a job candidate at my small liberal-arts college, looked great on paper but gave a mediocre presentation. She was clearly ill at ease. At the end of the day she asked the nonpregnant faculty member who had escorted her around the campus: "When is the baby due?"

Nervosa committed the ultimate social faux pas, but is that sufficient to throw her out of the pool? I am especially sensitive to this particular gaffe, having been asked the same question by one of those socially inept, downright goofy visiting professors that seem to litter our campus. Perhaps I'm not objective.

A: Ms. Mentor concedes that some academics are not always nice, kind, and generous—and some love the pratfalls of others. "Faux Pas," a popular game among some academicians, consists of inventing crass scenarios in the spirit of that legendary question from 1865: "Apart from that, Mrs. Lincoln, how did you enjoy the play?"

The game was accidentally inspired by a famous novelist who thought he was being ferociously witty when he described a colleague as "Moses among the Hottentots." Dr. Moses (not his real name) did not speak to the novelist for some twelve years, and new faculty members were warned never to invite the two of them to the same committee meeting or dinner party. It was an awkward time, pregnant with the possibility of endless faux pas, real or imagined. The tenured professors loved it.

But for job and tenure seekers, a faux pas can kill a career. Consider the legend of untenured young "Ferdinand," who reportedly found himself in a tavern competition with English department colleagues, all bragging about "the most important literary classic you've never read." The game finally escalated to the win-or-die round: "the biggest-name literary classic you've never read but have taught."

Young Ferdinand named *Hamlet*, and won the game—but was soon resoundingly rejected for tenure. His more staid colleagues decided he was just too ignorant to be kept on.

Ms. Mentor hopes there is no real-life original for this mythic tale (which David Lodge adapted in his novel *Changing Places*, for a game called "Humiliation"). Ferdinand was the victim of hazing, and his real sin was the same as Nervosa's. Both were trying too hard to fit in, to bond with their elders.

Men often bond by boasting and one-upping. Young men are supposed to jockey to find a place in the hierarchy. With seminal publications, eventually the most successful may become the Biggest Elk on Campus (or at least the dean). Women are more apt to bond by sharing domestic or personal details—yet those can also be treacherous twigs in the groves of academe. At job interviews with female candidates, there is often the dance around couple status (Dare we ask? Is she wearing a ring? Will her partner need a job?). Discussions of children can create bonds or evoke stereotypes ("She's a mommy first, and she'll always love them more than she loves us").

Some women bond with diet talk (a crashing bore, says Ms. Mentor). Women routinely compliment one another, and even at job interviews, it is not uncommon for women to retreat to the bathroom and find themselves looking in the mirror at the same time.

That can be the most dangerous time for a faux pas.

"Great haircut" is safe to say, and so are compliments on scarves or jewelry, which show the wearer's taste. But comments on body size and shape are almost certainly going to offend.

"You're so thin" is not necessarily a compliment, since weight loss can come from cancer, eating disorders, or depression. "You're so short" sounds disparaging, and even "You're so tall" is a comment on one's genes, not one's achievements. Compliments on hair color are also risky, since that shade of red may not be intentional.

Tact and professionalism require not noticing what is readily apparent in the gym, if not on the street. Everyone in a job interview should be considering brains and accomplishments, not bodily configurations.

Yet even polite Americans often lose all their manners when they spot a pregnant woman. They poke, they pry, they recite clichés or horrific tales. A woman who is visibly pregnant suddenly seems to be everyone's property.

Which brings Ms. Mentor back to Nervosa, who was trying to be chummy when she, in effect, said to a possible future colleague, "You're fat."

Among sensitive women, that is the most egregious faux pas of them all, and there is no way to apologize oneself out of that.

What could Nervosa have done differently?

If being flustered led to her blunder, she might have been more prepared for her interview. She should have rehearsed her presentation many times, including in front of her dissertation committee and fellow students, if she could get them to assemble. Even a cat is not a bad audience.

If Nervosa had felt more self-confident about her research, she might not have blurted out her fatal comment to the substantial but not pregnant woman who escorted her.

But is that remark enough to "throw Nervosa out of the pool," as the letter writer wonders? Ms. Mentor would say no, but she does not know whether Nervosa was ultimately hired.

Faux Pas games are safe for the entrenched faculty, who can snicker wickedly in the privacy of their own homes. But public behavior, especially among the untenured, has to be thoughtful behavior—and perhaps the youngsters will eventually inspire increased civility in these barbarous times.

Ms. Mentor can hope.

The Home Team Advantage

Q: Asked at a recent on-campus interview in the Northeast: "How d'ya like the Red Sox?" I was perfectly honest, and said I think sports are boring and infantile. I haven't heard back from the school. Did I err?

A: Well . . .

I'm Perfect, So Why Won't Anyone Hire Me?

Q: I've spent literally years seeking another faculty position. I've reworked my CV and revised my references. There isn't anything I haven't done professionally, from committees to writing articles to writing books. My teaching evaluations for over a decade are completely flawless, with not one negative comment and dozens of positives. My interview presentation is flawless. I have no problems with appearance, hygiene, clothes, attitude that would make me objectionable. There literally is nothing else I can do to make myself competitive. Yet every time I'm rejected. The only places that express any interest in me are remote locations where they obviously cannot get anyone else and, in the end, they also reject me. I've done some fifty on-campus interviews, and several hundred phone interviews. Is there anything else I can do?

A: When Ms. Mentor receives an epistle like yours—one with a mystery—she is always intrigued. Should you be propitiating some gods, making an animal or vegetable sacrifice, cursing fate, changing your name? All your geese are in order, all your eggs are in your basket, and yet—nothing hatches. "Surely in that time you could hoodwink somebody?" remarked one of Ms. Mentor's consultants.

Ms. Mentor read and reread, pondered and wondered, until—"Eureka!"—she found clues in two of your words: "flawless" and "remote."

We live in an imperfect world in which our most engaging interactions are often spontaneous, even goofy. Possibly you are focusing coldly on yourself—on your flawlessness—instead of reacting to the warm, living interests of your audience. Perhaps you're not making eye contact, or not listening carefully to those who speak to you. You may have a manner that discourages questions.

Your audience may want a responsive speaker with humor and information, but you may be giving them a slick and well-rehearsed monologue.

Hiring committees may also notice the geographical bias ("remote") that you cannot conceal from the all-knowing Ms. Mentor. Thanks to e-mail, phones, and airplanes, few institutions are really undesirably "remote"—unless you are among those academics who feel that every place outside of New York, Boston, and San Francisco is peopled by peasants and savages. Ms. Mentor is still surprised by the tactless and ignorant candidates who visit universities in the Deep South and say, "How can you stand to live . . . here?"

Ultimately, we must live with ourselves, and constant frustration ("I'm better than this") will do little but make you feel gnawed-upon and ulcerous. You can certainly rehearse enough small talk to seem spontaneous, and you can conceal your loathing for the boondocks—but to what end? Ms. Mentor presumes that you have tenure where you are, and she suspects that you do not sufficiently appreciate the colleagues who voted you in. Shouldn't you want to remain with people whose judgment is flawless?

Do I Brag?

Q: I've had eight job interviews, but only one offer, which I took. Do I have to tell people that I lost out, or can I say I'm deliriously happy to get my first choice?

A: Delirious.

Love and Sex in Academia

In medieval times, we are told, the life of the mind was disconnected from that of the body. Monks, celibate, could contemplate. Nuns, celibate, could serve others. But of course men often loved men then, and nuns in the convents often loved one another deeply, and only recently have scholars uncovered the rich, varied, passionate, ennobling, and beautiful stories of same-sex love.

Gossip mongers, meanwhile, know all too well the grisly story of Peter Abelard, the tutor to the brilliant linguist Heloise in twelfth-century Paris. After she gave birth to their child, her angry relatives castrated Abelard. The lovers were separated, but their yearning letters are still read and cherished more than eight hundred years later.

Teachers and students still do cross boundaries to be together. And a long-term relationship between two smart, sexy people is still tough to maintain.

Today's academic novels are rarely romantic sagas of raw, unbridled passion breaking through conventional boundaries. Like Richard Russo's *Straight Man*—the favorite among Ms. Mentor's readers—the novels are much more apt to be about middle-aged, mildly melancholy, male English professors. Sometimes they wind up attempting inept sex with women half their age.

Women in academic novels by women fare better. Instead of sinking into midlife despondency, their women protagonists imitate real-life women: they find new ways to spread their wings. The feisty English professors created by Carolyn Heilbrun, Joanne Dobson, and others have to take charge—because someone has to solve those pesky strings of murders that erupt periodically in English Departments.

Robert B. Parker, creator of the Spenser detective series, is a former academic, and a few Ph.D.'s are romance writers, among them Jennifer Crusie, Mary Bly ("Eloisa James"), and Deborah Gonzales ("Sabrina Jeffries"). But for most academic writers, sex is about irony and unfulfillment, more bumbling than baroque. That may also be true of academics in real life. Or so Ms. Mentor's mail suggests.

Isn't It Romantic?

Q: Can Ms. Mentor share some of her perfect wisdom for lovelorn and love-seeking academicians?

A: A few years ago, Ms. Mentor invited comments about romance in academe—and got just one reply. "Amelia," a librarian, wrote that she married the first academic man who actually listened to her without pawing the ground impatiently and snapping, "Uh-uh, uh-uh, uh-uh," until he got to speak. (Later another librarian, "Flavia," shared her dating history, including a lively medical student, a dull computer-science professor, and a physics professor who was a marvelous dancer and showered her with roses. "He was a rare one," she says.)

Ms. Mentor's other readers may have been too busy, for time is a great obstacle to academic romance. While civilians think scholars "work" just nine or twelve hours a week, with summers "off," in-the-trenches academics know that there is little rest for the ambitious. Besides grading, planning, office hours, research, and committees, successful scholars also fit in rumor-mongering, character assassination, placating, and such survival activities as cooking, cleaning, and reproducing the next generation—which may not be as easy as it sounds.

According to one well-published scholar, there is only one possible attitude for graduate students to take if they imagine their professors in carnal congress: "Revulsion," writes James R. Kincaid in an essay in *The Erotics of Instruction*. "It's a wonder the highly-educated propagate," he writes. Nor does promotion add glamour, he adds, for deans and presidents "enter another species altogether, a reptilian order."

But Ms. Mentor digresses. It is indeed difficult to have two bodies and two careers in academe. Obsessive researchers could easily spend years reading up on how hard it is to have a romance, without ever emerging to see if it's true.

How does one find a soul mate? Academics do have daily free time to go to bookstores, laundromats, and blood banks. They can attend out-of-town conferences, volunteer for committees, and take part in community activism. Couples have met at Amnesty International meetings, whale watchings, wine tastings, and receptions for obscure dignitaries from tiny nations. "Diane" and "Nancy" bonded when they found themselves side by side, gossiping and snoozing, at a meeting of the commission on the status of something.

Many an academic has met a partner, or at least a lively date, online, in dating sites or chat rooms or listservs. Academics are great online conversationalists, and their inhibitions (Am I tall enough? Do I look dweebish?) all vanish. Verbal dexterity scores.

Once academics meet in person, public-speaking ability helps: They can try out a rip-roaring discourse on an esoteric subject, and see who refuses to flee. Professorial types have commonalities (ugly cars, uncertain fashion sense). Lunch is easy to arrange and coffee is even less fraught, Ms. Mentor used to think—until she read a wildly dramatic *Chronicle of Higher Education* forum thread in February 2006. A married woman posted, wondering: What does it mean to have coffee with an attractive, married male colleague?

Academics live to interpret. For five days, nearly eighty posters gleefully theorized. Should she tell her husband? Is a coffee date "racy"? Is any tête-à-tête suspect?

When the man in the scenario sent a jovial e-mail ("Have a great day"), scholars pounced. Was there a sexual subtext? Oh, no, nothing's "more neutral" than a meeting of research colleagues, claimed one faction: "You women worry everything to death." Another poster recommended that they all read *He's Just Not That Into You*, by Greg Behrendt and Liz Tuccillo—which Ms. Mentor also recommends, for a dose of reality. Still another wanted to know if "Have a great day" now means "I want to suck your toes."

When the poster finally had coffee with her colleague, he pooh-poohed research talk and launched into a lugubrious whine: "Oh, I am so sad. My wife doesn't understand me. But you . . ." How gross, posters thought. How trite, added Ms. Mentor.

But she continued her scholarship, Googling together "professors" and "romance"—mostly turning up Romance-language departments, although there was also a list of romance novels featuring professors in love. Googling "professors" with "sex" turned up a list of "Hottest Harvard Professors," many articles on sexual harassment, and a Nigerian exhortation to faculty members and students to eschew "intergenerational sex."

But many American academics meet their mates later in life—after a "starter marriage," after divorce or widowhood, or after coming out or going into the closet. Ms. Mentor wonders how mature scholars handle sentiment, for much of academic research is devoted to debunking romance. Literary scholars talk about "performativity" rather than feelings; anthropologists record odd courtship rituals; and psychologists wonder how much of what we call "love" is merely physiology.

Yes, academics in love are apt to be self-critical and ironic, and the best-known academic novels have little love talk and few happy sex scenes. More often there are flamboyant flirtations followed by shrieking escapes, as in Erica Jong's *Fear of Flying*, which starts with a psychoanalysts' convention. There are multiple partners, as in David Lodge's *Small World: An Academic Romance*, but revenge, greed, and schadenfreude evoke more passion. The late May Sarton wrote academic novels about women, among them *The Small Room*, but (probably constrained by the homophobia of her day) did not include sexual expression. In older academic novels by the likes of Mary McCarthy (*The Groves of Academe*) and Bernard Malamud (*A New Life*), there are predatory faculty wives; in Jane Smiley's *Moo*, everyone—including professors of Spanish and agriculture—has an agenda.

But no one seems to have sex in those books just for the fun of it. Ms. Mentor suspects that academics distrust the idea of fun. They tend to be introverts, and academe allows people to be socially gawky for their entire lives. Scholars are supposed to be strong and individualistic, without emotional needs.

Some grow so used to lecturing that they utterly forget how to listen—and so they lose out on one of the wickedest and most delightful activities ever invented: reciprocal gossip. Ms. Mentor urges all frustrated romantics to learn to eavesdrop and collect (without snarky comments) the juicy details of other people's lives and work. Then you'll always have something to talk about—and you can claim you're merely doing your homework. Your research.

It works for Ms. Mentor.

Keep a Little Lust in Your Heart?

Q: If I yearn for someone I cannot have (my tarty student worker, my hot provost), should I confess my love and throw myself on his/her mercies, or is it better to suffer in soulful silence and sublimate my feelings into teaching and research and writing and getting tenure and moving on with my life?

A: Yes.

My Friend Has a Boy Toy

Q: A dear friend is in her first full-time teaching job at a community college. She is also having an affair with one of her students. He's twenty-six, so it's not illegal and "not against the rules," she keeps saying. Since the fall semester is over and he's no longer in her class, she says I shouldn't object—but I do. I think she's starting her career in the worst possible way.

Background: Her degree is from a school where the writing professors have been sleeping with students for years. One serial offender is department chairman now, and openly living with his latest young thing. But those are male professors, and the rules are always different for women.

Is there any possible way to talk her out of this? She is teaching a heavy course load of writing classes, she doesn't know very many people in her new location, and I think this affair is her only source of fun. I don't want to be a pill, but I don't want to watch her torpedo her career, either. Oh, also, she's a poet, if that makes a difference. I suspect it does.

A: Some poets are romantic, some are pigheaded, and some are saintly. They're a lot like other people, full of trembling emotions and inconsistent principles that collide and sweat against each other—especially about "sexual harassment" or "fraternization" or "true love at any age." Even nonpoets can be pilloried as heartless prudes or hopeless romantics.

Ms. Mentor chooses to be a fuddy-duddy.

She thinks teachers and students shouldn't touch each other with anything stronger than their own minds.

Underaged students should always be protected, especially now that female teachers and their boy toys have become sensational media fodder. *Notes on a Scandal* is an elegant, chilling book and movie about an art teacher and her teenaged protégé. In real life, art teacher Mary Kay LeTourneau went to jail for statutory rape, did her time, and emerged to marry her former pupil who, at thirteen, had fathered her child.

Ms. Mentor is unmoved by the usual excuses: "I was lonely" or "I'm a free spirit, and rules are for fools" or "I couldn't help myself. S/he's so hopelessly hot." Some male professors argue that "I was teaching her about men, introducing her to the best that life has to offer." If the experience is so enriching, Ms. Mentor thinks, then why isn't Professor Playboy required to have sex with all his students?

Ms. Mentor believes that students deserve to be taught, not groped— but some artistic souls, mostly men in certain avant-garde and very high-tuition programs in woodsy areas, have always viewed students as their "playground." Yet what seems like paradise to certain philandering men can be a pit of jealousy, grief, self-loathing, and wrist-slitting, especially for vulnerable young women—the ones most likely to be poets. ("A woman who writes feels too much," wrote the gifted, suicidal Anne Sexton.)

Perhaps there's no such angst going on with your friend (call her "Miranda," since she needs her rights explained). One could argue that Miranda is generously bringing to a community college the free-loving mores of elite, artsy colleges. But vulnerable students at Artsy U. usually have family money, access to therapy, and ways to escape from painful emotional cesspools. They can graduate or drop out, leave town, and start anew.

Miranda's young man probably doesn't have those escape hatches. He presumably lives in the community, has family and friendship ties—a chorus of people to cheer, judge, and hoot about his romance with Miranda. There may also be awkward and serious class differences which can't be ignored.

But the young man in this scenario has not asked for Ms. Mentor's advice. Nor has Miranda, who should have—because professors should know better. Especially for female professors, dignity and discretion matter. Lawsuits and scandals loom. And after a bitter breakup, anyone can be driven to stalking, threats, middle-of-the-night phone calls, and brutal sidewalk confrontations.

You, Miranda's friend, asked for the magic words to get through to her. You're faced with what it means to be a good friend. Can you watch your friend hurtle toward what looks like a wildly exciting train wreck?

You can recommend books and movies and counseling. You can suggest that Miranda sublimate her desires into frenzied, excited grading of student compositions. (Yes, Ms. Mentor knows that won't work.) You can pass along Ms. Mentor's advice to stop now, before you create a trail of rumors that will tag along behind you for the rest of your career. ("Helen," who routinely seduced her teaching assistants twenty years ago, still hasn't been promoted to full professor, despite a huge publication record . . . maybe because people whinny and blush when her name is mentioned.)

There are few secrets in academe, and a reputation for sexual harassment can keep one from getting another job, or grants, or a relatively serene life. One can be addicted to the excitement, but it is a far, far better thing to regard it as literary material. Countless poems have been wrung out of emotion recollected in tranquility.

Yes, scholars do "date" and marry students. Some have successful long-term relationships. But some end very badly.

In the short run, you may have to decide whether you can be Miranda's confidante. Sometimes tough love means leaving the scene until the storm stops swirling. If her life makes you ache and shudder, you have to protect yourself first.

And, yes, there will always be people who consider you a hopeless meddler and busybody, trying to force your ideas on others, as if you have superior wisdom.

Ms. Mentor doesn't listen to them, either.

Should Your Private Life Be Public News?

Q (from "Lavinia"): Because I teach courses on the history of sex, my students want to talk about their unfinished business—particularly date rape and sexual assaults. I'm a sexual-abuse survivor myself, but I don't talk about that in class. I wonder how open I should be with students who hesitate to go to therapists and prefer to confide in me.

Q (from "Matt"): I'm a grad student contemplating an academic career. I also practice S-and-M, responsibly and carefully. If I get a college teaching job, what are the chances that this will cause some dreadful scandal?

A: Ms. Mentor sighs and recalls the sage counsel drummed into all her age-mates, during the late Victorian era: "Don't do it in the road. You'll frighten the horses."

The subject is discretion: What to share with whom, and whether your private life should be up for discussion. While doing her daily deletion of e-mailed ads for nude celebrities, Ms. Mentor observes sourly that sex has become the most public subject in American life—yet one with the fewest clear rules.

Lavinia is wisely considering the power and propriety of a professor's role when students want to talk about intense and painful personal problems. Many a newish faculty member revels in that kind of sharing, the chance to mentor those not too much younger. It can be one of the thrills of teaching.

And yet faculty motives are not all pure. Lavinia may be warm and compassionate, but other young professors may be seeking ego boosts at their students' expense. Even Lavinia, as she admits, is not a trained therapist. This does not mean that she is unable to help: a listening ear is a gift. But Lavinia may not recognize psychological patterns that a trained therapist would see, and she cannot prescribe anything.

In worst cases, too, universities have been sued for not providing adequate psychiatric help for students who ultimately took their own lives.

Ms. Mentor suggests that Lavinia seek out compassionate and trained counselors on her campus, or in town—at, for instance, battered-women's programs. Invite counselors to come to her classes as guest speakers, so that students will know who is available and approachable.

While Ms. Mentor knows that rape crisis centers would not exist without the brave speak-outs and consciousness-raising of women's groups in the 1970s, she now believes that a certain distance should be kept.

But if Lavinia is teaching older students in a community college in a big city, then she may decide to trust her good instincts and find a discreet balance between the professor and the helper. Informally, in her office, she may want to use the standard formula for talking about oneself without talking about oneself: "I have this friend who had a problem . . ."

As for Matt, he, too, must be infinitely discreet if he insists on practicing his sadomasochism. Ms. Mentor feels that his sex life is not her business, or anyone's, if he is doing whatever he is doing with consenting adults. But he should not be doing it with students, *ever*, and he should not be flaunting it in college towns and scaring the horses.

Young faculty members are often horrified when their students perceive them as graders and judges, rather than as human beings with all the essential drives. Teachers who step outside the reward-or-punish role to become friends with students may enjoy a fulfilling camaraderie, especially in sports.

But if you become a sexual partner, or a comrade in confessions, or a fellow participant in odd rituals, you have overstepped the boundaries that allow students to make their own choices. You have interfered with their intellectual growth for your own purposes, and that is wrong.

Sometimes it can become reptilian.

Professor Pelvic Practices His Thrusts

Q (from "Joanne"): My best friend ("Karen") has a thesis adviser who kind of creeps her out. Yesterday they were in his office, discussing her first chapter, when he stood up, threw around a few couch cushions, and asked if she minded if he stretched out on the floor—because he has back problems, and that would make him feel better. Though she thought it was odd, she went on discussing her work.

But a couple of minutes later, she noticed he was doing pelvic thrusts. "This really helps my back," he said. "I hope you don't mind the informality." Of course she did mind, a lot. He was also looking up her skirt. "Let's reschedule," she suggested, but he refused. Is this all weird? What could she have done?

Q: (from "Karen"): I know my friend Joanne's already written, and I wanted to add that my thesis adviser has never made direct inappropriate comments to me. (I don't consider the pelvic thrusting direct, because he did give the old "I have a herniated disk" excuse.) He also kept apologizing for his informality. But I think he should have told his student (me) to wait outside while he stretched his back.

I have always had this uncomfortable vibe around him, and so do other female grad students. One even filed a complaint against him, and found out that there were similar reports from previous years. But the other faculty members don't seem to care, and I don't think I can do anything. I need his knowledge for my thesis now, and I'll need his reference letters for future jobs. Wouldn't it look odd if I didn't have my adviser's recommendation?

It's hard to focus on writing and seeing this through, because I really want nothing to do with him. Of course I'll finish, because my topic interests me, and I need the degree for my career. But is there anything else I can do?

A: Ms. Mentor is warmed by the knowledge that Karen is not a lonely planet in the academic universe. Joanne is a loyal listener, and Karen wisely tells her all about the peccadilloes of "Professor Pelvic." When victims remain silent, and when friends do not rally, sleazy behavior proliferates and cross-pollinates, and everyone winds up covered with slime.

Unlucky Karen is indeed a victim of "inappropriate behavior" by Professor Pelvic. He is a teacher, entrusted with her intellectual growth. He should not be mounting a bump-and-grind sideshow. While he has not made a direct sexual overture, his shenanigans have limited Karen's ability to focus on her tasks. He has, therefore, denied her equal educational opportunity—at which point some of Ms. Mentor's more fire-breathing readers will shout, "File a grievance!" or "Sue his pants off!" (A few may even mutter darkly, "Where's Lorena Bobbitt!") These readers will cry for justice. And revenge.

But Ms. Mentor urges them to take deep breaths, shake themselves, and look again. Karen is at a fork in the road, with two choices—or two narratives, or two paradigms.

The high road—the dashing road, the sweeps-all-before-it road—is the narrative of justice, or the pursuit of revenge. Karen may choose to cast herself as a gallant knight, righting all wrongs. If Karen chooses to gallop down this fork, she will file a grievance against Dr. Pelvic, probably for creating a "hostile environment."

Then she will meet with other professors in her department, learn how to write up official paperwork and memorandums, consult human-resource specialists, and perhaps hire a lawyer (almost certainly at her own expense). Eventually she'll have at least one hearing before a university disciplinary committee.

Karen will wind up surrendering her thesis time. She will be fighting instead of writing. Certainly she will embarrass Dr. Pelvic, but it is unlikely that he'll be punished in any other way, for what he did is not a "crime." Academic committees are rarely courageous, and they usually side with the entrenched one, not with the outsider.

A fire-breathing Karen will also have to answer naysayers and belittlers: "Well, he's just an unusual guy. What's the big deal?"

Most teeth-gritting of all: Karen will have made a life's enemy of Dr. Pelvic. She will lose his intellectual guidance, and if he writes recommendation letters for her at all, they'll be lukewarm ("Karen completed her thesis"). To future employers, it will seem as if Karen has done something to alienate or enrage her own mentor.

It will look like Karen is impossible to work with. Does Karen want to be a martyr?

The other fork is less morally satisfying. To political activists, and to academic revolutionaries, it will seem to be a repugnant sellout. (The word "careerist" is already springing to some fevered lips, Ms. Mentor knows—and she herself is tempted to stamp her foot and throw a rock.)

Nevertheless . . . Karen needs Dr. Pelvic's knowledge, she needs to finish her thesis, and she needs his recommendation. How can she achieve those goals?

She needs a cool head and a plan. She must make appointments with Dr. Pelvic only during the busiest school hours. She should bring a friend, who'll wait outside his office. If he starts to close the door, Karen can call, "Joanne, I'll be just a minute!"

To insensitive souls like Dr. Pelvic, Joanne may seem to be a chaperon—even a duenna. But Karen knows what else she is: a potential witness.

Karen has already been impeccably professional ("I'll come back later"). If Dr. Pelvic begins his thrusts, Karen can say, crisply, "Oh, I see this isn't a good time. I'll call for an appointment later on." And walk out.

Maybe this kind of tacky melodrama can be character-building, Ms. Mentor observes wanly. Dr. Pelvic's crude behavior does force Karen to set schedules ("We'll discuss Chapter 2 at 1 P.M. on Thursday, agreed?"). The presence of an ogre does goose grad students to finish faster, to escape his foul clutches. What Dr. Pelvic puts out is a whip rather than a carrot—but both can make a grad student think, write, move, and finish faster.

Every profession has its peculiar characters, with whom nonweirdos must learn to cope. Karen and Joanne are learning to protect their intellectual integrity and keep their eyes on the prize.

They will not be defenseless, ever.

The world's Dr. Pelvics do fear exposure and paper trails. Karen should find out where she can file a confidential complaint—so that there'll be a record, but not one that Dr. Pelvic can use for retaliation. She should check the student handbook; ask at her women's center or women's-studies program; and consult her university's human-resources office.

But Ms. Mentor exhorts Karen, and Joanne, not to make it a crusade to persecute Dr. Pelvic (although he deserves it). Research, not revenge, has to be Karen's theme. She and Joanne may also find it energizing to put up, everywhere they can, posters of Xena, Warrior Princess and Buffy the Vampire Slayer. Fierce is good.

Once Karen is a professor herself, she'll be in a position to prevent future Dr. Pelvics from being hired and tenured. Justice delayed is not always justice denied. And Dr. Pelvic, by forcing Karen to strategize, is motivating and molding her into a wise professional.

He's being, of all things, a mentor.

—

Reader Response: One reader wrote to rave about pelvic thrusts ("They cured my back!"). Another blamed Karen for wearing skirts instead of pants. Several reported similar incidents in their own careers, and a few insisted that Karen drop Dr. Pelvic as her adviser, immediately. But Dr. Pelvic is the only professor in Karen's intellectual area, the only one qualified to direct her thesis. If Karen dumps him, she will have to change her field, junk her research, and pursue something far less engaging. This is sex discrimination of the rankest kind—a throwback to the days when female medical students were kept from studying urology, because men did not want women poking around their nether regions.

If Dr. Pelvic's bad behavior means that Karen cannot study his field, he will have won.

My Colleague Sleeps with Students

Q (from "Catherine"): Newly hired at "Roseflower U.," I find that a colleague ("Floyd") is sleeping with one of his students. Roseflower has strict rules against these relationships, and I'm wondering what, if anything, I should do. I've encouraged those with firsthand knowledge to speak to the ombudsman, but graduate students are terrified of "Hurricane Floyd," who routinely berates and humiliates them. I dread being stuck with him for the next thirty years, but he comes up for tenure before I do, and he'll be voting on whether I get tenure.

A: Ms. Mentor praises conscientious Catherine for doing what she can through official channels: evidently the ombudsman is supposed to defend student rights. Catherine herself, new and untenured, has no powerful swords of her own to brandish. But no one can stop her from asking senior colleagues, innocently and frequently, "Why does Dr. Floyd yell so much? Is there anything we can do to make him less angry?"

Concerned students might also want to post the sexual-harassment/fraternization policy everywhere around the department. Maybe under Floyd's picture, on his office door.

If Floyd is known to be overbearing and embarrassing, students will shun his classes, parents may complain, and colleagues certainly won't want him around for thirty years. He won't get tenure, and Catherine and future students will be spared. There is power in chatter.

Randy Likes Priss

Q (from "Randy"): I've come back to town as a full-time staffer at "Little Religious College," and I'm very attracted to "Dr. Priss," who taught a poetry course I took a few years ago. Even though I'm still a (nontraditional) student, is it OK to tell her I admire her, and want to meet her off-campus?

A: Ms. Mentor suggests that you do your homework: consult Little Religious College's handbook for the rules against sexual harassment and fraternization. For you, an illicit tryst might be an adventure. But for her, a romance with a student might be the end of her career.

You can, however, honor Dr. Priss by rereading passionate poetry. A lesser man might fume that he's been thwarted. But a truly passionate soul, one who earns the approbation of Ms. Mentor, will find that the bittersweet poetry of renunciation springs to his lips and heals him. "I could not love thee, dear, so much, loved I not honor more" strikes just the right note.

You should recite it to yourself, renounce your longing for Dr. Priss, say, "Screw it," and go have a beer.

My Mentor and My Lover

Q (from "Hilda"): My mentor, a brilliant woman who may rival even Ms. Mentor in her acumen, is pushing me to apply for jobs only in the top programs in my field. But those are all far from where I want to live, with my partner. My mentor says I must not de-prioritize my career for a relationship, as so many women do—but my partner wants me back home, living with her. How do I choose between a gifted mentor and a cherished partner?

A: You are trying to please two mistresses, with your mentor and your partner. One represents the public world of work and esteem; the other represents the private world of hearth and home. And we all want nurturing love and meaningful work. And virtually every sage, including Sigmund Freud (*Civilization and Its Discontents*) and Mick Jagger ("You can't always get what you want"), has told us that we must choose.

Ms. Mentor will not choose for you, but congratulates you for having both an esteemed mentor and a beloved partner. You have a richness in your life that few women possess.

Hovering Hubby

Q: My spouse wants to come to my on-campus interview with me, so he can see for himself whether he'd like the place and the people. Since I haven't been offered the job yet, will a hiring committee (a) welcome my husband, or (b) dismiss me as an unprofessional little woman who's the tool of a busybody control freak?

A: (b).

I Can't Do the Faculty Wife Thing

Q: My husband is finishing grad school and will go on the market this year. Assuming he gets a job, he will be wading into the murky waters of academic protocol, and I am concerned about my role. I am disabled by mental illness and agoraphobia, and I'm getting treatment, but I'm afraid that my inability to attend (or host) gatherings will be held against him. How much are spouses still expected to participate in the social aspect of an academic career?

A: Lurking behind your question, Ms. Mentor knows, is the Angel in the House, that vicious Victorian image of domestic perfection. The Angel is that siren in your head that shrieks when you put yourself first. The Angel sneers at live-and-let-live housekeeping, calls you selfish for wanting a career, and faints when she learns that your children, like those of the late great Erma Bombeck, send Mother's Day cards to Colonel Sanders.

She makes women feel guilty and inadequate, and she's trying to do that to you.

But, in fact, you are a perfectly lovely person who wants to do right, and what's troubling you is the nature of the game. Luckily academia has changed since the days when there were but two images for a faculty wife, both rudely incarnated in Edward Albee's play *Who's Afraid of Virginia Woolf?* You could be Honey (Sandy Dennis in the movie), the whiny, self-sacrificing little woman who devotes her life to upholstering hubby's ego and papering over his faux pas. Or you could be Martha (Elizabeth

Taylor), the randy, drunken harpy who gets all the best and meanest lines while torturing an ambitious young prof and his little wifey.

Both are overwrought dramatizations, but they are a window into what faculty wifeys of the past had to do. They were expected to raise bright, perky children, welcome stray students, and bake pies at the drop of a homesick tear. They were supposed to contrive exquisite, homemade meals, served on antique silver with napkins stitched by twelfth-century French nuns. And then, in the after-dinner glow, all the wives were to listen attentively, passionately, to the pontifications of husbands and their male colleagues. Nancy Reagan, with her adoring gaze, was the paragon of the perfect wifey.

After dinner at some colleges, there was also—supposedly—"wife swapping." But Ms. Mentor has never been able to obtain the videos.

All that wifey work has faded, to the joy of women everywhere. Universities that once bragged that they didn't do partner hires ("we choose only the best") have lost their best and brightest to places that caught on first ("make 'em happy and they'll stay here on weekends and not put the moves on their students"). Ambitious women who can be cardiologists, computer whizzes, and corporate attorneys won't twiddle their thumbs as "captive spouses." Foreign-service wives and university upper administrators' wives may still have to do the elaborate hostessing. But for faculty wives and the rest of womankind, Ms. Mentor is happy to say, Hillary Rodham Clinton as First Lady was much more the norm—a wife with a life of her own.

Which means that your disabilities need not disable or derail your husband's career. At the junior (assistant professor) level, few departments expect to meet a spouse or partner before hiring a candidate. Many departments will help with finding a house, but hubby's house hunting by himself is not all that rare. Nor is hubby's going to social events alone, as long as he's sociable. He should make friends with his new colleagues—have lunch with them frequently—and make himself liked. It may be useful to have a cover story—"My wife is very shy" or "My wife has migraines"—for, as you and Ms. Mentor know, there is still a stigma attached to mental illness. And while it's useful to educate people, you might want to wait until he's established in the department.

As a twenty-first-century wife, you have no ironclad obligations. Extremely charming partners can help a career, and extremely surly ones can harm it, but most are neutral. If you can manage a small dinner party, four to six people, that would be welcome—but no one expects big bashes. If you bake cookies for hubby to take into the department office, everyone will be delighted. If there's a choice, you'll do best at a large public university in a big city—for small, churchly private colleges do expect a more traditional family image. Beware, too, of gossip networks in small towns, where medical confidentiality can be a myth.

But the world is far more open for faculty wives than it was in the 1960s, and you needn't be the Angel in the House or Honey or Martha. You can be yourself.

Am I Married to an Academic Failure?

Q (from "Daisy"): When "Chuck" and I married, I was a nurse in Well-Known City, with lots of money, friends, and self-confidence. Chuck was a plodding, nerdy grad student with a lot of potential. By the time he finished his degree and got a tenure-track post at Semi-Rural U., we had two small children. I quit my job to raise them, thinking we'd make a lovely nuclear family. We do—except that I never see Chuck. I'm coming to think I don't miss him.

Chuck is in a very demanding field (he says), and he's in the office day and night, working on articles that he hasn't sent out. When he comes home, he's tired and snarly. I thought summertime would be for rest and reconciliation, but now he's taking a student group to Australia, a place with no connection to his research, and no brownie points toward tenure. He wants to impress "Professor Big"—but even Big says Chuck needs to publish, not travel. Big has also called Chuck a "wimp" for not taking stands on department issues. Chuck seems to be alienating everyone.

It looks like I have a husband who's not apt to get tenure. What should I do?

A: Ms. Mentor sees some old and familiar life patterns: disillusionment, overwork, geographical discontent, and what Chaucer called the "wo that is in mariage." And it's all happening so fast.

Within the five pretenure years, Chuck has to get great teaching evaluations (or at least passable ones, if he's at a large research university). He has to do enough publication and research to impress his colleagues as well as peers at other universities who'll write tenure support letters. He has to do enough service (committee work) to seem energetic and committed to his department's "mission" (which may or may not be evident). And he has to be viewed as "collegial"—bright, cheerful, easy to get along with.

Ms. Mentor knows that many an adviser would tell you, Mrs. Chuck, to "Get off his back" or "Get up and invite his colleagues to dinner, at least." Indeed, there are always rumors—and academic novels—in which the loyal, hysterical faculty wife offers favors to the boss "if you'll give my husband tenure." You shudder.

But "this, too, shall pass," cooler heads will tell you. Once Chuck is tenured, they say, you'll have back the gawky love bunny you married so happily a decade or so ago.

Ms. Mentor is not so sure. Having observed countless human pratfalls, she does not believe in total transformations of character (except, maybe, from miraculous or horrific encounters with drugs). The priorities, the pacing, the social skills that one has in grad school—those are what people are.

So what is Chuck? By your account, he's nerdy—which Ms. Mentor takes to mean socially inept. Most academics are, so he does fit in. But he also seems to be academically slow, toiling endlessly instead of writing up and sending out the smallest publishable unit. Chuck may be a single-minded perfectionist—and right now, you and the little ones aren't really on his screen.

'Tis a melancholy fact that the pretenure period, like the prepartner stage in a law firm or the residency stage of a medical career, can be all-consuming. There is something to be said for a monkish dedication to career and career alone at that time in life—except that biological clocks won't allow it.

And so the children are with you, and Chuck is not.

You can, of course, nag Chuck (by e-mail, since you don't see him). Maybe you can get him to go to counseling. You can hope that he'll find another academic job after this one implodes. Or that he'll find something outside academe. You can offer him physical or emotional bribes. You can go home to Mother.

You can also recite Ann Landers's well-known question: Are you better off with him or without him?

Ms. Mentor thinks you know what you must do, to save your sanity and your security.

You must go back to your nursing career, at least part-time.

Academia can erode the self-confidence of graduate students, assistant professors, and their families. But with less financial pressure, and with a wife who has an outside life, Chuck may pull himself together. Or he may not.

But you cannot simply wait and hope, for your youngsters need you. Academic tenure may come or it may not, but the happiest people are those whose moms made them feel loved and safe. That's lifetime security, and it's the best tenure on earth.

—

Reader Response: "You're a moron," several readers wrote to Ms. Mentor, or words to that effect. "It's obvious Chuck is having an affair." Ms. Mentor does not admit to being a moron, but she concedes that Chuck's lack of attention to home life suggests—attention elsewhere. She does not know what finally happened with Chuck and Daisy, whose problems she wrote about in 2004.

Etiquette for Academic Couples

Q: Would you consider riffing for a bit on etiquette for dual-career couples, especially those who are in the same department? Some of us share one position; others were brought in as part of a partner/spouse's deal and are leery of stepping on toes. Aside from the obvious pitfalls (calling each other "honey" or "sweetheart" in the mail room, for example), could you help academic couples chart a path together, so that both people wind up being valued departmental citizens?

A: For Valentine's Day and every other day, Ms. Mentor proffers this advice for all academic duos sharing romance and work:

Couples of the world, untie!

Ms. Mentor does not mean that all couples should divorce, annul, move out, take vows of celibacy, form nonmonogamous groupings, or denounce one another on Fox News. She is a tolerant soul who will permit couples to live together and even have the same children. But on the job, they must individuate.

Ms. Mentor, in her perfect wisdom, knows what evils lurk if they fail to do so. To wit:

- "Delphine," a brilliant historian finishing her Ph.D., could not understand why she got no job interviews, while her husband, "Robert"—competent, but not outstanding—scored half a dozen. And then Delphine's mentor checked her dossier, in which "Professor Tradition" had written: "Mrs. Jones is quick, yes, but Mr. Jones, in his quieter and less flashy way, will make a far better scholar in the long run. You really should hire him."
- "Howard" and "Rose," both Ph.D.'s in the natural sciences, applied for jobs at the same universities. Several departments expressed an interest in Howard, and added that Rose would make an excellent research associate—"paid for through Howard's grants, of course."
- "Estelle" and "Ralph," both psychologists, were hired at the same time by Small Town College. Four years later, Estelle had published six articles and won a teaching award. Ralph had published only two. But when it was suggested that Estelle be put up for early tenure, several department members objected: "Think what it will do to Ralph's ego."

Are men's egos really more fragile than women's? Are women's talents really less worthy than men's? Ms. Mentor groans and moves on to strategies.

Ms. Mentor's Don'ts for Academic Couples

- Do not take anyone else's last name. Careers last much longer than marriages in our interesting times, and you should never surrender your identity. Besides, you want your high-school classmates to eat their hearts out when they know it's you, up there with your Nobel Prize.
- Try not to share an office, for that evokes dark, conspiratorial mumblings ("they'll vote as a bloc on curriculum revision"). Among

older colleagues who think all young people look alike, you won't be recognized as separate creatures (you'll be "Fran-and-Tony" and "Bill and What's Her Name"). Moreover, if you're in different offices, you'll be able to collect twice as much gossip and department lore—to share at night, in secret orgies of collaborative research.

- Do not ask for special privileges, such as dovetailed schedules.
- Do not fight each other's battles, nor engage in supportive sulks, feuds, or whispering campaigns.
- Do not indulge in public displays of affection, even handholding. If endearments such as "cutie pie" or "hot bunny" do slip out, a few colleagues will chuckle, but young students will be horrified. How could anyone as old as their parents possibly have a sex drive?

Ms. Mentor's Do's for Academic Duos

- Do play on the department's softball team together, if you're both good athletes.
- Do volunteer for different committees, preferably visible ones where your diverse skills will be recognized. This is especially important for trailing spouses ("coat-tailers" or "captive spouses").
- Do vote differently on department issues, especially the unimportant ones.
- Do loosen up a bit after tenure, if you can. "Prudence" and "Preston," two earnest souls who were known for discussing department bylaws in bed, finally learned to make fun of themselves: "Do you really want to put a comma all the way in there?"

But, Ms. Mentor, what about same-sex couples?

Often they have extra burdens, as interracial couples did in the past. There will be colleagues who believe that their partnership should not exist. But their job responsibilities are the same as those of straight people: teaching, research, and service. They should not have to defend their relationship, *ever*.

Finally, what about the couples who meet on the job—who catch each other's eyes across the crowded department meeting room? Well, as countless melodramas and lawsuits have shown, there are risks: sexual harassment, conflict, and heartbreak.

Far be it from Ms. Mentor to deny the lure and the lust that animate human hearts. And yet it is a sign of the times that, just before Valentine's Day one year, one of Ms. Mentor's most eloquent correspondents sent along the following proclamation:

"I am following the advice of my sister, who said, 'Never screw anyone you work with, in any way, shape, or form.' "

Her Partner Stole My Job

Q (from "The Patsy"): I've been skunked, and not for the first time, by an academic couple.

I made the shortlist for a tenure-track job at Very Good School. But the position was yanked to create a job in another subfield for "Tommy," a known mediocrity whose only merit is being married to "Trish," a prodigy who's won teaching awards and research grants. Knowing that "Tommy" got my job sticks in my craw and fills my soul with bile.

I remain an angry adjunct. Besides starting an Academic Assassins for Hire franchise ("Murders by top Ph.D.'s only!"), what can I do?

A: Ms. Mentor believes that Academic Assassins for Hire, while it has a certain Darwinian charm, is not a good career move. Nor are spouse or partner hirings always evil. A few examples:

- Before the wife of "Dr. Nobel Prize Winner" joined him as a professor at Big Ivy, Dr. Prize Winner had been taking off for three- and four-day weekends, leering at young women, and losing his students' research proposals. Once the Prize Winners were together under one roof, she had time to finish her book and Dr. Prize Winner regained his zest for attracting grant money and sharing it with the best and brightest students.
- Whenever "Dr. J. Crackerjack" moved to a higher administrative job at a new college, she insisted that the history department hire her husband, who was studying academic bureaucracies. He was a great raconteur with a historian's extraordinary memory, and he was full

of academic gossip that delighted students and made him the hit of every dinner party.

But "The Patsy" needn't fear the Crackerjacks or the Prize Winners. Her competitors are the Twinklers, people who may rise to stardom—or burn out ignominiously, sometimes over thwarted romances. Of the thousands who meet in grad school and fall in love with each other's minds, Ms. Mentor wonders how many know how hard it will be to combine love and work. Most will never again be academic peers on the same campus.

Some colleges make gracious accommodations. When "Evelyn" got a tenure-track job, she negotiated an instructorship for her "Everett," also a Ph.D. He volunteered to be the department Web master, and is now one of the top "computer guys" on the campus. Flexible and adroit, he built his own ladder and climbed it.

Others try but fumble. "Kyle" and "Kathy" were both hired at Half-Great U., where Kyle was tenured first—but his boorish behavior so annoyed his colleagues that they voted not to tenure Kathy. Both eventually got jobs at Minor U., where Kathy is still bitter and Kyle has found another woman. And so has Kathy.

Ms. Mentor's point is that no one can predict how Twinklers will turn out, nor whether they'll stay together. And if they do, will they form a voting bloc to do egregious or sadistic things?

Meanwhile, hiring frenzies are not universal. Bidding wars are rare at regional universities, and almost unknown in community colleges. Hiring may also vary for different kinds of couples: Ms. Mentor hopes that Margaret and Mitzi, or Bill and Bob, would get the same considerations in the recruitment game as a straight couple, but she has doubts.

As for Ms. Mentor's original correspondent: "The Patsy" did apply in good faith to Very Good School—where administrators cancelled one job, created another they did not advertise, and handed it to "Tommy Mediocrity," because he's married to "Trish," a fledgling star. Ms. Mentor trusts her readers to comment on whether this is legal. She questions whether it is moral.

If Very Good School is in a rural area, perhaps Tommy and Trish can double as de facto house parents and advisers. If it's a religious college, they may be role models. Tommy may eventually make an excellent daddy.

Yet he lacks the academic expertise that Patsy has. If she does not get a job, she will be lost to the world of scholarship forever. Students won't be able to study her subfield nor share her research.

Dual-career couples do struggle, everywhere. Hockey great Wayne Gretzky left the Edmonton Oilers to be with his ambitious wife, Janet Jones, in Los Angeles. Julia Roberts and former husband Lyle Lovett reportedly split up because they never saw each other. Yet some marriages survive because the principals live apart, and meet only for romantic weekend trysts. There is no longer one model for a family, nor for a successful scholar—and Ms. Mentor wonders if Patsy, living alone and focusing on her career, might do more for students than someone whose tasks include shoring up a mediocre partner.

Ms. Mentor has received hundreds of letters on "the two-body problem," the most popular subject in her mailbox. Among the best sources are Constance Coiner and Diana Hume George, *The Family Track*; Robert Drago, *Striking a Balance: Work, Family, Life*; and Mary Ann Mason and Eve Mason Ekman, *Mothers on the Fast Track: How a New Generation Can Balance Family and Careers*. Ms. Mentor also encourages vociferous public discussion (besides the usual scheming and backbiting) whenever a "spousal hire" is suggested.

Some might point Patsy toward a lawyer, but Ms. Mentor wants her to persevere in her writing, for publication is the only tangible step toward stardom. Work is also consoling, while thoughts of revenge simply rile up the stomach. Ms. Mentor cheers The Patsy for her sense of humor, her independence, and her feistiness—qualities admirable in academics, and in real humans as well.

—

Reader Response: "I would contend that King Charles I got more from his executioners than Patsy did from you," wrote one furious reader. "You should stop sage pontificating and pious clucking, and go to battle with the cult of mediocrity, narrow-mindedness, and downright stupidity that permeates the U.S. academic world."

Ms. Mentor welcomes suggestions as to how to do so.

The Best of Times, the Worst of Times

Q: Are there right times in an academic career to have a baby? To tell a hiring committee that you're part of a couple, and you'll need a job for your partner? To tell a hiring committee that you're pregnant, and need time off, and a job for your partner? To tell anyone that you're gay?

A: The best time to have a baby, many academic women say, is in graduate school, when your time may be more flexible. After tenure is often too late, and the rush to tenure is too stressful. Other women think being an "oops" teenaged bride "takes care of it, and then you're ready to roar."

Mothers in academia do pay a penalty. As Mary Ann Mason's research has shown, "maternal profiling," or being seen as a mom, can cost a woman her tenure-track job.

Most job candidates bring up the need for a partner's job during an on-campus visit—sometimes before, sometimes after, they've been offered the job. It takes intricate maneuvering, and it is rarely satisfying, especially for those in the humanities. Academic couples often wind up living and working apart.

Pregnancy, unless it already shows, needn't be mentioned until contract negotiation time. This is a good time to check the university's parental leave policies, which should be on the school's Web site or in the faculty handbook. Most schools can postpone the start of a job for a semester.

When to come out? That often depends on whether you want domestic partner benefits. Many candidates just say casually, "My partner's coming with me," and drop in the correct pronoun just as casually. If you don't have a partner needing a job or benefits, your private life is no one's business—but while you're on campus, you can ask to meet with directors of women's studies or gender studies or diversity, and ask about the local gay community. You can check the course listings for queer studies, and look in the phone book for student and community organizations. With the Internet, it's far more possible to suss out a community, look for legal rights, and find out the local lore—or discover the nearest large city where there will be bookstores, bars, activism, and more. But the best resource is always people—the gossipers and networkers who want to share.

Too Late, Baby

Q: According to the latest U.S. Department of Education figures, the average assistant professor is forty-three years old. Should we still postpone childbearing until after tenure?

A: No.

You're Hired!
Early Years in a Strange New World

When Should You Grab a Sword?

Q (from "Hotspur"): Because I wanted to get a jump on my new life, I moved to "Midsize University" in July. I'm a brand new assistant professor.

But in my very first week, I had a huge fight over a twenty-dollar purchase with my department chair, who informed me very rudely that I was "off to a bad start." Since then, "Dr. Chair" has tried to keep me in the dark about how the university operates, so he can maintain power over me. He micromanages endlessly and refuses to believe we need a secretary for our department (seven faculty members), which means that I have to do all of my own clerical work. He disparages everyone outside our department, and many of the people within it.

It's gotten so bad that even before classes started, I went to talk with our campus dispute mediator. I couldn't talk to any of the senior faculty members, who have bad blood between them. Until I found out about the mediator, I had to keep all this bottled up inside myself.

One possibility the mediator mentioned was having a different chair, which would improve things for me. But I worry that by going through mediation and forcing a change, I will be hated forever by Dr. Chair. Should I get out as quickly as possible?

Q (from "Harriet"): Though I'm a lowly graduate student, I've been made the coordinator in charge of the "Intro to Psychology" sections at my university. The professor who usually runs them ("Dr. Usual") is on sabbatical, and when no other professor wanted the job, it fell to me.

I'm in an awkward, fairly powerless position, especially because I also have to plan the course with "Dr. Counterpart," the coordinator on our sister campus. He's a tenure-track professor, and this semester it's his turn to come up with "Intro to Psych" experiments and exercises for both campuses.

The problem: The new teaching materials Dr. Counterpart sent me have major statistical flaws. When I asked about them, he said I'm wrong and he's right. And so I've consulted with Dr. Usual, who says she just ignores him, rewrites the experiments, and runs them correctly on our campus. She has been doing it this way for years.

I have stuck my neck out and done that, and am ready to be damned with the consequences if Dr. Counterpart finds out.

But I can't help thinking about the hundreds of students on the other campus. They are being taught wrong statistics, and I'm horrified at the way their papers are being graded. I can't sleep at night.

A: Ms. Mentor knows scores of academics who like to imagine themselves as powerful knights, sallying forth to right all wrongs and remove all ignorance from the land. It is a shiny picture, and far more heroic than the image of oneself as dissertation drudge or lab rat.

But it is not always clear what the battle is, or who should be fighting it. And so those who grab their swords prematurely can make themselves into gory and unpleasant spectacles.

Ms. Mentor knew, for instance, the notorious "Dr. Genghis," an assistant professor who burned with a fever against all injustices, including onerous forms, parking rules, and anything from his boss, "a craven tool of the crypto-fascist university administration." Since e-mail hadn't yet been invented, Dr. Genghis spent hours pounding out caustic memos on his sword-equivalent, a manual typewriter. By the time his colleagues voted not to renew his contract ("Who needs all this aggravation?"), Dr. Genghis's memos filled an entire shoebox. But he had no publications, no allies, and no job.

Hotspur is in the Dr. Genghis mold: slash first, ask questions later. Establish your turf, and fight all encroachments.

Yet there is a big difference between a deadly missile and a misfiled piece of paper. Many newly hired scientists do find that their lab space isn't what they were promised, and they have to take fighting stances.

Computers, library resources, and class size are all significant professional matters, and it is never belligerent or unseemly to say, "I need these to do the best job possible."

But Hotspur should not have drawn his sword over twenty dollars. Nor should he have proclaimed himself an expert on personnel management ("We need a secretary"). Nor should he be proclaiming that Dr. Chair is plotting "to maintain power over me." Nor should Hotspur file a complaint so early. That's the bureaucratic equivalent of declaring war: "Now I'm really gonna stick it to the king."

Hotspur has, in fact, stuck it to himself, and his wild scheme—to dethrone Dr. Chair—drives Ms. Mentor to pound on the table. She advises Hotspur to be silent; find stress-reduction exercises; do the best he can to make friends; and quietly look for another job. He has almost certainly poisoned his own well.

Ms. Mentor does not mean that new faculty members must swallow all insults or be silent when real injustices appear. Massive dishonesty, sexual harassment, racism, and homophobia should not be allowed to flourish unchallenged. But a sword is only useful when there is a genuine battle, and where the sword wielder has some hope of winning.

Goliath cannot be defeated by a toothpick.

Now, unlike Hotspur, Harriet is a good academic citizen. But she has become (as so many women do) a responsibility magnet. She has taken on an enormous chore that should never have been given to her in the first place. Ms. Mentor blames Harriet's university for putting a professionally vulnerable graduate student in charge of a major general-education program, instead of paying a faculty member to do it and allowing Harriet to continue her studies. "Looks good on the vita" is no excuse for exploitation.

Still, Harriet has been wise enough to get advice from Dr. Usual. Harriet has ensured that her students will be taught correctly. She has done all that she has the power to do. And yet . . . Harriet cannot sleep nights, for evil still exists in the world. She yearns to grab a sword and take off after the errors on the other campus.

Ms. Mentor does sympathize with Harriet: one does not like to think that students will be taught things that are not true. Yet youngsters cope with the knowledge that Santa Claus and the Easter Bunny are fakes. Chemists-in-training learn that Boyle's and Charles's laws don't really work. Historians now acknowledge that history doesn't happen only to white men. Moreover, the debates that excite chemists, historians, and other academic professionals usually bore, confuse, or repel students taking general-education courses, such as "Intro to Psychology."

Harriet may be comforted to know that few students remember much from "Intro to Psych." Unless it's titillating and spectacularly wrong—such as the concept of penis envy—much of what's taught is forgotten after each exam. Harriet has Ms. Mentor's permission not to grab her sword.

Often the best weapon is patience.

—

Reader Response: Soon after her story appeared in Ms. Mentor's column in 2000, Harriet wrote that Professor Counterpart turned out to be a fraud. He had failed his dissertation defense and had been claiming a Ph.D. he did not possess. Alerted by an anonymous tipster, the local newspaper gleefully pursued the story, and Harriet, although feeling a "bit soiled," was able to concentrate on finishing her Ph.D. Three years later she was happily ensconced in a tenure-track job, and "I sleep the sleep of the just."

How Do I Make a Good First Impression?

Q: I'm a new assistant professor who's worried about how to behave. Is it possible to mess up so badly in the first semester that your career never recovers? What are the unforgivable sins?

A: Poor fashion sense isn't one of them, Ms. Mentor is happy to report. "Jeff" attended his very first faculty meeting wearing a wrinkled, raggedy shirt, buttoned wrong. And so, when he stood up to be introduced as the department's golden boy, a shiny new Ph.D.—his round, hairy tummy was the first thing everyone noticed.

But Jeff was a mathematician, hired by people who pride themselves on keeping their heads in the clouds and ignoring mundane reality. After a round of mild chuckling, Jeff got the hint to look down, and rebuttoned himself. The show was over.

Other faux pas, though, can linger, fester—and eviscerate a career.

No one is invisible at that first, fateful department meeting in late August or early September. The entrenched senior professors are rested and gazing about, testing their new bifocals on whoever's new or diverting. Mid-level professors sit, drumming fingers, aching to get back to their labs or their libraries or those great new sites on the Web. The caucus of malcontents—every group has them—is alert for new recruits, new people who'll "see through it all" and throw themselves into feuding and sniping. The department weasel is ready to make excuses about something, and the mom (who may be any gender) is primed to smile beatifically ("there, there").

But you, new on the job—you're in a frenzy. In the last six months, you've defended your dissertation, moved to a new part of the country, placated or junked relationship-mates, dealt with child and elder care, struggled with landlords, stood in line to register everything, tried to remember dozens of new colleagues' names, and developed new allergies hitherto unknown to humanity.

You also can't digest the local mussels, and the hard water leaves a scummy film in your hair. You thrash around half the night, obsessed with your syllabus and your courses and what to wear. You're convinced that you don't know enough to be a college professor. You'll be unmasked as a fraud. Everyone will see your tummy.

But on that first day when everyone's watching you—you must try to look like you fit in.

Unless you're at an artsy place, dress conservatively and professionally. Don't sport nose rings, skimpy shorts, or huge peacock tattoos. Don't be the young sociologist with the untamed beard who never lived down his first-week nickname ("Wolf Man"). And definitely don't wear a T-shirt saying, "English teachers do it with class." You'll never be taken seriously.

You also need to show that you're "collegial"—friendly, knowledgeable, good company. Even before the first meeting, introduce yourself to everyone you see in the halls of your building. If you're shy, practice your name with a smile, handshake, and conversational tag: "I'm Jane Tolliver, a new assistant professor in art history, and I've just come from Mid North Central State."

You'll keep getting the same reactions: "Where's that?" and "Great football team" and "Oh, yes, do you know old Percy Ravenswood?" But each chat makes you memorable, as a pleasant individual with a life history. It's even better to have a lively story about your colorful new neighbor or what you've already enjoyed in your new town. Stifle any impulse to be weepy or smutty.

In your first semester, your job is not to opine, but to listen. Avoid taking sides, since you don't know who's feuding with whom, or why. Get yourself a mentor, or several—senior professors who'll decode the academic enterprise for you, and tell you that words that seem distant and uncaring ("uncollegial," "inappropriate," "not germane") are in fact strong condemnations, not mealy-mouthed euphemisms.

A good mentor will also tell you about past department feuds and minefields, so that you don't naïvely rave to Professor E about the accomplishments of Professor R, her philandering ex-husband, to whom she hasn't spoken in five years.

Ask privately about department procedures. Never use meeting time to display your own ignorance, and don't make invidious comparisons, however tempting. Everyone already knows there's no good bouillabaisse to be had in your small town. Never say, "Why, at Elite Private U., my grad school, we had so many more computers on campus. This place is soooooo backward."

Maybe so, but you must assume that your new colleagues have been resourceful with the money and space they've been given. You weren't hired to be a savior, scold, or instant expert.

In your first year, you're a sponge, a grateful guest, and an anthropologist studying the lore and habits of the natives. Accept all offers of help, social events, and food, and be an enthusiastic recipient. Be the one charmer who adores Professor Francophile's snail salad.

Meanwhile, start your Tenure Diary at home, putting in all contracts, memoranda, and professional documents. Include your school's tenure and promotion policies, and study them. Quietly, nonconfrontationally, keep track of whether the rules are being followed. If things go awry, you'll need proof.

Your Tenure Diary is also the safe haven for your raw, unvarnished opinions: "Professor Q is very thoughtful, but Professor R works hard at seeming befuddled—what a clever ploy to avoid committee work!"

Create a Tenure Box for the big paperwork you need to save: publications, syllabi, reviews, grant proposals, new course requests, committee reports, student evaluations. Those are the materials that will always run and hide when you need them most.

Study the people who've recently gotten tenure. Use them as role models and learn about their teaching and research. Ponder these scenarios that Ms. Mentor finds in her files:

- "Russell," who came from a culture of complaining, was used to bemoaning, belittling, and satirizing. In his first department meeting, Russell groaned and rolled his eyes during the chair's announcements. At the reception afterwards, he groused loudly about "this hick town we're stuck in." His new colleagues felt wounded and insulted.
- "Nelly," overwhelmed by newbie anxiety, threw up three times on the morning of the first faculty meeting. When she was introduced, she stood up, smiled, and had to race from the room again.
- "Jared," who exuded self-confidence, snagged the seat next to "Cherie," a lovely and newly tenured associate prof. He couldn't resist smirking while a much older professor at the front of the room deplored all the outrageous salary discrepancies, unfair teaching loads, and perfidious deans. Jared leaned over and murmured kissingly to Cherie: "Who's the old goat?" She smiled glacially. "He's my husband."

Rude Russell went on to alienate so many colleagues that he was never even invited to lunch—a sure sign that he was being frozen out. After three years, his contract was not renewed.

Nervous Nelly grew calmer, because she had senior colleagues who cherished her and wanted her to succeed. They got her into a writing group, with deadlines, rules, and stern criticism; they protected her from too many committee assignments; and they shared teaching strategies and portfolios. By the time she got tenure, Nelly was beaming and self-confident.

As for Jared, he immediately became the butt of a thousand jokes—but his faux pas was so hilarious that it also became a beloved part of department lore. Jared's high spirits made him popular with students, and he was wise enough not to date them, ever. By the time Jared's contract was renewed, he'd grown a goatee, and happily announced that he looked forward to becoming an old goat himself.

In short, Jared and Nelly were good and cheerful department citizens who learned from their mistakes. Russell was annoying, boring, and apparently unteachable.

Ms. Mentor needn't mention that you can kill your career spectacularly—through felonies, for instance. Or you can watch it ooze away, as Russell did, because you don't know enough to learn as well as teach. Being a little clumsy or naïve can be charming. Thinking you know it all is unforgivable.

I'm New and I'm Wretched

Q: I've wanted to enter the gates of the Ivory Tower since the tender age of eight, and I've made it: I'm a tenure-track assistant professor at Large Research University with Solid Reputation. And I'm miserable.

None of the faculty members noticed that I arrived in town, much less invited me to lunch. Parking is expensive and hard to find. I'm not teaching any classes within my area of interest. Support staff are surly, unhelpful, and downright mean. The pay is low, the cost of living high, and my tribulations are met with sympathetic yet strangely gleeful laughter from my elder peers. I wonder if I really want to do this.

A: Ms. Mentor's diagnosis: Precocious Burnout, the new people's malaise. All professions put newbies through unpleasant and disillusioning apprenticeships, with low pay, snarly coworkers, wildly inappropriate assignments, and bad parking. Meanwhile, most new job holders also make horrific mistakes: the exasperated telemarketer, for instance, who ordered a customer to "Please pay promptly, peckerhead." Or the brand-new hospital nurse who lost a patient's head. "Dang, I know I put it down somewhere," she told her boss.

No such disasters will befall you in your first semester, especially if you watch more than you speak. You've landed in the one profession that rewards continual thinking and continual learning, at whatever level you're teaching. Be patient. The parking gets better with seniority, too.

To Know Him Isn't to Love Him

Q: "Professor Magnanimous" has been lying about himself in published columns, claiming he's much more popular, sincere, and generous than I know him to be. How can I choose between roaring laughter and vomiting bile?

A: Don't.

This Brings Me Nothing but Heartaches

Q: Three years after getting my Ph.D. in a scientific field, I finally landed a tenure-track assistant professorship at Big National U. The problem is that it stinks here. The facilities are poor (which I knew going in, but can't change). The graduate students are mediocre to uninspired (although I haven't any of my own, anyway). The faculty in my area ignore me when they aren't asking me to deliver guest lectures in their classes (I've never been to any of their homes). I'm on my third secretary, and this one isn't any good, either.

But that's not the bad part—which is that I'm buried in paperwork, an endless stream of forms for purchases, travel, time sheets, recruiting and outreach expenses, office furniture. Often I have to complete the same form two or three times because it routinely is misplaced by the business office or the dean's office or Lord knows where they go.

I can't get any face time with the department chairman (he says to talk to the senior colleagues). I'm so miserable and pessimistic that I can't bring myself to write what really counts: my research papers. Am I crazy for hating Big National U. and wanting to leave?

A: Ms. Mentor, who likes to find a flower in every sludge pot, gamely congratulates you on not getting sick: most wildly overworked first-year faculty get pneumonia or a killer flu. But you seem to have all the other common maladies: melancholy, fury, hatred of those above, and loathing of those below. No doubt you also have murderous impulses and you want to weep and you're always tired.

In short, you're mostly normal.

Scientists like to see themselves as hardheaded realists who emphasize researchable, provable facts, and fidget at any popular talk about feelings. (Watch Oprah? Never!) Unlike literary scholars who revel in irony, hidden meanings, and scandal ("Dentist Fills Wrong Cavity"), scientists are trained to ignore grief and anger, and never admit to schadenfreude. Emotions are taboo.

And so scientists can be thoroughly unprepared for the blues that come when they finally land a post, and should be singing odes of joy.

You've probably been uprooted from a community where you were known, where they put up with your snarling and found it endearing. You may be with people who don't behave like those you've known before: easygoing Californians, taciturn Midwesterners, gossipy Southerners full of raunchy wit. Certainly you don't know the culture of your own university and the social and logistical expectations.

Ms. Mentor can tell, because you seem to have made some big mistakes.

You seem to have packed a negative attitude, a black cloud. As you expected, Big Nat's facilities are inadequate. The students must be dolts, even though you don't have any. Your rude colleagues and your boss shun you, paperwork disappears, and staffers flee—and yet you don't see the common story pattern. It could be a nightmare or a monstrous conspiracy, but it seems to Ms. Mentor that you've made enemies by—alas—being yourself.

On a typical day, do you scowl at the first friendly "How are you?" and go on to describe your mound of boring paperwork, your insomnia, your intestinal malfunctions? Do you greet everyone in the hall outside your lab—or do you stride by with furrowed brow, lab coat flapping, in deep thoughts that you cannot possibly interrupt for social froth?

Are you friendly and smiling with staffers and maintenance workers—or do you bark orders at them while not bothering to learn their names? (This is not uncommon in academe, and it makes Ms. Mentor furious.) Do you have coffee or lunch with colleagues, telling them entertaining stories while asking for advice and department lore—or do you lock your office door and brown bag it alone? Do you ask your colleagues to read over grant proposals and thank them warmly for suggestions—or do you argue with their criticism until you've worn them down? Do you make eye contact and listen intently to others? Do you remember what they said and follow it up later? ("How'd the game go?")

Besides your research, can you talk about many other things—or just sports? Do you imagine other people's points of view? (If you can't decode the meanings ["stories"] of others, Ms. Mentor recommends *Difficult Conversations: How to Discuss What Matters Most*, by Douglas Stone, Bruce Patton, and Sheila Heen. Many a scenario will be familiar.)

But most important, are you consistently upbeat, especially on gray and wintry days? No one wants to be around a constant carper. Smiling makes your face happier. Buy cookies. Wear something red.

You need to schmooze. You need to be liked. And, yes, good manners and professional smarts do mean having contingency plans and forgiving others' trespasses. Keep second copies of everything, swallow your doubts, and trust secretaries to handle your papers. Impatience with others' "incompetence" makes you seem sour and difficult, and encourages your underlings to "forget" and "lose" things. You must cherish administrative assistants and clerical workers and let them mentor you, for they know how bureaucracies work. They also know the staff in other offices, and together they can make your paperwork an easy ride—unless you irritate or patronize them. Then your paperwork empire will turn into a living hell.

Finally, if no one likes you, you're unlikely to get tenure. Such decisions do involve "collegiality"—whether your colleagues want you around for the rest of their careers.

Right now you may believe that A Bigger Better School will give you perfect facilities, brilliant students, appreciative colleagues, a supportive boss, and a smooth and invisible bureaucracy. You may want to test the hiring waters again. But Ms. Mentor knows that the only behavior you can adjust is your own.

As you start your second year at Big Nat you may feel that looking on the bright side is a sappy sellout, and you'd rather "be me." Charm is for sissies. But charm is also rare and therefore exceptionally winning in the halls of academe. If you cannot sincerely be interested in the lives, health, or feelings of others—then fake it. The job you save, and the psyche you improve, will be your own.

The Young and the Pointless

Q (from "Venerable"): Why is it always assumed that older professors are stagnant, and young ones au courant? How about giving older profs equal time to share impressions of younger colleagues?

We could start with semiliteracy and poor listening skills and then move on to those who want (and feel they deserve) to be the department chair yesterday, although their experience and speaking skills ("like, like, you know, I mean, like . . .") fall short.

And let's not forget simple civility or good manners or finding conversational subjects other than me-me-me. These are Professor Gen X characteristics, right?

A: Oh, but you are far too narrow. The qualities you describe are the vices of every younger generation, according to their elders. And so Ms. Mentor's first prescription for you is some good junk food, a trashy novel, and a glass of wine. You need to relax, dude.

Ms. Mentor concedes that older folk do have valid gripes. She loathes booming car speakers and cell phone addictions. But she urges more compassion for academics fresh out of grad school or postdocs or adjunct positions. They're awash in the newest lingo and theories—which they really do know well, although some do name-drop, brag, or sneer. Some even think their elders are cute ("What a sweet little old lady, and she knows her queer theory!").

Yet these new professors have had to be self-centered. They are the survivors of an intensely long and grueling boot camp. Only half of those who start Ph.D. programs finish their degrees—and of those in the humanities, no more than half will ever get tenure-track jobs.

Venerable's young colleagues, in their grandiose moments, may consider themselves the crème de la crème. But at home, weeping with exhaustion and overwork, they write to Ms. Mentor, wondering why they are in such a demanding and hate-filled profession. It is not easy to be the last soldiers left standing.

Often the newbies—call them "Portia" or "Paul"—have been treated as nuisances by professors much more interested in their own research. Some senior profs have to be nagged just to write letters of reference for their charges, whose self-confidence plummets. In grad school, Portia and

Paul learned they could never do enough or read enough. Now they're sure they'll be exposed as frauds.

Those who have refused romances, gone deeply in debt, or waited too long to have children also wonder if they've missed the message telling them to drop out and have real lives.

Still, they've slogged through, and after a quarter-century in school, they've Arrived—whereupon they find Professor Venerable, teeth ready, sharpened to bite.

Portia and Paul need to be respectful. They should introduce themselves, smiling, to Venerable and other elders. They should invite Venerable to lunch, resist the urge to chatter about themselves, and ask him the department's strengths (be upbeat). If Venerable decides to share some crabby or lurid gossip, they should remember every detail—but not spread it around the department.

In department meetings, newbies must not complain about the town, the students, or the facilities. Newbies don't know the department history and culture, and they don't yet speak or understand "departmentese," Kathryn Hume's term for the language of self-interest. ("We need to hire someone dynamic to add to our strength in colonial history" may mean that the current occupant reads from yellowed notes, bores students senseless, and stopped doing research in 1978. But it is never admissible to say "Clyde Colonial is a catastrophe.")

Newbies should never refer to anyone as "an old goat," for that may be someone's husband. Or wife.

As for Venerable's other complaints, Ms. Mentor wonders if new faculty members are really semiliterate poor listeners who string together sentences with "like, you know, I mean." Venerable may be confusing young teachers with young students (they do sometimes look alike). And of course, newbies without much teaching experience may flounder and stammer when they speak publicly. They haven't the self-assurance or the store of pertinent anecdotes that Professor Venerable may believe he's always had. And of course they haven't yet read enough. And they're sure that students are laughing at their clothes.

It takes years of lecturing to sound as stentorian and secure as Ms. Mentor.

Meanwhile, Venerable may find Portia and Paul useful as interpreters and translators. When his students say, "And I'm, like, omigod," Venerable's young colleagues can reassure him that the students really mean "I'm cognizant of the poet's sophisticated uses of floral marginalia."

Ms. Mentor enjoys a rousing rant, and she is not without sympathy for the Venerables of this world. It is tiresome to be patronized or tuned out because of one's age.

Perhaps all faculty members would be better off teaching with bags over their heads.

Disguised as a Grownup

Q: I'm a small, young-looking, new faculty member who's often mistaken for a student and brushed aside and even cussed out. May I get geeky glasses and frumpy clothes to appear older and more serious?

A: Yes.

I Know the Department's Secrets

Q (from "Cassandra"): I've been at my school for two decades. Because I've paid attention to power politics, I know which colleagues are decent and helpful, and which ones are dishonest, even dangerous. Should I share those stories with more vulnerable, recently arrived colleagues, on the theory that they deserve to know where the bodies are buried? Or is that unprofessional?

A: Ah, a question dear to Ms. Mentor's heart. What, indeed, do we owe the new and the naïve? Should we spew what we know and risk being pushy, disloyal, or unsporting? Or do we keep a demure silence, freeing the young to learn about minefields and treachery on their own?

Sad to say, there's no shortage of those experiences. Some new hires are coerced into joining hostile department factions: theory versus practice, tradition versus trendiness. Other newbies have been assured they'll get tenure if their partners are well-liked. Or they've been solemnly informed that their gender, ethnicity, and/or sexual orientation will work for them, or against them, or both: "They're watching who you have lunch with."

Ms. Mentor calls that rumor-mongering bizarre and unfair, for it muddles the minds of new faculty members who need time for teaching and scholarship. They shouldn't be ambushed in their offices by lonely colleagues whose "Got a minute?" can easily stretch into an hour or more—leaving hapless newcomers scrambling to keep up with their own lives.

Still, generous elders like Cassandra should be warning the newcomers to avoid, politely, certain department types:

- The satyrs: Sexual harassers always have a sordid history, and potential victims can be told—in a friendly way, over lunch or coffee—that Professor L is something of a Don Juan (and a fiendishly clever one, who's never been caught). "So keep your office door open, be an ostentatious workaholic—and write down anything he says that doesn't seem quite right." Newbies should also be advised to record any untoward remarks, including warnings, in the Tenure Diary, kept at home.
- The sadists: Most colleges have a cadre of tenured cynics who hang out in local bars, lambaste their more productive colleagues, and dispense cruel predictions, such as, "You'll get tenure when muskrats get wings." Incumbents should advise new recruits that the barflies are one of many social groups in the department with different views: "We have a colorful variety here."
- The satirists: Usually housed in English departments, these learned worthies sometimes compose serious political essays—but they specialize in wickedly witty and crude lampoons and e-mails.

How does a new faculty member react to an e-mailed ditty called "Old McDonald Had a Funny Farm," when the provost is named McDonald and the clucking animals are all recognizable colleagues? Ms. Mentor suggests locking your office door, laughing until you cry, and then forwarding "The McDonald" from your home computer to close friends in other parts of the country, and never mentioning it to anyone until after tenure. In later years you can explain to newbies that "some of us are gifted writers in many genres."

Bland and upbeat is best for senior mentors, and so is straightforwardness about social arrangements. Entrenched faculty members should make a point of telling fledglings who is married to whom, and which pairs or groups may be living together. Novices also need to be told about past relationships if they affect how the department functions (J and V, once a couple, have feuded for years, ever since he found her in an intimate embrace with K).

Past attempted secessions and coups should be revealed if the combatants are still bruised or sulking. Recent embezzlements may explain a lack of travel money, and grade-change scandals may explain the elaborate procedures now used for student records.

But if the passionate and painful events happened fifteen or twenty years ago, and most of the bitter enemies are gone, senior professors should resist the urge to recite the story. Such fogy folklore may give the impression that your colleagues will never get along, which could propel the best recruits to begin job hunting again.

For newbies, elders are the models for professional behavior, including respect, tact, and loyalty. Newcomers ought to emulate those good department citizens who teach enthusiastically, pursue scholarship with lively curiosity, and need no prodding to do the ethical thing, as Cassandra is endeavoring to do.

Unmentored, uninformed fledglings may wander astray, and become too enmeshed in others' trivial or spiteful plans. Newcomers can see the intensity, and it's up to such incumbents as Cassandra to explain that most of the stakes are truly small.

Will I Drown in Committee Work?

Q: My department expects a great deal of committee service from its faculty. I'm untenured and want to make a good impression. And yet you, Ms. Mentor, have sometimes claimed that committees get mired in drooling and trivia. While I know that your wisdom is always perfect, I wonder how to reconcile your pearls with the bauble (tenure) dangled before me if I follow my department's wishes.

A: Ms. Mentor does not thoroughly disdain committee work. She would enjoy the literate and somber deliberations of, say, a Nobel Prize Committee, or the vicious wranglings of the Pulitzer Prize Committee. But she would shun the sixth-century Council of Mâcon, at which a committee of bishops allegedly debated whether women have souls.

Ms. Mentor grimaces.

It is a melancholy truth that time spent on nonessential committees is gone forever. Ms. Mentor recalls "Harry," an industrial chemist who toiled faithfully at his research, nine to five every day, for some twenty years—until he became an academic. Suddenly he was attending daily meetings about equipment repair, overflowing wastebaskets, bylaws, curriculum changes, flowers, and human-subject rules—although the only human subject he'd touched in twenty years was his wife.

Harry found himself lobbied vociferously to give the Top Student Award to "Marvin," a ne'er-do-well perpetual student, because Marvin's mentor was a powerful professor before whom the others quailed. Harry listened to vigorous debates about where to hold the annual banquet. He survived a four-hour meeting about the wording of an urgent resolution to be sent to a smaller subcommittee to be revised before it was submitted to a council of deans, after which it would rise to a university-wide committee, and eventually land on the chancellor's desk, where it would languish for seven months.

"Why doesn't someone else take care of this stuff, the way they do in industry, so I can do my work?" Harry finally asked his chair, who said, "We've always done it this way. Collective decision-making is the lifeblood of academia." Harry felt as if he'd been set upon by vampires.

But Harry was a full professor with tenure, who learned he could hide in his lab and say No. For nervous newer professors, committee burdens have been the ruin of many a poor girl or boy. "We need new blood" is chilling enough, but "We need a woman on this committee" or "This committee shouldn't be all-white" means that people of color, and women in nontraditional fields, are chronically picked for committees. "Louisa," a new African American Ph.D., found herself on eighteen committees, representing "diversity," in her first year at "All Things U." By the second, she'd fled to a small historically black college ("Here I'm not some kind of weird token").

Enough stories, you're thinking: What about me?

And that is exactly what you should be thinking. Too many newish professors, especially women, are seduced into thinking that without them committees will die, their sacred tasks undone. Committees do need someone to show up and ratify decisions, and few women can resist that siren call: "You are needed" (the academic equivalent of "You are loved").

(Yes, Ms. Mentor knows that men need love, too, but not in this column.)

But you, whatever your gender, must resist frittering time on things that do not really matter. Ms. Mentor is glad to know that during the September 11 attack on the World Trade Center, people grabbed their cell phones to say "Goodbye" and "I love you." They did not attempt to write one more memo.

Ms. Mentor urges you to think about what will make you happy and what will get you tenure (sometimes they are the same thing). Are your department's committee expectations written somewhere—or are you relying on rumors from committee workhorses, people whose social lives revolve around meetings? What about the star profs who publish, do research, do outreach? Most departments have both, but the stars get raises and prestige. If you want tenure, or if you want to move on to another job, reach for the stars as your role models.

Yet Ms. Mentor knows that you do need to be on committees—to be a good department citizen, and to learn how the university works (few corporations are so arcane). The best committees, if you have a choice, have a finite task with a deadline. They meet infrequently, are well known, and include professors from other departments, so you'll get to know people.

The worst are standing department committees that meet every week, generate endless paperwork, and will continue to do so, world without end. If they also involve salary recommendations, you can easily make enough enemies in six months to kill your tenure possibilities forever.

Do not hesitate to ask for advice from your chair and from senior professors. Take them to lunch and ask what committee work they did in their early years. See if they remember—and if they don't, that will teach you about the importance of committees. Keep asking polite questions. People love parading what they know and advising the young, and you'll pick up bureaucratic gossip. (Really lurid scandals are rare in academia. Most people have to settle for inflated travel vouchers or mild treachery.)

How can you avoid being devoured by committees? Set aside specific planning and writing times (Mondays and Wednesdays, 3 P.M., say), and decline to meet during those hours. Do not cite family obligations, lest you look unprofessional. But Ms. Mentor encourages you to schedule medical appointments at times that conflict—oh dear—with going-nowhere committee meetings. If all else fails, claim ignorance. You can't, for instance, be on the time-consuming awards committee if you don't yet know the faculty and their strengths.

Some professors do have administrative strengths. They are well-organized, precise, and eager to create new programs and structures. Ms. Mentor lauds them, and if you are one, you are a rare breed that should be honored and cultivated. But if you are the more usual sort of academic—a lab rat, a library nerd—you should be hoarding your time and spending it only on the best person in your untenured universe.

Yourself.

My Head Is Exploding

Q: My neighbor just left a tiny kitten on my porch and fled. I'm grading three sets of papers, writing five grant and conference proposals, trying to finish my dissertation, and waiting for the job listings, so I can send out half a hundred personally crafted applications. I still teach, but I never cook, rarely eat, and have no social life. On the good days I comb my hair, drive on the right side of the road, and remember my name. How do academics survive October? And what do I do about the kitten?

A: October is the cruelest month, and it starts, for academics, on or about September 17.

In August through mid-September, there's a fresh aroma of possibility, while by November and December there are holidays (sleep days) ahead. After a bleak start, second semester gets cheery, with Mardi Gras and St. Patrick's Day and Easter eggies. The sun shines. Life is good.

But October means dark days, dark clothes, and the year's longest chilly stretch without a break. Too many grant and paper proposals are due. Too many conferences are scheduled. Weary midterm graders jostle each other in LAX, DFW, and O'Hare, where they're at the mercy of uncertain weather, overworked air-traffic controllers, and enraged fellow passengers.

Meanwhile, ambitious new academics—unless they're properly mentored—may make their own Octobers more onerous. To wit:

- "Gilda" somehow committed herself to two conferences in one weekend, in Albuquerque and Minneapolis. Instead of networking and sharing ideas, she was careening through airports, panting and starving.
- "Terence," in his first tenure-track job, stayed home, but wasted his October applying for fellowships and grants that go only to famous, well-published people. (He suspected as much, but was afraid to ask.)
- "Imogene," a dedicated teacher, gave her students imaginative but very complex assignments throughout October: field trips, daily journal entries, weekly quizzes, individual meetings. She went to work in the dark and came home in the dark—chilled, hoarse, and shaking with exhaustion.
- "Milburn," in mid-October, was found marching back and forth outside the department office, muttering to himself, trying to remember where he was supposed to be. Students skittered away—a loony? someone going postal? —until his mentor gently called the health center for sleep medication, canceled Milburn's afternoon class, drove him home, and tucked him into bed with his teddy bear.

October, in short, is Exploding Head Syndrome Month.

Maybe you're so attuned to school deadlines that you think you must do everything perfectly, NOW, or you'll flunk. You're racing everywhere, your tummy aches, your nose runs, and your head feels like an engorged pumpkin.

DESIST! Ms. Mentor barks.

If you live alone, keep the kitten. It'll be good company when you take a sick day, unplug the phone and computer, and just sleep. You cannot neglect children or elders, but your partner must do at least half the housework, while you study ways to cut corners:

- "Alice," a superb cook, wanted to entertain her new colleagues, but desperately needed to finish a conference paper. She invited a herd of people to a simple, exquisite buffet, but hid most of her chairs—so no one would stay too long.

- "Burl" "lost" his cell phone, so he couldn't be reached.
- "Chris" got a low-maintenance haircut.
- "Dudley" put in a standing order for pizza delivery every night.
- "Tillie" gave up ironing.

They all did their routine errands in four hours, once a week, in the same shopping center where they bought groceries. They lowered their standards, and when the unvacuumed dust bunnies got too big, everyone ate by candlelight. ("Can't see the corners," Chris bragged.)

"Okay, Ms. Mentor," you're growling. "I can live with a filthy house. But what about my teaching and research?"

To get those articles and books finished, Ms. Mentor recommends writing groups and daily page or hour quotas. You have no time to wait for the muse, who always goes on sabbatical in October. Install your kitten in that role.

Simplify your teaching by making students active learners, not passive note-takers. Assign them to discussion or research groups; have them share writing drafts and field notes and make joint in-class presentations. You'll learn from them, while you decide whether this is the October to start the dreaded job search.

Last year, "Robert" was only halfway through his dissertation when he dove into the Modern Language Association's October Job Lists. Fighting a head cold, he still managed to send out fifty applications. Many of them required dossiers, costing him hundreds of dollars.

Then he waited by the phone and checked his U.S. mail twice a day and his e-mail every hour. Nary a nibble. Everything grew colder and darker.

In December, he got one call from a hiring committee chair: Will you have your Ph.D. in hand for the MLA convention? Robert said No. The caller snarled, "Don't waste my time"—and hung up.

Meanwhile Robert's concentrated writing time was dribbling away, forever. He was competing, intensely and unnecessarily, with his classmates, and his parents were nagging: "Heard anything yet?"

Ms. Mentor could have told Robert that tenure-track jobs hardly ever go to the unfinished. He had misused his last October as a student.

Ms. Mentor would also have pushed Robert—and you, and everyone—to do something for the one upbeat rite of October: Halloween, the official end of That Month.

Ms. Mentor recommends a mask and a costume. Be a witch. Be that devil you always wanted to be. Run wild in the streets, at least in your imagination. Flap your wings and be batty. Find out what it's like to be a Real-World Person, not an academic.

But do not emulate the stressed-out Johns Hopkins grad student who took a quick shower one Halloween night, donned his big black executioner's hood, and hopped onto a Baltimore city bus—only to discover he'd forgotten his pants.

Sometimes in October, you're better off just staying home and howling.

—

Reader Response (from someone signed "Assistant Cockroach"): "The proper scientific name for the phenomenon you describe is 'Imploding Head Syndrome.' The pressure bears in from all sides upon the hapless first-year tenure-troller (this writer being same). The effect could be simulated in a campus laboratory by putting one's head through a course of treatments in an eighty-ton hydraulic press."

I've Been Exiled to the Provinces

Q: I am starting my fifth year as a tenure-track assistant professor at "Southern Regional U." My partner and I do not really like the community we live in. I can't say I much enjoy the people that I work with, and I want to apply for other positions. Any advice?

Q: I've taught for four years at a small liberal-arts school where the students are as dreary and flat as the local landscape. I want to quit. Even teaching part-time in New York would get me back to civilization.

Q: My husband and I, new faculty members at Village College, have seemingly been adopted as best friends by another faculty couple who seem a bit conservative by our New York standards.

Q: Finally I have a tenure-track job—in a snake pit. After three months, I've figured out that maybe eight of the thirty faculty members are truly competent. Meanwhile, everyone lives in dread of the Mighty Duo, two powerful senior professors who keep up a running feud with our chairman, a nice liar.

My research is stymied, too, since I've been studying flora and fauna in a different geographical region. I could go away during the summer to continue—but it's been hinted to me, by these extremely provincial Southerners (I'm a New Yorker, as if you can't tell) that taking my research elsewhere will cause big disapproval. But if I refocus and work with the Mighty Duo, the department's deadwood will hate me.

I've considered complaining to the dean about the endless whispering campaigns. But when I complained earlier about my teaching load, his advice was to lay low, take the garbage handed out, smile, and stay out of the politics. My inability to repress my tongue may be another problem. How does one lay low, get research done, and cope with being stuck here?

A: Oh, the yearning and churning Ms. Mentor hears from some academics. Like latter-day Romantic poets, they look before and after, and pine for what is not. Or they imagine themselves as brilliant flowers, wasting their sweetness on the desert air.

But Ms. Mentor reminds her readers that the Romantic poets had a habit of dying young—which made them poor candidates for tenure. New academics might prefer to consider Lenny Bruce's blunt advice: "Time to grow up and sell out."

More gently, Ms. Mentor exhorts fledgling faculty to ponder which is more important: the place or the profession? Rare is the soul who can get both. Will you move to wherever a tenure-track job surfaces, or would you rather be a barista in Seattle than a professor in Saskatoon?

Some sunny souls adapt happily to volcanoes or igloos, palm trees or prairies, as long as they have the libraries and labs they need. Others model themselves on Ovid, Victor Hugo, or Lenin—producers of poems, novels, political broadsides, and endless gossip from exile.

Some urbanites delight in places where (according to "Gerald," a new instructor in the heartland) "they're not shooting at you, the dogs are calm, and you're not commuting among cutthroats for two hours a day."

Others revel in what seems exotic: potato bowls, jambalaya festivals, tractor pulls. They learn to make lutefisk, grits, and boudin.

But some academics, especially those from the Northeast, refuse to blend in. They're the ones bellowing, "Hurry up already!" in Pocatello, or blasting all of Iowa as "cornfed and white bread," or stereotyping the entire South as racist. (Ms. Mentor reminds her readers that there are more African American elected officials in Mississippi than in New York.)

Some dedicated malcontents do return to New York, but usually as adjuncts—teaching six different courses at three different schools, commuting by subway, and earning maybe $15,000 a year. But many weep with joy anyway. They're back in the Big Apple.

Ms. Mentor thinks theirs is a perfectly rational choice. So is leaving academia, for those who cannot imagine living anywhere except San Francisco or Philadelphia or Boston. What is not rational is to fritter away one's life waiting for a call from the Sorbonne or Austin or Madison.

Nor is it useful to fume all the time. Ms. Mentor's last correspondent, above, suffers from first-year faculty disappointment, department feuds, regional malaise, and reluctance to be tactful or strategic. But astute academics are ones who pick their battles. They shrug off rumors, ignore petty issues, find nonacademic friends to laugh with, and welcome the chance to have the Mighty Duo mentor them.

To all her correspondents, Ms. Mentor recommends scheming rather than moaning. Think "How can I get my teaching and research done where I am, without making deadly enemies?" and "What can I learn here that's valuable and challenging?" Or, if you must: "How can I save enough to live in New York on my sabbatical?"

Sometimes, too, lost souls find other answers. One winter night, two Texans spied each other across the crowded room in the only Mexican restaurant in "Icicle City," a college town in the Upper Midwest. Over burritos and quesadillas and margaritas, the two really got an earful of their own endless whining and ranting—which finally made them giggle, then guffaw, then roar.

A year later, a contented and well-fed couple, they are superb teachers who've published more than anyone else in their departments and have been recommended for early tenure.

Sour souls would say they're stuck in Icicle City forever. But Ms. Mentor says they're happy.

I Thought I Mentored Her, But . . .

Q: I'm not the person your advice is usually aimed at. I'm white, male, middle-aged, tenured. I'm also committed to sharing advice and publishing opportunities with new faculty members. My past successful mentees have been of both genders, but all of them have been white, because of the demographics in our field.

Our most recent hire, "Dr. Nouvelle," is a young black woman. During her first semester, I suggested on a dozen occasions that the two of us go out to lunch or that she join me and several others for lunch. The purpose was to talk about what it takes to make tenure. She always sounded enthusiastic, but always backed out. At first, I asked once a week, and then every few weeks, and now it's been months since the last time I asked. I can only handle so much rejection.

Recently, at a faculty meeting, Dr. Nouvelle suddenly launched into an impassioned speech about how she's been left alone ever since she's been here, twisting in the wind with no one offering any help. I believe everyone in the room was shocked by her feelings and the passion with which she expressed them. She's said to be on the job market again.

I feel as if there is some detail I've left out that would explain everything, but I can't figure out what it could be. What should I have done?

A: Ms. Mentor salutes your commitment and is glad you are no Maundering Mentor with old war stories: "When I was your age, we walked barefoot uphill both ways in the snow to get to the Faculty Senate . . ." (Epidemics of eye-rolling among the young.) Yet there is, indeed, some perfect wisdom you're needing. Ms. Mentor will supply it.

Few white people, however well-intentioned, know how deeply racism pervades the lives of African Americans—from random name calling, to assumptions of prowess in music and sports and nothing else, to routine police harassment just for being in certain areas ("driving while black"). By the time someone like Dr. Nouvelle is hired at a university, she will have endured constant insinuations that she got where she is through affirmative action, not through her own merits. She will also have been told that racism is no longer a factor in academia. (Ms. Mentor calls this "epistemological solipsism": If I don't know about it, it doesn't exist.)

Dr. Nouvelle will have dealt repeatedly with wrongheaded assumptions about poverty, drug use, and sexual availability. At the Modern Language Association conference a few years ago, a new Ph.D. standing outside a hotel room, nervously awaiting her job interview, was accosted by a hotel detective who suspected she was a prostitute: "Well, you're young and black and a hottie, and it's the middle of the afternoon," he told her.

When, in Dr. Nouvelle's new job, a middle-aged white man invites her to lunch, she might very well feel uneasy. Bluntly, she may have thought you were hitting on her—making a sexual overture—and she wanted to avoid an unpleasant scene. She may have interpreted repeated invitations as harassment from a powerful white man. It's also possible that she could not afford to go out to lunch. Like many African American professionals, she may be part of an extended family, and responsible for aged or disabled relatives. Black faculty members at most universities also try to "give back to the community"—give time and money to each other, to students, to troubled children. Everyone should do so, Ms. Mentor believes—but it does clash with the career-at-all-costs mentality that makes ambitious people "successful."

Or Dr. Nouvelle may genuinely not have known that "doing lunch"— networking—is vital. Most graduate advisers do not discuss the politics of an academic career, and few students know that whether They (the senior colleagues) like you will make the most difference in your tenure prospects. Most African American graduate students, in particular, are not mentored. Too many are passed on, without constructive criticism or serious engagement with their work. African American faculty members often find themselves patronized or bullied, but few are mentored about hidden agendas and processes.

Perhaps, Ms. Mentor suggests, it will help to think of Dr. Nouvelle as a foreigner in the land where you've been comfortably ensconced all your life. Dr. Nouvelle's speech may have seemed especially impassioned, or even out of place, to people not familiar with African American women's more assertive cultural style. White women are more apt to speak deferentially, with apologetics and qualifiers. Or perhaps Dr. Nouvelle's speech was a cry for help, in a world that seems hostile and mysterious.

Ms. Mentor urges you to be explicit about your intentions: "Let's have lunch to discuss tenure procedures." Use unquestionably professional language: "Let's meet over lunch," not "Let's have lunch as a couple." And when you suggest lunching in a grubby school cafeteria, it will be clear that your intentions are not romantic.

Avoid awkward emotional climates, and do not emulate "Dr. Science," the department chairman who, one Friday afternoon, called a meeting of the tenured faculty (all male) and the three untenured women. They all sat down, and Dr. Science abruptly told each woman to select a mentor from the assembled professors. Some of the men straightened their ties, while others looked away ("don't choose me"). All were embarrassed—and once the women, reluctantly, chose their mentors, the losers were angry for the next four years.

It is much better to have faculty volunteers, like yourself, officially assigned to mentees—for when mentoring is formal and institutional, it's not seen as a quirk of personality or misread as some kind of stalking. Women can also be encouraged to serve as mentors for each other.

Ms. Mentor is heartened by your letter, for not enough senior professors think about how to be ethical and generous academics. You have, in fact, mentored Ms. Mentor's readers. You are a mensch.

—

Reader Response: Ms. Mentor got one snarky response from a critic who insisted that the word is "mentoree," not "mentee." Ms. Mentor reminds readers that the right words are the words that she uses. A few months later, the original correspondent got his college to set up a formal mentoring program, with meetings and workshops, so that new faculty would be explicitly told what was expected of them. Ms. Mentor applauds.

Squelching an Upstart

Q: Starting a second year as the only tenure-track woman in my department, I'm continually irritated by a vocal and disaffected grad student I'll call Mr. Upstart Whelp.

We're both on the hiring committee to replace Upstart's adviser, who is retiring—but only Upstart, of course, knows how things should be done. Upstart also knows that his is the only significant subfield in our discipline. Mine (which he knows nothing about) is "boring" and "nowhere near cutting edge." Upstart is loud and argumentative, and his ill-formed opinions are a waste of time.

And, well, he pisses me off. He peacocks at seminars, and purports to know "how to succeed in grad school" ("faculty act like they're busy, but they don't really do anything, so you should make the rules"). He's bought into the department's sexism, trying to curry favor by criticizing my ideas in public. I'd like to rub his nose in the news that I have a Ph.D. and a job, and he doesn't. I also have wicked fantasies about giving him a Jackie Chan-style kick in the face.

Yet I also have some existential angst and self-doubts about being in a position of power. Must I comfort myself with fantasies, or is there a way to stop this guy from being such an arrogant prick?

A: Ms. Mentor can hardly deny you your revenge fantasies. They are the refuge and the delight of every geek, nerd, lab and library rat. They are the solitary vice at which academics are most proficient.

For instance, what if . . . you took martial-arts lessons, rented *Crouching Tiger, Hidden Dragon* a dozen times, memorized all the moves, and then seized the floor during a committee meeting and kicked/thwapped/slapped the Upstart into senseless submission?

Or what if you decided to contribute dramatically to Upstart's literary education? You might leave about a copy of *Macbeth*, open to Act 4, Scene 2, in which Young Macduff calls a murderous intruder a "shag-eared villain." The intruder, his self-esteem obviously wounded, cries out, "What, you egg! Young fry of treachery!" and kills the noble but misguided upstart pup.

Upstart might get the message that one ought not to piss off the people with knives: profs with tenure, and those on the track to get it.

You could, of course, tattle on Upstart to your department chair, who might sympathize with you as a damsel in distress. But he might also wonder whether you're up to the rigors of tenure.

And so Ms. Mentor suggests you do nothing in particular.

She knows, in her infinite wisdom, that all Upstarts eventually slip and fall on their own banana peels. They lack the radar to know they've offended; they lack the cunning to fake being charming to those who can benefit them.

Instead, Upstarts labor under the delusion that everyone wants to hear their opinions. They are, yes, the ones who peacock—who strut and fret and ask the laborious and irrelevant questions at department seminars. They are the ones who mortify and harangue job candidates.

You, though, should be taking notes on Upstart's boorish behavior. Keep a notebook with you at department meetings, and write down (in a coded shorthand) what he says and does that is offensive, especially to you. Keep a duplicate copy of your Upstart journal safely at home with your Tenure Diary. If there's ever any question about harassment, or a pointed discussion about whether he should receive departmental goodies (awards, honors), you will need facts, dates, and particulars.

You can also goad him to look worse in the eyes of the tenured professors who decide on recommendations and assistantships. "Tell me why you feel my subfield is useless and boring," you may ask innocently. The more he orates, the more he tightens his own noose, and the more the tenured professors will find him insufferable. They will rise up in wrath, squelch the Upstart, and view you as a marvelous and moderate presence.

Serenely doing little or nothing also frees your mind for your research and teaching. If Upstart dominates your thoughts, he will have diverted your energy and attention to himself and stolen it from you. He will have won.

Finally, Ms. Mentor exhorts you not to wallow in angst or guilt about possessing the power you have. You have earned it, and you can teach through example. You can teach, publish, and get tenure. You can even list Upstart in your acknowledgments, if his presence has pushed you to excel.

Eventually you may choose to be the tenured professor in your department who handles political problems and social tensions, the one who tells loudmouths to pipe down.

That will be the best mentoring they'll ever get.

The Fine and Quirky Art of Teaching

Victor and Galina: A Comparative Case Study

Victor is shy.

On his first day of teaching, before his very first class, he lost his breakfast. On the way to the classroom, he broke into a sweat that left him bathed in ice-cold clothes by the end of the period: He had to lean against the wall as he struggled to walk, and colleagues kept stopping to ask, "Are you OK?"

Once he got into the room, with twenty-five young students in their first college composition class, he sat down at the teacher's desk, barricaded himself with books, and did not move for an hour. He said, "Hello, class," in a croaky voice, and began lecturing.

When Victor came up for tenure, several colleagues observed his teaching. "Try to speak up," one suggested gently. "Students don't seem to be hearing you." Another wrote that "Victor was obviously nervous about having visitors, and that may be why he did not do his best." A third observed that "Victor's teaching needs improvement, but he has a fine mind and the makings of a promising scholar."

Victor did eventually publish one highly regarded book. He was a major scholar in his subfield, spoken about with awe at scholarly meetings—which he rarely attended. Crowds frightened him.

On his last day of teaching, thirty-two years later, Victor skipped breakfast, as he had for most of his career. He wore a jacket, because his newly washed shirt would be bathed in sweat by the end of class. He limped on the way to the classroom—he now had a cane—and once there, he barricaded himself behind his books, pulled out his yellowed, well-honed lecture notes, croaked "Hello, class," and began his hour-long lecture, which had never been interrupted by student questions. No one dared, and no one truly cared.

And then there was Galina, hired about the same time as Victor, a frisky young woman with a mysterious Eastern European accent who danced into the classroom, calling everyone "Dahlink." She had no notes, sometimes remembered to bring a book, and seemed to be thoroughly spontaneous. She would tell long, involved, comical stories in her native Helvetica, which no one understood. But students knew the stories were funny—and naughty—because she would announce in a stage whisper that "Now, this is really *smooty* [smutty], and is it all right if I tell you?"

The students would roar their approval and she would continue, interrupting herself to laugh hysterically. The students did not understand any of it, but by the end of the smutty story, they would be laughing so uncontrollably that tears streamed down their faces. Many of them left the class with wet shirts.

Years later they figured out that there was no such language as Helvetica—that it's a typeface. They were not sure what language Galina had been speaking—something of her own invention? And whenever they thought about her, they laughed their heads off again, until tears ran down onto their shirts.

Victor's students rarely remembered his name. "The guy who hid behind the books and mumbled," they called him. They remembered nothing of his careful, learned lectures on intricate grammatical points and word derivations.

Everyone remembered Galina, and every syllable she'd spoken in English, and every nugget she'd presented on social and political matters, and every dotty observation she'd made about "you Amerrrricans—you lack the soul of romance. You get and spend. You do not loooove."

Which one was the better teacher?

Discuss.

What Do College Teachers Do?

Once upon a time, well-respected professors—we're told—lectured to worshipful young students who eagerly wrote down and cherished every pearl of wisdom. In Europe, students vied to carry the professor's briefcase.

The world is different now. More paperwork, more students, fewer good readers or mathematicians, and many more distractions. Students work full-time jobs; they're in debt; they're pregnant; they're coping with disabilities and traumas. In class they're fidgeting with cell phones, surfing porn on their laptops, eating, drinking, text messaging, playing with themselves.

If Johnny's at an expensive school and doesn't get an A, his helicopter parents will call up his professor—and his dean—and the college president, and bully and bluster. "I'm paying $40,000 a year for this, and my kid deserves an A!"

Socrates also ran into parental opposition, but not quite of this kind.

Ms. Mentor urges her flock—teachers and would-be teachers—to take stock of themselves once they begin teaching. It can be the most rewarding and enriching job on earth, and the most challenging. Nietzsche felt that it was humiliating to be required to "think in public about predetermined subjects at predetermined hours," but many academics thrive on the give-and-take. No other professions, except maybe courtroom law and standup comedy, pay us for constantly thinking, and for keeping our intellects sparklingly alive.

But college teaching is not for everyone. The bureaucracy has grown, safety can be worrisome, and tenure as lifetime security is eroding. Nowadays Galina would still enjoy the theatrics of teaching. But Victor should have examined what else he might do. Nowadays he might consult Susan Basalla and Maggie Debelius's *"So What Are You Going to Do with That?" Finding Careers Outside Academia*, or, before that, Dorothy Bestor's *Aside from Teaching, What in the World Can You Do?* For Victor was not temperamentally suited to the job. He was a loner who could not fake being an extrovert (he was also twice divorced). Library or archival work would have suited his scholarly talents and preserved his digestion.

When Ms. Mentor gets anxious letters about teaching, she wants to hug the young ones and tell them to "Fake being self-confident. Be loud, be blunt, dress as if you're twenty years older than you are, and have a stern syllabus with inflexible deadlines and schedules. Be tough, be smart, and be a leader. Your country needs you."

Then she feels a little silly. But not entirely.

I Don't Need Those Silly Credentials

Q: I want to teach writing at a community college, but my M.A.'s not in English. I'm currently doing adjunct teaching in developmental writing and composition, but I'm told I have to get at least an M.A. in English, and maybe a Ph.D., to get a secure position. As someone who quit the business world to move into teaching, this scrambling to get degrees makes me angry. The decision to hire should be based on what kind of teacher the person is, just as in the real world. There are people with degrees who can't stand in front of a classroom and teach. They just read the book at you. I've seen them all.

But getting a Ph.D. would take ten years. I don't have ten years of my life to devote to something that, once I get it, will pit me against every other person with the same degree. I am thirty-five and getting older fast, and I'm bitter about all this baloney. What should I do?

A: Well . . . some might say that you have a very healthy ego. Lesser mortals need to take courses in the subjects they teach—but you don't. Other weaklings may need to follow the rules and learn professional norms and methods—but not you.

Ms. Mentor, more gentle, will point out that there are reasons for degree requirements: to make sure that the individual knows the subject, knows the research, uses the most current teaching methods, understands the theoretical jargon, and can share the rules of the field with students. (Would you trust a mentor who had never been an academic?)

Certainly there are inept teachers. And like all veterans, Ms. Mentor is sure that ineptitude is far more widespread now than it was in her golden youth, sometime before the Peloponnesian War.

But you do not make a case for your own eptitude. Nowhere in your letter do you mention any talents, skills, or achievements that should induce employers to ignore your lack of credentials. At elite universities, people without traditional degrees sometimes do teach—but they are usually Nobel Prize winners, or novelists with fifteen books, or film makers or artists with distinguished records.

What, Ms. Mentor asks you to ask yourself, have you done lately?

She suggests that you calm down and consider this: Would you hire someone with a lot of drive, but no traditional degrees, to be your neurosurgeon? (Remember that doctor in Florida who amputated the wrong foot?) Or—if you think that classwork and training are not needed for teaching writing—then perhaps you have a low opinion of the field in which you hope to work?

And then there's the matter of collegiality. Teachers' lives are not independent. Every teacher is evaluated repeatedly (even chronically) by peers and students; courses have descriptions to follow; and faculty members who wish to stay must be "collegial"—meaning they must work and play well with others. Hothead critics get axed.

As for time: thirty-five, the age of the average American today, is hardly old. The average graduate student in English is over thirty. "Bad girl" Courtney Love is well over forty, and "bad boy" Mick Jagger is in his mid-sixties. It is too late to be a teen idol, but most of the rest of the world is still open to you.

Ms. Mentor has been accused of being relentlessly bourgeois, but traditional middle-class values will serve you well here. Study the field, follow the rules, amass the grades and credits, and work hard to achieve your goals.

And if Ms. Mentor were not the soul of tact, she might assign you another morsel for thought: If you feel that you don't need professional training, and that having the drive is what matters most . . . then why not go for a really well-paying, glamorous job? The Rolling Stones usually hire a few extra younger guitarists and backup singers when they go on tour . . .

They've Got Me Team-Teaching with Bozos

Q: What happens when one teacher has to work with two others, "Bonehead" and "Moppet," who are amazingly incompetent? They seem constitutionally unable to write a syllabus, plan a course, or create lesson plans. They cover up by bullying other teachers and students, or by filling class time with videos. ("Live interaction is wasted on the young," they claim.)

When anyone challenges these two, they proclaim that they are superior to the rest of us. The administration refuses to take action. Have you seen this type of insane behavior anywhere else?

A: Ms. Mentor has seen everything. Some teaching-learning partnerships are ideal: Mentor and Telemachus, Marie and Pierre Curie, Annie Sullivan and Helen Keller. The medieval scholar-lovers Heloise and Abelard were doing splendidly until her disapproving relatives had Abelard castrated.

Ms. Mentor knows that collaborative teaching can produce other nasty surprises:

- "Bertrand," team-teaching the history of architecture, suddenly discovered that Notre Dame Cathedral had been dropped from the course. "Who needs all that old stone?" said his colleague.
- "Roberta," team-teaching with a sensitive, neurasthenic soul ("I can't bring myself to grade exams"), wound up doing all the grading herself. But Roberta knew enough to consult her department chair, who tactfully assigned her a grader. That gave Roberta time to publish and to apply for jobs elsewhere.
- "Oswald," aching to make his third of the team-taught course a "really serious learning experience," assigned a triple load of reading. Even the most dedicated students couldn't keep up. They wrote scorching evaluations, and Oswald got a tongue-lashing ("Learn to be a team player") from his department chair.
- "Virginia," team-teaching a biology of sex course, had to insist to a man thirty years her senior: "No, we can't leave out the clitoris. It's not a frill."

As for your plight, Ms. Mentor's advice is simple: FLEE! If you have any way to extricate yourself from Bonehead and Moppet, you should do so.

But Ms. Mentor assumes that you're an untenured newish faculty member, sentenced to team-teach with two entrenched, burned-out older professors. You're wondering how to survive this melange of nastiness and nuttiness.

Ms. Mentor, in her infinite wisdom, exhorts you to analyze your role dispassionately, with trusted off-campus friends. Do not whine, "What did I do to deserve this?" because you know the answer: "I'm in the wrong place at the wrong time." Do ask yourself:

- What really has to be covered in the course?
- Can Bonehead and Moppet be charmed into doing some work?
- Must I be the responsibility magnet who does it all?
- How can I salvage my self-respect?
- How can the students get something useful out of the course?
- Is it possible that Bonehead and Moppet are actually doing their best?

Ms. Mentor knows you shriek at the last possibility, but that can make you stronger and more compassionate. If they pick a quarrel, it is far, far better to smile and say, "Thank you for sharing."

If, as your letter implies, you've gone over their heads to complain to the administration, you've already made enemies. Everyone loathes tattlers ("there she goes, yammering about injustice again"), and your bosses may blame you. It is much easier to get rid of you than to change Bonehead and Moppet. You, not they, may be in danger.

Do not shrivel. Be shrewd. Invite Bonehead and Moppet to lunch and make a charming offer they can't refuse: "Let me try drafting the syllabus. I'd like to learn to do one well. I'll put in any changes you'd like, and we can all teach what we know best."

Then create the plan that is most pleasing—or least galling—to you. Award yourself the plums. Assign Bonehead and Moppet to teach only when their specialties must be covered. Praise their insights. If they show videos, offer to arrange group discussions afterward.

If Bonehead and Moppet do propose time-wasters, pick out (for yourself) only the most egregious, and cheerfully offer a substitute. Do not fight, and never offer unsolicited advice. If you must watch truly terrible teaching, devise a code in which to write yourself satiric notes. Compose odes to your own magnificence and magnanimity—and hide them at home in your Tenure Diary.

Remind yourself that collaborations are like semesters: they end. If you have wisely chosen your battles (those you can graciously win) and ignored the rest, you will seem to be serene and saintly. Once you've acquired that aura, it will be hard for anyone to refuse you anything—such as rehiring, raises, and tenure.

And best of all, a course of your own.

My Grad Students Terrify Me

Q: I am the youngest and the only untenured professor in my department. My colleagues seem to like me, and I love my undergraduate teaching and find it affirming. But I'm tormented to the depths of despair by the graduate seminars I have to teach.

Although the students are very respectful and friendly, I feel like a stupid, useless specimen under surveillance. They have so much drive to succeed and be the best in the profession, and I am just too overworked to know how to teach them properly. I feel like I lead a double life. By day, I'm a success with my undergrads. By night, in my seminars, I am an ugly, deformed monster.

A: Ms. Mentor knows you're not monstrous, but very likely hyperconscientious—a common malady among academics.

Professors, after all, were the perfect students who got the science and spelling and literary awards. In college they made the dean's list and won all the fellowships. School was a joy and a treat.

Grad school did prick that bubble a bit—for it's the boot camp where one learns that one doesn't know everything. Some profs specialize in disdainful remarks: "How could you possibly construct a credible argument without the theoretical modalities of Axolotl of Potrzebie?"

You were the kind of student who'd Google this overlooked authority, get his books, and teach yourself Furshlugginer, the best-known of the sixteen indigenous languages of Potrzebie, so that you could read him in the original. The following week, in seminar, you would quote him: "As everyone knows, Axolotl of Potrzebie, the major theorist of fricative evasion. . . . "

Even your professor would look impressed, while you flushed with pleasure and swelled with self-love. Among the scholarly minded, the opportunity to learn is sublime. And so is the chance to shine and show off.

Then the most diligent and talented—and lucky—find themselves teaching, almost always at less prestigious institutions than those they attended. Many will seethe about "watering down" what they learned and taught at Elite Grad U. Most will find their students less academically adept than they were, and more hormonally alert (yes, grad school can dry up the sex drive). You may be lucky if half your undergraduates faithfully do the reading. Some won't be able to, because they haven't the vocabulary or the math skills, or they're sleepy from their other jobs.

Still, you are in a dream situation, and—like most mortals—unhappy anyway. ("What a sorehead," Ms. Mentor hears her readers muttering.)

Ms. Mentor wonders if you're a perfectionist who's afraid of spontaneity. You think your graduate seminar must always be intense, theoretical, jargon-filled, and professionally perfect. You're wildly researching all the time, terrified that grad students will ask questions you can't answer. (You could always snow them with obscure Furshlugginer names, but you have integrity.) You're sure your ratty underwear is showing, and you're a charlatan and a fraud.

Such feelings are entirely normal.

In fact, the best graduate teaching is done by newer academics, who know the minutiae du jour. They've actually read the right journals and worked with grant getters. They know what's hot and what sells and what everybody in the know is twittering about. New faculty members are, by far, the best mentors to indoctrinate grad students into the academic world, with excitement and urgency.

Senior professors, Ms. Mentor believes, can contribute most to large survey courses. They know the whole sweep of Western civilization. Some even went to school with Plato and remember when the earth was flat. They remember scientific hoaxes and romantic old names. They know a military quagmire when they see one.

Senior professors are also more at ease in front of a large lecture hall, since they (usually) no longer care whether their students find them fashionable or attractive. If their underwear shows, so what?

Ms. Mentor believes that you are well qualified to teach graduate seminars in your department. If you don't know something, you can train students to go to the library and the Internet to find it. Your willingness to learn new things is a gift to your seminar. Make the students your allies in the pursuit of knowledge, and you will become their finest role model, the young intellectual who approaches the subject with verve and curiosity.

They will not throw things at you.

—

Reader Response: A few readers did not want to throw their sympathy to this letter writer. Some scoffed: "You think you've got it bad? Try grading hundreds of papers at my community college." Others moaned: "You know, we aren't all academic powerhouses." One veteran professor still smarts at the memory of the snide young profs who taught him: "Colonial Overseers, from the country of All Things Worthwhile, sorting through the poor, moronic natives to determine who might be worthy to serve as flag bearers in the Queen's Overseas Regiment. . . . I'd take an older, more secure professor over a Bright Young Bloated Ego any day."

The original letter writer reported later that he'd decided that he preferred teaching general-education courses to working-class undergrads. He moved to another job where he is happily doing that.

The Plague Spreads

Q: I notice that most of the people inveighing against cheating nowadays fail to spell "plagiarism" correctly. How does this bode?

A: Ill.

The Smell of Misplaced Priorities

Q (from "Henry"): I'm an assistant professor at Midsized U., where my best M.A. student ("Stella") wants to apply to top Ph.D. programs. Stella is very bright and capable, with great potential—but she also has a substantial case of body odor. If she's in my office for five minutes, there will be a lingering unpleasant smell for half an hour.

I'm on good terms with professors where she will be applying and would like to alert them to Stella's application, but her pungency is no small matter to visit upon my peers for the next five to seven years. I am, therefore, reluctant to sing Stella's praises too strongly, lest colleagues treat future recommendations from me warily.

If I'm forced to choose, my relationship with my colleagues will count more than my desire to help Stella. Is it appropriate for me to alert her to the professional implications of a casual approach to hygiene? If so, how?

A: Ms. Mentor is reminded of "Margaret," an enormously talented student teacher whose third graders loved her laugh and her lilting voice. They flocked about her after school, had to be shooed away and sent home, and wept for days when she finished practice teaching and left them.

But "you're much too fat to be a good teacher," her supervisor told her. Margaret was a big, round woman who had been plush and pillowy all her life. "You have to get skinny," her supervisor ordered. "Join Weight Watchers and get it off, or I won't write you a recommendation." Knowing she was naturally fat and could never be a twiggy, Margaret quit teaching. That was the end of her lifelong dream.

Her supervisor was irresponsible and cruel—as is any adviser who destroys a student's career because he doesn't like her looks, or her race, or her hygiene.

Any third grader knows how to handle Stella's case badly: deodorants dropped on her desk, anonymous lampoons and e-mails, and graffiti about "Stinky." If Stella has had this difficulty all her life, she has endured all that abuse.

There are also adult cowards—people who think that since odors are a delicate subject, Henry ought to enlist the nearest female professor, or the department administrator, or the director of women's studies, to chat with Stella about her "issue." Woman-to-woman, goes the thinking, the conversation might be less awkward—a point of view that Ms. Mentor finds sexist as well as irresponsible.

It is Henry's job, not his colleagues', and women should not be dragooned into handling situations because men feel uncomfortable. Henry needs to take it like a man—and talk to Stella.

What to say?

For his homework, Henry might read *Difficult Conversations: How to Discuss What Matters Most*, by Douglas Stone, Bruce Patton, and Sheila Heen. He might also peruse Dale Carnegie's classic *How to Win Friends and Influence People* for ways to use a positive spin while delivering bad news.

To Ms. Mentor's readers who are already objecting—No touchy feely! No sensitivity palaver!—Ms. Mentor points out that the ability to discuss anything at all with compassion is the mark of a good teacher as well as a good human being.

If Henry wants to consult an expert who won't make him feel queasy/twitchy, he might call an international-student adviser. Some institutions have handbooks for foreign students about peculiar American habits, such as frantic showering to erase one's natural animal smell. Henry can find out how the experts talk tactfully about deodorants to foreign students who do not want to violate American sensibilities (although many of them also know what a Scotsman once told Ms. Mentor: "You Yanks smell ridiculously floral").

But Henry's biggest challenge will be how to broach the subject. Ms. Mentor suggests a private talk about "career development," beginning with great praise for Stella's achievements. "Your work is excellent, and you should have an outstanding career, but there's one thing that may be a professional barrier. I don't want you to be turned down for any fellowships or opportunities, but right now there's a bit of a problem with, well, an odor that comes along with you . . ."

It is lovely to be suave, of course, as in the tale about the queen of England, who, to put it bluntly, broke wind at an official event. She apologized to the soldier nearest her, who said blandly, "I wouldn't have noticed had you not spoken about it, Your Majesty. I assumed it was the horse."

Few people can aspire to be so smooth, and you needn't try. Awkwardness and apologetic language may, in fact, come across as more considerate of Stella's feelings. It could be that she's unaware, or too busy to do laundry, or she could have a medical condition. But your role is to let her know that you support her and want her to succeed, and you don't want any irrelevant problems to prevent her from using her talents and pursuing her dreams. Ms. Mentor feels you must speak up.

Finally, Ms. Mentor finds it troubling that you seem to worry most about what your peers will think—instead of concentrating on how to help a student have a brilliant career.

That doesn't smell quite right.

Don't Teach So Close to Me

Q (from "Carla"): Is it weird and cheesy for professors to be on Facebook, sending social notes to their students after a long day at school?

My colleague ("Brando"), in his mid-fifties, has a Facebook site connected to the sixty students we see every day in our very intense program. I wonder how Brando has time to "play" with students like this on the Net. Is this a newfangled ploy to establish popularity and "coolness"?

I struggle to make students understand that I'm not instantly available by e-mail. Brando's site undermines my efforts, and students haven't a clue as to how sad this really is. In our big university (eight thousand), he is the only faculty member on Facebook.

Students learn professionalism from us, which should include keeping away from time sinks and temptations. One of our troubled graduates was recently arrested for chatting up underaged students online, and it turned out he also had a cache of child porn—all of which makes me even more uncomfortable with my colleague's activities. He says he understands my position but keeps up his Facebook activities anyway. Am I a hopeless prude?

Q (from "Luanne"): Teaching at a community college, I create open, friendly relationships with my students, who feel comfortable sharing personal problems. We bring food, I appreciate them and their cultures, and I share my personal experiences about challenges they also face, such as financial difficulties, relationships, and violence against women.

Students always volunteer to help me carry equipment, but last semester, "Nosey" abruptly asked if something was going on between me and another student, "Ray," because "Ray's always following you to the computer center and here and there." A few weeks earlier, someone had stolen my work ID card in class, and Nosey said Ray must've done it, because "he's always after you." I told Nosey there was nothing going on between me and Ray.

But it was close to the end of the semester, and I got panicky and angry. When Ray came late to class and said his grandmother had died, I told him he had to stay in class and do some work if he wanted to pass. He did, but started using his cell phone. I got upset, raised my voice, and stopped all discussion. Ray left, slamming the door, calling me paranoid.

During the final exam, he cursed me, claimed I was harassing him, and threatened to report me to my boss, which he did.

I was not hired to teach at the college the following semester ("unsatisfactory performance," they said). What went wrong?

A: Mulling over these scenarios, Ms. Mentor wonders if "closeness" between professors and students is ever really needed. Maybe we are not meant to be pals.

Yes, she knows the histories of bundling and coupling (Socrates and Plato were probably more than friends). She's also heard about schools where faculty members reportedly view students as their "playground." But now, please, she would like to drop the subject of professor-student sex with just one word: Don't.

Be friendly, but be a grown-up, says Ms. Mentor.

Consider your institution's culture. At small liberal-arts colleges, profs are supposed to be socially available and invite students to their homes. At universities, customs vary, but at community colleges, professors are less likely to share their personal lives. Many students at two-year colleges are working adults, and many faculty members are part-timers themselves, racing from one job to another. As for online teachers, the fastest-growing faculty group: most never see their students at all.

In between, though, are many micro-decisions. If students come to your office hours, do you keep the door open? (Most faculty members do.) If students want to talk about their personal tragedies, should you try to solve their problems? (Probably not, but offer sympathy and the name of a good counselor.) If students send you very passionate or suicidal e-mail messages, what do you do? (Tell someone, quickly.)

Even the youngest instructors, those fresh-faced twenty-five-year-old prodigies, are officially grown-ups. They must cast off childish things and hang out with their elders.

That usually does not mean Facebook.com, a cheerful, teenagey venue in which students create groups ("Metaphysicians Who Barbecue"), post photos, and leave greetings on each other's "walls." Ms. Mentor does wonder why Brando, some thirty years older, is hanging around in that playground. Ms. Mentor thinks he should be playing with people his own age, rather than appearing to be desperately lonely or in need of some illicit lovin' that could wreck his career and derail the aspirations of students.

Since his colleague Carla cannot stop his "weird and cheesy" behavior, Ms. Mentor will direct him bluntly: Knock it off. Now.

As for Luanne's saga: At first it looks like another "No good deed goes unpunished" story, with an innocent and generous professor targeted by malicious Nosey and troubled Ray. Luanne's last and biggest mistake was certainly her in-class meltdown. When you lose your temper, and the warmth that makes students care for you, there may be nothing left but grief and anger.

Still, "what went wrong" may have been Luanne's approach to the job. Luanne seems to have tried to be a mom or a sister—instead of a teacher. Her classes sound like parties or support groups, evidently with international students who may have misinterpreted her. To a lonely young man, thousands of miles from home, an open and friendly American woman may seem to be inviting romance. And while Nosey and Ray were vying for Luanne's attentions, there was an ID card thief in her classroom, and Ray was failing the course.

Ms. Mentor wonders if Luanne misunderstood her own role as the teacher. Maybe she was also lonely. But it isn't up to students—or faculty members—to fix each other's lives, or to keep each other wildly entertained or romantically fulfilled or well fed.

The job description is really a lot simpler: "Teach and learn."

—

Reader Response: Ms. Mentor was roundly lambasted ("fogy!") by over a dozen readers who do not share her amused, detached view of Facebook. com. It is not merely a teenaged playground, her correspondents insist. They love it for sharing pictures and news with friends and family, "but we always use privacy settings."

Ms. Mentor was feeling archaic until, within a few days, a Maryland sorority was put on probation for drunken Facebook photos, and a Maryland university president had to apologize for tacky Facebook vacation photos (including a nude tapir) that were not supposed to be publicly available. Now Ms. Mentor wonders about Maryland as well as Facebook.

And then one of Ms. Mentor's faithful readers began writing and sending comic poems about tapirs and college presidents. Ms. Mentor is keeping the poems in a special place. She is not sure why. They really belong on Facebook.

As Blog Is My Witness . . .

Q: A very outgoing young man in my class ("Aidan") keeps a blog (Internet diary) about his schoolwork, partying, and politics. As I read his entries, including his grousing about my class, I tell myself that I am not eavesdropping, and that he is entitled to write whatever he likes in a public forum. Yet his field is public-school teaching, and I think his openness about his life might hamper his chances of getting a job. Should I warn him or let it go?

A: Ms. Mentor salutes Weblogs ("blogs") as modern wonders. They encourage fluid prose, creativity, gobs of writing, humor, and gossip—all the qualities that make words worth reading, and life worth living.

In fact, Ms. Mentor warmed up for this column (in 2003) by Googling herself, linking "Ms. Mentor" and "blogs" and finding herself in such venues as "Invisible Adjunct," "Defender of Mediocrity," and "A Frolic of My Own." She also found herself occasionally mocked, misunderstood, and personally blamed ("clueless dupe") for all the ills of academia.

She had no idea she had such power.

"Aidan," too, is probably unaware of his power to disturb. No doubt he believes that all his opinions are interesting and valuable, and that he has a sacred right to express them (which he does). Though her ox is sometimes gored, Ms. Mentor cheers the bloggers' right to "be me," to invent their own spellings, fabricate their facts, and even wear white shoes after Labor Day.

The only requirement is to grab people with your writing—and what could be more sublime?

And yet—what if tight-laced profs and future public-school employers are reading Aidan's blog? Aidan may consider himself a political animal, a judicious critic of his own education, and a bon vivant—but less worldly souls may read him as a dangerous radical or an empty-headed party boy. Irony and satire are often misunderstood, and public-school teaching is one of the few professions left in America where one's moral tone may be scrutinized.

Conservative educators could fear that lovable Aidan will teach political positions they disapprove of: legalization of marijuana, same-sex marriages, removing U.S. troops from Iraq (all good causes that Ms. Mentor supports, but definite feather-rufflers). If Aidan writes glowingly about his own drinking and partying, many schools will wonder if he'll buy beer for students—or drive drunk to a basketball game. If he mentions sex . . . well, some communities are only now extricating themselves from that ludicrous experiment called "Abstinence Education."

Aidan may assume that he can erase his blog whenever he needs to. But many people who've been photographed in illicit circumstances now know that no juicy stuff is ever fully destroyed. It's all lurking on some server, somewhere.

But what about Aidan's professor, awaiting the next juicy installment of Aidan's blog? How does one say, "I've been reading your diary and I noticed . . ."? Rather than an embarrassing tête-à-tête ("I do not really assign four thousand pages of boring reading" and "my lectures are not always snoozers"), it is far more tactful and educational to give the whole class a short lecture on "fitting the image of public-school teachers—do's and don'ts." Even better, the professor can bring in a guest speaker to talk about job applications, self-presentation, and legalities.

Once he's informed about the consequences, Aidan may decide not to be in a profession that requires him to be silent about some things dear to his heart. Or he may, like many a young rebel before him, move effortlessly into being a narrow-minded grump himself. But Ms. Mentor, who treasures free spirits, hopes Aidan will not desist from blogging, and that his professor will simply show him how to be more canny and pseudonymous. Ms. Mentor knows how to do that.

The Torment of Teaching Evaluations

Q: I work twice as hard at teaching as anyone I know, but I still can't get good student evaluations. I've tried outlines and keywords on the board, handouts, individual meetings, midterm evaluations, peer observations, lecturing more, lecturing less. Some student comments are so harsh and demoralizing that I put off reading my evaluations until school breaks, when I have time to be depressed. Is it possible that my low evaluations stem from personality issues that I can't do anything about? Am I alone?

A: No, you're not. Ms. Mentor's mailbag is full of complaints about student evaluations—none of them from students. Faculty members feel that they are cheated, mistreated, and misunderstood. They're right, for most evaluation forms are so vague and perfunctory ("Concerned about students—rate 1 to 9") that they do nothing to improve teaching. Instead, they become weapons to get rid of untenured profs who have made enemies. No one has ever really agreed on what makes a "good teacher," and Ms. Mentor still grieves for Socrates, who taught his students to question everything, and wound up dead instead of tenured.

But your risk is smaller. You just need good evaluations, and Ms. Mentor can tell you how. (Naïve and idealistic souls may wish to stop reading at this point.)

Simplest of all, you can give higher grades, which do correlate with student ratings. You can use more hand gestures, modulate your voice more, and walk while you talk. Students give higher evaluations to teachers who are good-looking or very dramatic. This is called "the Dr. Fox effect," named for a hired actor who purported to be "Dr. Fox" and who gave a nonsensical university lecture in a wildly entertaining style and got outstanding student evaluations for his brilliance.

In one notorious study, those who saw just a thirty-second soundless video of a teacher in action gave him virtually the same ratings as the students taking his course—who'd spent a semester reading, writing, thinking, and talking with him. Smile warmly for the first thirty seconds of the first class in January, and you'll get good scores in May.

(Ms. Mentor directs doubters to grab the nearest search engine, type in "Teaching Evaluations," and seek research by Nalini Ambady and Robert Rosenthal; Ronald H. Naftulin et al.; Wendy M. Williams and Stephen J. Ceci; Elizabeth M. Lieux; and Susan Basow.)

You'll also get better evaluations, Ms. Mentor knows, if you put on a more entertaining show. Skip the top-down or banking model of teaching, where you pump the knowledge into the students' heads and have them parrot back what you've fed them. That doesn't sell now, except for the rare charismatic lecturer who's chock full of gossip, humor, and new information.

Study standup comics to learn how to open a class. Troll the Internet, television programs, and newspapers for current references you can make to crazed celebrities, moral issues, songs, food, gadgets, heroes, goats. Encourage students to be problem-solvers: You're a Civil War general whose army has no shoes: What are your alternatives? You're a celebrity who wants to help poor single moms: what can you do? Can Bill and Melinda Gates cure malaria by throwing money at it? (Ms. Mentor hopes so.)

Your story and follow-up questions can be entertaining, or explosive: "Was Saddam Hussein worth the number of Americans and Iraqis who've died?" Get students to be active learners, talking to each other—not just writing down what you say.

Learn students' names, create discussion circles, make chat rooms, assign hands-on group projects, require in-class presentations, encourage role-playing. Today's students learn by doing—making a Civil War–era quilt from a pattern found on the Internet, writing a sonnet, cooking the quail in rose petal sauce from Laura Esquivel's *Like Water for Chocolate*. You may fear that you're denying your students access to The Expert (you). But if they're teenagers, most would rather interact with each other than listen to you.

That may be especially true if you're a woman professor. Students expect women to be nurturers, and men to be authority figures. Your mean-spirited evaluations may be from students who regard you as a gender-role violator. But if students feel loyal to their small groups and committed to their work, they're more apt to rate you highly, as the one who made it possible: "I really worked my butt off and got an A. Hurrah for Professor Jane!"

Is this pandering and coddling? Maybe. But it's less blatant than toting wine and cheese or a glamorous guest speaker on the day the evaluation forms are given out. And it's less corrupting to the conscience than giving everyone A's and being prominently featured in Pick-a-Prof.com, which publishes professors' grade distributions.

Suppose you do the gesturing, the smiling, the small groups, the food bribes, and the inflated grading, and you still get bad teaching evaluations, which may mean you won't get tenure . . . and you still approach the classroom in a state of terror and dread? In that case, Ms. Mentor gives you permission to quit.

No one has to teach.

Your energies and talents may be more appreciated in business, for instance, where you're interacting with task-oriented adults instead of restless, hormonally charged teens. There is no shame, Ms. Mentor decrees, in moving on. But there is shame, and waste, in making yourself miserable.

That will always get you a bad grade from Ms. Mentor.

—

Reader Response: Ms. Mentor expected bilious and vituperative retorts to this column. She expected to be kicked for cynicism and pilloried for pandering, and one grad student did proclaim (as the young often do) that "Good teaching is good teaching." But mostly, Ms. Mentor received plaudits, especially from the victims of evaluation vendettas. "Had I known then . . ." several mused.

This column has had the most requests for reprints, and has become a standard reading assignment in centers for teaching and learning throughout the Midwest.

One dissenter accused Ms. Mentor of having received poor evaluations herself (never), and claimed that his evaluations are always high because he is "handsome and dramatic." Were anonymity not promised to all writers, Ms. Mentor would direct readers to check the photo on his Web page, as she did.

Ms. Mentor also heard from one spy whose university requires students to fill out evaluation forms just three weeks into each term, because that's most convenient for the computer center. The forms are filed away until the end of the semester, when they're sprung upon the instructors, who've had no chance to see or learn from them. This practice strikes Ms. Mentor as bizarre, and she encourages victims to print out her column and leave it when it might help the most.

A Fraud or a Great Teacher?

Q: My colleague "Phoebe" is a fraud, and the rest of us in the department have known it for years. Her dissertation, which she claimed was original work, is actually a translation of another scholar's dissertation in an obscure language, with a few extra pieces thrown in.

But no one confronts Phoebe, because she does what we don't want to—she runs the language lab. She also does it superbly, serving as a mentor to countless students. Still, she doesn't have an honest Ph.D., and some new colleagues believe we ought to expose her to somebody—her grad school, our department chair, our human resources staff, our dean, the local sensationalist paper.

We suspect that the dean and other administrators already know, but don't want to be bothered. She's now coming up for contract renewal—but if we get rid of her, we may wind up with someone who won't run the language lab so conscientiously and cheerfully. Maybe we should just continue our silence, since we don't have tenure, and the only reason to speak out is for Justice and Fairness, things that we've seen don't exist anyway.

A: Ms. Mentor hears a chorus of her readers bellowing: "Fire Phoebe!"

After all, if Phoebe is a vile plagiarist, and if we condone such academic dishonesty, we are violating the most sacred canons of truth and original inquiry and throwing offal on the ivory tower.

But . . .

Phoebe does her job magnificently, and the world of language teaching needs Phoebes to inspire students. Would an outsider with a pristine Ph.D. do better?

Ms. Mentor, in her perfect wisdom, sees two competing ethical systems in your letter. One is the role of rules in academe, the abstract absolutes that are supposed to govern our lives. The other is the ethic of care for others, the responsibility to students. (Scholars of ethics will recognize these competing beliefs from Carol Gilligan's *In a Different Voice* and Mary Field Belenky et al.'s *Women's Ways of Knowing*, as well as Portia's speech on justice and mercy in *The Merchant of Venice*.)

If Phoebe is fired, the rule-mongers will be satisfied—but students will lose.

And yet, can you simply ignore what you know about Phoebe's dissertation?

You already have. Stringent academics might view you and your colleagues as accessories, handmaidens to a cover-up. If you do decide to denounce her, how can you explain your silence in the past? And won't the bad publicity make your dean very, very angry? And if your dean is the punitive sort, and you come up for tenure . . . ?

By now Ms. Mentor's readers are frothing and fuming in all directions. She urges them to sit down, have a cold drink, think deep ethical thoughts, and ponder parallel situations from the last decade or so.

Reporter Jayson Blair, for instance, famously fabricated stories about snipers, Iraq, and more in the *New York Times*. He was fired, as were his bosses.

Meanwhile Quincy Troupe, named as the first poet laureate of California, turned out not to have the college degree that he claimed—though he had published thirteen books and served as a mentor to hundreds of budding writers. He was fired as poet laureate.

Ms. Mentor agrees that Jayson Blair should have been bounced, but wonders about Quincy Troupe, sixty-two years old, with decades of accomplishments. Did a degree matter at that point? Why didn't his undergraduate college simply award him an honorary degree?

She returns now, more calmly, to creative solutions for Phoebe and the colleagues who know that her dissertation is less than original, but who value her contributions to teaching.

Phoebe is not exactly a plagiarist. She is an appropriator. Since her degree is in foreign languages, a field where translations are acceptable dissertation topics, it could be said that her dissertation is merely mislabeled. Instead of calling it an original piece of work, she and her committee should have called it a translation with commentary. Ms. Mentor wonders if Phoebe's graduate school would be amenable to such a labeling change.

Meanwhile, Phoebe's job may also be mislabeled. Since language-lab coordinators are not always required to hold Ph.D.'s, perhaps the job could be re-advertised as a master's-level position. Phoebe would then qualify as an outstanding internal candidate.

Ms. Mentor wants her readers to consider alternatives, and envision where each path will lead them. Often what seems to be the path of righteousness is also the path of shooting oneself in the foot.

Phoebe has made a mistake, but she may very well be a sinner worth saving for a higher good.

———

Reader Response: A chorus of readers called for Phoebe's immediate resignation, if not execution. Most of them, Ms. Mentor noted, were underemployed Ph.D.'s in foreign languages.

Ms. Mentor's respondents also have vivid imaginations. One envisioned Phoebe as "a perpetual grad student slinking around the language lab because she's uncomfortable hanging out with the big boys and girls." Another was convinced that Phoebe is "verging on the psychopathic." While Ms. Mentor enjoys meditation on the virtues and follies of others, she urges her readers to—well—read what's on the page. That is all that we know about Phoebe.

I Am Hot, Hot, Hot

Q: I know that pranksters sometimes put chili peppers (for "hotness") at random in teacher rankings on RateMyProfessors.com. But since I have four (4) chili peppers, may I assume that I am truly hot, even though it won't get me tenure?

A: Yes.

Working and Playing Well with Others

You've all been taught how to behave, Ms. Mentor knows. You are supposed to be generous, brave, and serene. You clean up your own messes, listen to other people without interrupting, and treat everyone with kindness and compassion until they really piss you off.

And then you write a nasty memo. And maybe you send it to the department e-mail list, but that was by accident. Really, it was.

Many academic incivilities appear to happen by accident—even if they aren't really accidental, such as treating female colleagues differently from male ones. Deirdre McCloskey, formerly the economist Donald McCloskey, noticed that after her sex-change operation, she was treated in very different ways. (McCloskey is one of at least fifty transgendered academics now teaching, among them biologist Joan Roughgarden, author of *Evolution's Rainbow: Diversity, Gender, and Sexuality in Nature and People*, and English professor Jennifer Finney Boylan, author of *She's Not There*.)

In her memoir *Crossing*, Deirdre McCloskey records an Aha! moment that took place when she was in an all-male academic group. What she said was ignored. Then it was embraced when "Harvey" made the same point a few minutes later.

"Wonderful," McCloskey thought the first time, "they're treating me like a woman." But the thrill faded quickly.

There are advantages to living in an ivory tower, Ms. Mentor often thinks. Unlike most women, she can never be interrupted.

Cat Fight?

Q (from "Hedwig"): I have a socially inept new faculty colleague who told a group of people—again and again and again—that she is far better looking than I. She certainly tries harder than I do, showing more cleavage and then some. Anyway, a senior faculty member said she is competing with me. (We're both untenured.)

I hate competitions of that kind. My question is: Do I just go ahead and compete? Do I ignore her like the annoying puppy she is and permit her to embarrass herself, again and again and again? Should I give her a link to your column?

A: Ms. Mentor's first reaction was to think "cat fight"—and to gird herself against it. She would cite *All About Eve, Working Girl,* Scarlett vs. Melanie, and *Heathers,* and recommend *Competition: A Feminist Taboo?* edited by Valerie Miner and Helen E. Longino. She would point out that Sue, the sometimes nice girl in *Carrie,* is the only one who survives the carnage.

Ms. Mentor can well imagine the old Hollywood version of your story. Your new colleague would charm and seduce every powerful man on the campus, even reducing student workers to cow-eyed blithering. You would be dressed in brown and cast aside, your memos unanswered, your students snarling and whining. In the cafeteria, you would have to eat your grubby lunch alone, while your colleague—bathed in bright gold lighting—would dine in the center of a throng of worshippers.

In the end, having lost everything to your golden rival, you would be trudging pitifully through the snow, clutching your moth-eaten coat about you. You would press your nose against a window and see "her" inside, surrounded by adoring sycophants and laughing in a merry cat-swallowed-the-canary way. She would stretch out her long, silken legs, and you would see that she was sitting at . . . your desk.

Ms. Mentor whimpers.

But that does not seem to be the movie you're in.

In academe, the roles are different. Your colleague may indeed be socially inept or misguided if she's chosen a common social role for women—to be sexy and flirtatious—over the more austere professional role and demeanor expected of female Ph.D.'s. Academe tends to be more

Middle American in style. Crisp and clean and competent are valued more than cleavage.

It is true that good looks may get you a chili pepper for "hotness" on RateMyProfessors.com, but those are student ratings. Students don't vote on your career path. In fact, according to research by Daniel S. Hamermesh, good-looking academic men may be rated more highly by students, but the evidence about women is equivocal.

Ms. Mentor thinks the evidence against your colleague ("Inepta") is also questionable. Is she truly some kind of scheming Jezebel, bragging and flaunting, trying to vanquish you through her clothes and competitive spirit? Should you be pondering revenge?

Or is Inepta-as-catty-colleague mostly the figment of someone else's imagination, maybe someone who has seen too many movies?

Ms. Mentor ponders the evidence. Inepta reportedly "told a group of people" that she outfoxes you. But who were those people? And why the use of "again and again and again," hammering home Inepta's alleged perfidy? Who is badmouthing Inepta to you?

Ms. Mentor finds one prime suspect in your letter. There is the "senior faculty member" who claims that Inepta is competing with you.

Why is Professor Senior telling you this?

Ms. Mentor sees a different scene. Two junior professors, you and Inepta, are both fairly new to academe, and understandably anxious. The issue isn't Inepta's appearance or yours. (And in any case, Ms. Mentor is sure you look fine.) Nor is it clear that Inepta is competing with you. Even if she were, what might she be competing for?

The rewards in academe go to those who teach well, who are likable and good department citizens and committee workers, and who publish and do research that meets the standard expected by their colleges. Certainly there are some unwritten rules in academe. But "Be hotter than thy colleague" is not one of them.

Ms. Mentor wonders if Professor Senior is the villain here, the one who is lurking, rumor-mongering, kicking up worries and dirt. Professor Senior may be a classic academic type, a crank who likes to foment discontent for his own amusement. He may be a faux mentor who, in the guise of being helpful, is making you skittish and hostile toward your peer. He is probably doing the same to Inepta ("Hedwig says you're a bimbo").

Academe harbors many talented, pot-stirring, highly verbal, and articulate meddlers. Mostly they are bored, midlife associate professors who find teaching no longer interesting or challenging, and who have lost whatever ambitions they once had for research. They may have failed to get grant money, or their articles may have been repeatedly rejected for publication. They measure out their lives in passionless meetings, full of repetition and posturing. Once upon a time, they used to find their low salaries, troubled students, and squalid offices galvanizing, even enraging. Now such things are deadening, part of a life of quiet desperation, until . . . Hark!

Strangers have come to town. Two young female strangers. Excitement and diversion looms. What if they're set against each other? Won't the fur fly?

That scenario is, alas, not uncommon in real life as well as in Hollywood. Cat fights are presumed—or fomented—whenever women work together, even though most women prefer to work harmoniously. In a crisis, as research by Laura Cousino Klein has shown, men have the fight-or-flight response. But women bond with one another.

And so Ms. Mentor suggests bonding and cooperation with Inepta. Your instincts are good, and you should not compete. You must treat her with polite friendliness at all times, and connect her with a reliable senior mentor if you can. You may, of course, give her this column, and you can be sure that Ineptas all over the country will be receiving copies, probably anonymously, from their own cowardly colleagues.

But the best thing you can do, Ms. Mentor opines, is to invite Inepta to lunch. Make it just the two of you, publicly in the cafeteria, discussing scholarship and teaching, obviously enjoying each other's company, and showing solidarity.

The meddlers and bad-mouthers will have to contrive a new scenario to explain all that. But you and Inepta will both be sitting pretty.

What Are the Real Rules?

Q (from "Cardozo"): I've read in your column that one is supposed to erase a blackboard before leaving a classroom. Where is that written? At least around here, there is no such obligation.

A: Ms. Mentor concedes that most rules for academicians are unwritten. But she has taken it upon herself to fix that.

Presumably we learn at home to share, to flush, to sauté the onions first, and to hurl a piece of pasta against the wall to make sure it's done . . . but how do we learn the rules for successful, or at least peaceful, life in academe?

Colleges in the United States do have rules-that-are-not-rules, true urban legends. Students everywhere believe that if the teacher does not appear within ten minutes of the official class starting time, they are free to leave—although it may be fifteen minutes if the teacher is a revered or grouchy full professor.

Among new faculty members, there's the myth that one cannot leave a department party until the most senior person has left. If you have a party-loving good old boy for a chair, you'd better engage an overnight babysitter.

Some campus traditions have died in recent years, such as public drink-and-run contests, or the expectation that faculty women will "pour" at the fall tea. What to wear is a vexing question for newly hired people for whom the general rule is: Be fairly formal until you're established. But call all your colleagues by their first names, even if they're old enough to be your grandparents. If they are, they don't want to be reminded. And never praise anyone for being "spry."

But most of those are simply good manners, like not chewing with your mouth open, not depositing used chewing gum on the furniture, and not indulging in criminal activity unless it's expected of you. (The French ex-convict author Jean Genet was famous for lifting the service at chic intellectual gatherings, and people would watch and coo delightedly: "Oh, look, Genet's stealing the silverware again.")

Each campus, like each jail, does have its own culture, some of it revealed in the school's faculty handbook, which may hint at secrets while describing noble goals. Mission statements, for instance, always call for excellence, but Jesuit universities also mention justice and encourage peace and social activism. Some mission statements sound like promises: Clemson University aims to hire outstanding faculty and "compensate them at nationally competitive levels." Marshall University pledges to "provide a safe and secure employee work environment" and "enhance the quality of health care in the region," while Drew University seeks "intellectually prepared students who want to learn."

All of those statements—which Ms. Mentor found through a random Google search—are clues to the rules, and the challenges, at those institutions.

You should also read promotion and tenure policies with care and an alert imagination. If the policies are very detailed, they may have been redefined or smothered in jargon to protect the university from litigation. Where policies are vague and short ("excellent teaching, research, and service"), the unspoken factor ("collegiality," or whether They like you) may be the main criterion. If your school has no written policies, then the decision is all collegiality—and in religious schools, it may also involve piety.

Ms. Mentor reminds all untenured newbies to record in their Tenure Diaries whenever policies are followed, whenever they're ignored, and when anyone makes an unseemly comment or prediction. "Olaf," a worrier, once asked "Torvald the Tactless Senior Prof" about his tenure chances—to which Torvald replied, "Snowball in hell," and promptly forgot the incident. Olaf wrote it down, in case he ever needed evidence that the deck was stacked against him. But he also worked twice as hard on his publishing and teaching, did get tenure, and—with a show of suavity few people could pull off—invited Torvald for a celebratory schnapps.

And so Ms. Mentor decrees that two unwritten rules are "Be gracious" and "Be thoughtful"—to administrative and clerical staffs and maintenance people, as well as to students and colleagues. That means starting class on time, getting out of a classroom as soon as the session is over, not allowing students to leave food messes to fester, and smiling at everyone. It doesn't hurt, and they'll either like you or think you have a hidden agenda, which gives you the reputation for deep thought.

You may also need to teach students the rudiments of manners that some do not seem to know: no cell-phone use in class, no interrupting or erupting, no racing out while discussion's continuing, and no whining or eating carrots during class. Amorous students should also be discouraged from sharing their love publicly.

As for faculty: Ms. Mentor urges senior ones to help the newbies. You were young once, most likely, and you, too, were puzzled when you made an excellent suggestion in a department meeting and no one responded to it at all.

You violated a couple of unspoken rules.

As a newbie, you're not an expert, and you don't know what powerful interests may be for or against what you proposed.

Probably, too, you did not couch your idea in proper "departmentese," Kathryn Hume's term for the bland language that masks self-interest. Eventually you learn what must not be bluntly said. If you want to be heard, and especially if you want tenure, you must not say that Professor Rot has become a mule, incapable of teaching, research, or service, and ought to be sent to the barn. Rather, in departmentese, you'll talk about his fine mind, his long years of devoted service, and our desire to "continue his legacy" by hiring others who will (in reality) do the work he's supposed to be doing.

The study of self-interest, always fascinating, underlies the best and most vicious academic novels. What better laboratory than a department for studying rodents cooped up with each other for years, unable to shriek about what they really want, but still craving food, space, self-aggrandizement? Ms. Mentor is reminded of President Lyndon B. Johnson's wise counsel: "Don't spit in the soup. We all have to eat."

The rules are made by those who follow the rules, and department meetings can be exercises in the will to power. Notice who stands up, who filibusters, who fiddles while someone else burns with indignation. Meetings are carnivals, episodes in ongoing soap operas, and skits peopled with—yes—some atrociously bad actors.

Yet there is also beauty in order, the structure that you come to see as you study the architecture of academic life. There are serfs; there are dragons; there are definitely bats in belfries. Sometimes the longitudinal study of your colleagues—Devin Diffident, Sara Surreptitious, Barnaby Bluster—is the most entertaining and longest-running show you'll live with. It rules.

I'm Afraid I Made Some Enemies

Q (from "Arky"): I'm new in a department that's trying to improve our research productivity. As my contribution, I combed the citation indexes for publications by department members and distributed a chart showing how many times each piece had been cited. As it happened, one of my articles had been cited quite a few times, while those of some of my more established colleagues were cited rarely or not at all. Was this in poor taste on my part?

Q (from "Bambi"): I have had a messy but (I believe) unpublicized skirting-around romantic involvement with one of my dissertation committee members ("Polonius," thirty years my senior), who is now seeing another grad student. I have been wanting him off my committee for years, even though I have gotten a lot of academic help from him, but have been afraid that people would suspect the reason. What should I do?

Q (from "Carroll"): I'm a tenured full professor who recently had words with my new dean ("Deanna") about her policy on professional development. She suddenly said, "You don't believe me because I am a woman, and that tells me a lot about you." I felt offended and disrespected, and I sent her an e-mail saying so. She replied, "Have you realized that you challenged my words?" and added, "Have you done that with a male dean? I will be willing to work with you, but only if you treat me with respect, and I will treat you the same way." What is your advice about handling this?

A: Ms. Mentor rarely gets to tell all her correspondents that they've done wrong. But Arky, Bambi, and Carroll have all erred, with hot pen, hot tempers, and hot hands.

Arky has good political instincts. He volunteers to be helpful, and then realizes he's made a big boo-boo—for it is never good to make one's elders (and one's judges) look bad. And so Ms. Mentor advises Arky to backtrack—to find out what his elders are good at, and figure out how to compliment them for it. Since they've no doubt dedicated themselves to teaching and service, Arky can seek out their advice for teaching and department citizenship. They will be flattered and appeased, and Ms. Mentor can relax.

Bambi's professor Polonius has not been kind to others: he has loved unwisely, not too well, and probably too often. Ms. Mentor deplores romantic relationships between faculty members and students, and finds his conduct loathsome. He is entrusted with students' intellects, and to cross the boundary between mentor and lover is simply wrong. Bambi needs to expel him utterly, and she can satisfy herself and her battered heart by being inordinately gracious. She should tell the world that her dissertation "has gone in a different direction, and so I need a different committee. But I will always be grateful to Professor Polonius for his guidance."

She could have busted him for sexual harassment, but instead benevolent Bambi also makes prurient Polonius look good. He's apt to fume privately that she doesn't care ("heartless bitch"), but he can't ever say in public what she may, sometime down the line, want to whisper in private ("terrible in bed"). In a few years, Bambi may own the forest.

Carroll, meanwhile, needs a reality check from the impeccable Ms. Mentor. "Look what Dean Deanna did to me!" Carroll seems to be railing. But Ms. Mentor cannot get the whole picture. Carroll "has words," but what words? Carroll sends a furious e-mail, but what's in it? And, considering the dean's reaction, is Carroll a man or a woman?

If male, did Carroll interrupt his dean, as men frequently interrupt women? (Some 70 percent of conversational interruptions are committed by men breaking into women's speech.) Did he bellow and drown her out? Shake his fist?

If female, did Carroll expect Deanna to show solidarity with women or be confidential in ways that Deanna can't or won't be? Did Carroll want to bond with a female dean who insists on an academic pecking order?

Or is Carroll simply a typical tenured academic, a ranter against all authority figures?

Once you become an administrator, one recent correspondent reports, you instantly become "disliked, misquoted, gossiped about, and maligned." Oh, the rants Ms. Mentor has seen.

Still, Carroll has deeply erred. For Carroll can control only his/her behavior, and s/he should not have sent a nasty "poor me" or "you're mean" e-mail message. Such messages can and will be forwarded, archived, and remembered for eternity. Interpersonal and emotional communications should be handled face to face, in a respectful and conciliatory way. Carroll should not make accusations ("You always—I never"), but should try, "I think maybe we got off on the wrong foot." An apology is never amiss.

Even people with tenure do need to work and play well with others.

The Perpetual Peacock

Q: My colleague is a chronic peacocker. When we have visiting speakers, his first "question" is always a disquisition on his own research, whether relevant or not. When we have job candidates, he tries to outdo them with rants about his own research, whether relevant or not. We all eye roll when he starts, and some of our more courageous members snort, whisper, or sigh—but that has no impact on his strutting, preening, and peacocking. Since we're far too polite or cowardly to try ridicule or confrontation, are we saddled with his behavior forever?

A: Yes.

Mispronunciation or Manipulation?

Q (from "Professor Stickler"): "Dean Titan," a very senior administrator at our U., insists on pronouncing "collegial" with a hard "G" in every one of his impassioned perorations to our faculty. That has led to a bitter division among the faculty, with the more sycophantic members following his pronunciation while the rest of us bravely resist. Who is right, and do you have any suggestions?

A: Ms. Mentor often hears from the victims of academic malefactors, but never from the perpetrators. She would love to know why they commit their harassments, their whispered vilifications, their butcheries of the English language. She wishes the offenders would explain their crimes. She seeks only to understand.

She also marvels at the will to power among academics. After all, they've chosen a profession that will prevent their ever getting most worldly recognitions—such as piles of money, fabulous cars, or tabloid-worthy flings with beautiful people of low intellect. Academics ought to get satisfaction from sharing ideas and opening the minds of the young to truth and beauty. Many do.

But others seek power, or at least individuality, by fomenting rebellions, being ridiculously chic, or interpreting others' utterances as highly meaningful and probably malevolent.

Which brings Ms. Mentor to Professor Stickler's question. How is "collegiality" pronounced, and should the dispute produce rival factions who hiss at each other?

In American English, the preferred pronunciation is indeed "coll-eej-al," but it is linked both to soft-G "college" and to hard-G "colleague." The loyal Latinists who have never accepted English as the world's lingua franca might dig in their heels for a hard G.

There are also British speakers who prefer "collegial" with a hard G as an assertion of imperial privilege and differentiation from rude colonial Americans. In a similar vein, British scientists speak of amino acids as "am-eye-no," a word Americans pronounce as "a-mee-no."

In short, Dean Titan may merely be a harmless Anglophile. But that would be far too dull an explanation for Professor Stickler and his ilk. There must be a better reason! There must be Meaning! There must be a reason to take up sides!

After all, taking sides puts everyone in a category, and academics love to categorize. Whole subject areas are built on classifying, polarizing, separating, labeling, and dating. Subtle and unsubtle distinctions are the bread of life. If you are not a Platonist, perhaps you're a Freudian, a Marxist, a Whig, or a dendrophile.

But Professor Stickler's cohorts seem to have reduced it all to one question: Are you Dean Titan's toady?

"My natural instinct is to toady," said Isadora, Erica Jong's scholarly heroine, some thirty years ago in *Fear of Flying*—and souls more cynical than Ms. Mentor have applied that label to those who make it in the ivory-tower world. Indeed, academicians have a history of conformity. They followed orders, memorized the Periodic Table, did their homework on time, and headed their papers correctly. They just need to be told who's the head toad, and a-toadying they will go.

Dean Titan clearly is the head toad. But Professor Stickler and his gang want to express their independence of spirit, their refusal to knuckle under to power. They will rebel. They will soar. They will pronounce "collegial" as if it had a J.

Ms. Mentor confesses that she cannot get excited about their feud. She is far more engaged by the feud that took place between the Big-Endians and the Small-Endians in *Gulliver's Travels*: some 11,000 people "suffered death rather than submit to break their eggs at the smaller end."

Ms. Mentor is glad that Jonathan Swift was writing fiction. And she cannot resist mentioning that Swift himself was a dean—of St. Patrick's Cathedral, back when deans had some serious social prestige.

Which brings Ms. Mentor back to Dean Titan and his uncommon pronunciation of "collegial." Perhaps, like Gulliver among the Lilliputians, or Swift as an Irishman in England, he simply doesn't know the local rules. Maybe Dean Titan just doesn't know how to pronounce the word correctly. Perhaps he's more to be pitied than poked at.

Most academics do possess a barn full of passive vocabulary, words that no one but Ms. Mentor can pronounce with complete authority. Among her favorites are "behemoth," "scion," and "menarche," but she also likes "boustrophedonic" and "pinguid."

Ideally, teachers who advise and mold the young will look up those words and pronounce them correctly in public. But in the heat of the moment, while passionately lecturing, even the most staid may throw caution to the winds and follow Humpty Dumpty in Lewis Carroll's *Through the Looking Glass*: "When I use a word, it means just what I choose it to mean—neither more nor less. . . . The question is which is to be master—that's all."

Perhaps Dean Titan knows exactly what he's doing: Words are pronounced the way I pronounce them, because I Am the Head Nabob in Charge. And that is what it comes down to: Who is master?

Being "collegial" is important. Being liked can determine your academic future. And so, while Ms. Mentor knows you would like her to say that you should stand on principle . . . and pronounce the word correctly . . . and devil take the consequences . . . she, in fact, will offer you this advice: If you don't have tenure, pronounce the word "collegial" just the way Dean Titan does.

If you do have tenure, pronounce the word however you please.

Lilliputian Power Play

Q: Because our university president is vertically challenged, the microphone at public gatherings is always adjusted for him. Everyone else must bow their heads to use it. Is this silly little power ritual an example of no one's head being allowed higher than the king's?

A: Yes.

Why Won't She Behave?

Q: My question is about perpetual temporaries. Every department has them, with titles like "research associate" or "adjunct." They got their Ph.D.'s here years ago, but instead of moving on like most people, they stay . . . and stay . . . and stay.

"Marlene," for instance, would never be hired on a tenure track, due to lack of publications, but has been kept on anyway in low-paying positions, teaching a few courses and working in the lab I share with several other faculty members. I have had complaints from my students about Marlene's "bossing" them around in the lab and trying to "tell them" how to do their work. When I heard of this behavior, I immediately told the students that they report to me. I short-circuit Marlene's interference by maintaining a high presence in the lab, and by informing the students that if there's a problem, they should tell Marlene to talk to me. (She never has. I think she is frightened.)

My question is, will this person never leave? Why is she happy (?!) or at least satisfied with a low-paying temporary position? I refuse to hire Ph.D.'s to do technician work, but other professors keep finding small contracts or little bits of work that permit these people to keep hanging around. My opinion is that it is morally wrong to do this. We should kick them out of the nest and let them get on with their careers.

A: My, my, you do sound like an underappreciated film director ("These ungrateful actors have their own ideas! Don't they realize they're my puppets?"). You also remind Ms. Mentor of writers whose characters stubbornly take on lives of their own and argue with their creators ("No, Juliet, you cannot run away with him and live happily ever after, no matter how much you beg!"). Like auteurs and authors, you have very firm ideas about how other people should run their lives.

Ms. Mentor suggests that you try out Marlene's role for a moment, and consider a plot in which she, not you, is the central character. She is obviously competent and experienced, but she has chosen a very different path. Maybe she discovered in grad school that she'd rather be a bench scientist than an assistant professor who grinds out grant applications and journal articles, schleps to endless meetings, and presides over a little ant farm of researchers and students and helpers. Marlene may be someone who loves lab work, knows her own heart, and does not care about tenure or awards or big bucks.

Yes, Ms. Mentor knows that you think Marlene is a coward, unwilling to face the world. But Ms. Mentor suspects that Marlene's story is much richer and more complex. Marlene may have a life partner rooted in Same City, or she may be a single mom who wants Same City's innovative schools for her kids. She may have a disability treatable only in Same City. Or she may be a devoted daughter to aging parents, or a would-be musician, or a community activist working to change her part of the globe. Or Marlene may just love Same City too much to leave it.

In short, Ms. Mentor thinks you need to brush up on your imagination. The Marlene you describe is a drab character, without dreams or friends or personality—and when she follows her own bent, not yours, you get angry. Ms. Mentor wonders why.

Okay, okay, I'll be nice to Marlene, you say grudgingly—but Ms. Mentor wants you to rewrite your drama even further, making Marlene a solid supporting actor. A Marlene who knows everyone can warn you against hiring that incompetent technician who keeps getting fobbed off on new people. Marlene knows what works and why, and knows why you can't expect Professors Top and Bottom to collaborate on anything (Mrs. Top used to be Mrs. Bottom). Marlene is your institutional memory, the human database you need to be a wise and successful monarch in your own lab.

Marlenes in the lab are often nurturers, rarely backstabbers, and sometimes defenders against tragic or comical mishaps. A long-term researcher who knew about safety gloves (there are twenty-six different kinds) might have saved the life of Karen Wetterhahn, the Dartmouth professor who wore the wrong kind to work with mercury—and died, poisoned. Experienced research associates can keep novices from releasing dangerous viruses, breathing toxic substances, killing puppies, or burning down the lab.

Right now Marlene is mentoring students and sharing her expertise, while you are sabotaging yourself, undermining her, and fussing about her "behavior" (which makes you sound a little, well, adolescent). You're wondering why she can't be like you (what's her problem?), when in fact she's playing her role much better than you're playing yours. And so Ms. Mentor suggests that you applaud and reward Marlene. Give her a co-starring role. You both will shine.

Dr. Hissy and Dr. Prankster

Q (from "Rosie"): When my Very Annoying Colleague is having a hissy fit because he needs copies quickly but the copier needs a new toner cartridge and the secretary is home sick, do I have a moral obligation to inform him that I know how to change the toner? Or may I keep that knowledge to myself and enjoy the show?

Q (from "Mark"): I have an odd colleague who feels that by playing the prankster, he asserts his ethnic identity. (Don't ask. He has tenure.) His role as antagonist, "subverting the dominant paradigm," inspires him to cancel others' classes without their knowledge, show strange films unrelated to his subject, and berate and leer at random. He says he'll stop next month, that all this is an experiment. How should academics deal with nutty colleagues who have found a theoretical or ideological framework for acting like jerks?

Q (from "Julia"): I'm talented and tenured, tall, pretty, and very charming, and male administrators leave me out of projects lest people "talk." I work with computer geeks. What should I do?

A: All right, Ms. Mentor will admit it. Many academics do behave weirdly.

People in business can, presumably, model their behavior after CEOs who trumpet their profits on TV. Doctors can emulate furrowed-brow researchers who are interviewed with great respect. Lawyers can orate about injustice and seem quite photogenic.

But who, in our world of images, shows academics how to behave properly? Ms. Mentor's cupboards bulge with movies about nutty professors, absent-minded professors, and spinster schoolteachers. Every campus has some lore about a monomaniacal prof who, when his wife was out of town, forgot his lunch and ate his tie. (Ms. Mentor knew one of those in graduate school. His colleagues implored him to take up smoking.)

People who dwell in their minds are allowed to be a little out of touch with the prevailing mores and folkways of the "real world." But how far?

Rosie's annoying colleague, call him "Dr. Hissy," is a high-maintenance type who, if female, would be accused of "princess behavior." Ms. Mentor knows there must be a proper clinical term for someone who comes unglued at the slightest mechanical glitch. Researchers in the past have named all kinds of things common to professors, including "dysgraphia" (bad handwriting) and "prosopagnosia" ("face blindness," the inability to remember familiar faces), as well as "Asperger's syndrome" (social awkwardness, not looking other people in the eye, being astonishingly brilliant in one intellectual area).

In the real world, those behaviors may stamp one as "an odd duck," ill-suited to the schmoozing and communication needed to keep an office afloat. But in academe, the ability to focus completely on one task—while the rest of the universe is IMing, iPoding, and cellphoning—is a caste marker and a cherished ability. Academics can discuss ideas for hours without fidgeting.

However, Ms. Mentor has failed to concentrate on Rosie, who's still watching, smiling slyly, as Dr. Hissy froths about the missing toner. Should Rosie rescue him?

Ms. Mentor posed that question to a gaggle of academic experts at a recent conference, and their verdict was unanimous for tough love: Rosie should keep the knowledge to herself and "enjoy the show." Some experts were motivated by simple schadenfreude, the joy in others' misfortunes that may be the ruling emotion in academe. Others claimed loftily that if Rosie did change the toner, she would be "an enabler," preventing Dr. Hissy from being an independent "self-actualizer."

Still others, chuckling evilly, suggested that Rosie wait until Dr. Hissy gives up and leaves in a huff—then slip in and replace the toner. Once Dr. Hissy sees others happily traipsing by with new copies . . . well, maybe it will be a teachable moment.

Dr. Prankster, Mark's colleague, is a stranger case, a prof run amok. Whatever his ethnic fantasies (yes, Ms. Mentor is curious, too), Dr. Prankster should not be flouncing about, bedeviling his fellow creatures. Even a month with a self-appointed madman can make everyone else slightly insane.

Ms. Mentor would enlist the department head to scold Dr. Prankster, for academic freedom does not mean the right to go berserk and trample upon others' educations. Ms. Mentor hopes that such a warning would work. Grievances and interventions are messy, and a barrage of lunatic memorandums is rarely entertaining outside witty academic novels.

As for the beautiful Julia, Ms. Mentor sympathizes with a "Don't hate me because I'm beautiful" quandary, but sees no cure for the binary thinking of academics and civilians alike. Too many people believe that a woman cannot be both beautiful and brainy—as if there's some kind of conservation of virtues, and no one gets more than one.

Julia could uglify herself, communicate mostly by e-mail and phone rather than in person, or simply be pushy and insistent, along the lines of Dr. Hissy. If she develops some of his obnoxious traits, and possibly mixes in a few mild peculiarities from Dr. Prankster, no one will think she's beautiful anymore. She will be taken more seriously, and a whole new world of opportunity may open up. (Or maybe not.)

Eccentric and self-absorbed academics may find it humbling to poke around in the blogosphere, where colorful commentary flourishes among the pseudonymous. The blogger who calls herself "imreallyparanoid," for instance, has this to say about professors as social beings: "urgh! you guys i went to a faculty-dominant party yesterday and i must say, i was reminded again that the majority of academic men (and women) . . . is really rather unattractive. and i don't mean bone structure and style but the stuff under the skin, which is more important anyway. things like smiling and telling jokes that are actually funny and being able to talk about stuff besides yourself and your work. i guess most academics were socially retarded as children, but you'd think by the time you are in your 30s and 40s you would have gotten over those hangups, no? maybe someday i will write a self-help book on basic social etiquette for nerds."

Ms. Mentor is saving her money to buy it.

Should I Give Credit to a Freeloader?

Q (from "Edwina"): When I was hired three years ago, departments in my college operated as separate feuding entities. Wanting to change that, I created a popular joint lecture series between my department ("Oil") and another one ("Water"). The strongest opposition came from "Sylvester," a very competitive Water professor with a big mouth who loves to run everyone down behind their backs. And now Sylvester is applying for other jobs and claiming he's the one who created the lecture series. He even asked me to proofread his application letter. I really would like to expose him for the lying cheater that he is.

A: Revenge may be the single most captivating dream in human existence. Ms. Mentor cherishes Dorothy Parker's story, "The Banquet of Crow," in which the loser ends up chomping on a shiny, black-feathered thing. Other scholars have imagined yanking their enemies' nose hairs, or corrupting their spell checkers, or sending them to hoity-toity wine-and-cheese parties toting only Velveeta and wearing bunny suits. One dean advises his flock, "Teach your dog to piss on their feet."

Experienced academics know that most good deeds can double as revenge scenarios. You may, for instance, nominate your enemies for useless honors. Get them appointed to countless busy-but-powerless committees. Drown them in paperwork, while praising them for "service." Pass none of the reforms they suggest, and use their vitas for paper airplanes. Shred their documents. Lose their memos.

Lucky Edwina doesn't even have to scheme. Sylvester, the colleague without a conscience, does have the power to make her whole career a misery—but not if someone else hires him first. Wisely rising above her own principles, Edwina can offer to write him a recommendation letter, honestly praising his ambition and dedication to his job. She can also amuse herself by writing (and not sending) a letter telling the truth as she sees it: "Sylvester's intellectual accomplishments are exceeded only by his charm. While his leaving will create a void in my life, I have often wanted to tell him where he should go."

Bulldozed by a Moderator

Q (from "Pinky"): At our last national convention, I was on a panel with two other young scholars and a mature moderator ("Dr. Attila") who usurped forty-five minutes of our ninety-minute session with his "opening remarks," which included unrelated video clips and strange right-wing tirades.

When he finally introduced us (as "the unholy trinity," sans our names), we gave our truncated talks, but even then he interrupted and heckled us with questions. There was no time for audience reaction at all. Should we have murdered him?

A: Murderous musings are not uncommon at academic conferences, and they inspire some of our cleverest fiction. The first in Ms. Mentor's ken is

Deadly Meeting (1970) by Robert Bernard, in which the victim—bigot, philanderer, all-around wretched scholar—is dispatched at the Modern Language Association's annual meeting.

As Elaine Showalter shows in *Faculty Towers: The Academic Novel and Its Discontents*, academics revel in murder mysteries. By the time D. J. H. Jones published her *Murder at the MLA* (1993), she was tapping into a universal yearning, an impulse that Pinky obviously shares.

Things needn't be so terminal, Ms. Mentor thinks. Panel discussions, which began with Plato's Symposium, have taken many forms. The late *Crossfire* on CNN is one of the foulest in Ms. Mentor's files, but academic-meeting discussions are much more decorous. Shouting is rare, as are overt insults: "My esteemed colleague may have failed to notice" is more common than "Who gave you a degree, you pusillanimous pedant?"

In the sciences, what are called panel discussions are often—not. Usually they're consecutive lectures by half a dozen researchers in the same subfield, all clicking their PowerPoint slides. When one ceases, the next hops right up. The panel members rarely discuss much with one other, but they will take questions from the audience. They are generally not boors, though some do drone.

Of course, academic panels do take place in darkened, overheated hotel meeting rooms. One hears the light snoring of a few esteemed worthies—and the scratching of Ms. Mentor's quill as she nimbly takes notes for you, her readers.

Panels in the humanities may be more sociable—although the flamboyant disruptions and walkouts of the 1970s rarely happen anymore. (Yes, academe used to be peopled by giants.) Panels consist of four "papers" read aloud, in order. Audiences are always told that "we'll take questions at the end"—but that hardly ever happens. Most presenters love their own discoveries too much to confine them to a mere twenty minutes. And so the eager youngsters who want to know what the great elders are thinking rarely get to ask.

Ms. Mentor's favorites are the genuine panel discussions: unscripted conversations, sometimes called roundtables or fishbowls, in which a moderator serves up a question or case study for reactions. Sometimes the questions are distributed ahead of time, but Ms. Mentor finds it much more exciting when they aren't, and panelists have to improvise, blush, and squirm. Ideally, panelists are soon chatting wittily and wisely with one another, after which the audience is invited to join in. Roundtables work especially well at writers' conferences, where verbal dexterity is prized—unless there's a dominant narcissist.

And that might bring Ms. Mentor back to Pinky's query, if Ms. Mentor had a time limit and a martinet of a moderator, which she doesn't. And so she will expatiate on the hidden little skills that academics ought to be taught.

Everyone learns research methods. Many, especially in composition and languages, have formal teacher training. Most fledgling scientists learn about grant getting. But no one ever takes a tutorial on how to run a committee meeting, and no one, except maybe in student development, is ever taught how to be a good panelist or moderator—how to work and play well with others.

Panel members not born with exquisite tact may have to discipline themselves not to be Mockers, Interrupters, Know-It-Alls, or Attackers—types that Ms. Mentor finds in the excellent, idea-filled BlogHer Discussion Guidelines, available online: http://www.ashleyrichards.com/2005/08/06/blogher-discussion-guidelines/.

Meanwhile, moderators have to figure out on their own how to be Comics at first (opening with enthusiasm) and Devil's Advocates later ("How would you answer someone who says armadillos are the unsung geniuses of the animal world?"). Moderators, as the BlogHer notes, have to be Diplomats, quelling impossible arguments and changing the subject. But most of all, they're Traffic Cops. They keep time, nudge or pass notes to panelists ("two minutes left"), and courageously cut off verbose presenters in mid-sentence: "I'm sorry, but we need to move on. I hope we'll be able to return to that subject in the question period, or afterward."

There are also more forceful ways to enforce time sharing—such as using a "designator," an object indicating that someone has the right to speak. A microphone is the most common designator, but Ms. Mentor has seen other varieties used in small groups: plush pea pods, scepters, pitchforks.

Pinky and her colleagues might have smuggled in a pea pod, or seized the microphone—but Ms. Mentor thinks the best strategy is a well-oiled conspiracy. It can gain you allies for life. Pinky and colleagues might have networked with each other in advance, making a pact not to go overtime. They might have quietly consulted colleagues at other universities—not asking, "Is Dr. Attila a pompous bloviator?" but e-mailing (or better, phoning) to ask, "How is Dr. Attila as a teacher? A moderator? What are his strengths?" (If there is a long pause, that is a clue.)

They might have e-mailed Dr. Attila to confirm the time: "I notice my presentation, the first one, starts at 11:30. I'll be ready with my slides at 11:25. I hope you'll signal me if I go overtime." Just before the session started, they might have whispered genially to Dr. Attila: "I have fifteen minutes, right? How will you signal me if I go overtime?"

Yes, all this strikes Ms. Mentor as extremely tedious, like reminding a child to tie his shoelaces and stop drooling. But sometimes a show of deference makes a difference.

Once Dr. Attila roared into his "remarks," however, what might Pinky and the others have done? The one closest to him—or the one not on the job market—might have pulled on his sleeve or passed him a note ("It's time for me!"). Someone might accidentally kick him or knock over a water glass. Or—if the grapevine had suggested that Dr. Attila was inclined to wax poetic at great length and crowd out his underlings—a friend might be planted in the audience to shout: "Let's hear Pinky's presentation now!"

Ms. Mentor has seen only half a dozen such interruptions in her long, long career. She always finds them thrilling. Murder is not a good career move, generally—but learning to muscle in on someone's time and turf is great practice. And sometimes seizing the floor is not a coup, but a mercy killing.

For Want of a Bulldozer . . .

Q: At a panel discussion where I was the respondent, the Major Name Panelist took so much time that I could barely get out any of my carefully prepared remarks. But I did get a paid trip to the conference, a line on my vita, a lot of new knowledge from papers I heard, and some great evening hang time with new colleagues from other schools. Should I quit moaning and decide it was a good thing?

A: Yes.

I Want to Work Alone

Q: I have a personality that irritates people. I like to keep to myself on the job, without constant interruptions. I have a strong work ethic and have held many jobs, but I hate playing office footsie with people I would rather not be bothered with. I have about a decade left of work life and would like a meaningful position before it's too late.

A: Ms. Mentor is not much given to sighing for what is not, but she wishes you had been born in the eighteenth century, when you might have gotten on as an ornamental hermit.

Every English grotto back then had to have one: a robed, bearded figure who now and then emerged from his hutch to amaze guests with his visionary mumblings. Of course, ornamental hermits in effect had tenure: health care, room and board, free robes. They merely had to have a theatrical sense and perfect wisdom—which, as Ms. Mentor knows, was as rare then as it is now. But if you had it, you could make a career of flaunting it.

Jobs for smart misanthropes are harder to come by nowadays. Colleges do need all kinds of reliable staffers: career and financial aid counselors, math and writing tutors, physical plant and clerical workers. But all of them have to be calm and friendly despite others' ignorance, rudeness, or sloppiness. Those are not good jobs for angry, impatient people ("How many times today have I told someone to just read the parking rules?").

Most staff jobs are for the sweet and saintly—not for you.

What about faculty positions? Misanthropes have prospered in academe. Law-school professors, for instance, are famous for bullying their underlings. But academe is also the perfect citadel for even-tempered loners—self-motivated scholars who prefer their own quiet thoughts. As Anneli Rufus notes in *Party of One: The Loners' Manifesto*, true loners (who are not necessarily misanthropes) feel drained, not enhanced, by hordes of people. At parties, they are the ones skulking in back rooms or hiding in the conservatory with a candlestick.

Can you be a bookworm, a lab mouse, and still be a professor? Yes, you can teach without being a warm, fuzzy person. You can present well-prepared lectures with aplomb and wit, and be known for intellect rather than charm. (But you know your students' cell phones will go off, and they'll ask you strange questions, and you'll seethe.)

As for research: The lone mad scientist in the castle, creating monsters from bubbling vats, is now extinct (along with ornamental hermits). But scholars in such fields as mathematics, literature, and philosophy can still hunker down in solitary splendor—as did "Casimir," a philologist whose life's work was an ancient-language glossary. His office at Great Plains U. was paid for by a mysterious donor, and he was not required to teach or interact with anyone. Once Ms. Mentor, then a young duchess and unschooled in the ways of misanthropes, asked a colleague why Casimir never said hello to her.

"He never will," she was told, "because you don't know Hittite."

If you can find that kind of unique niche, you need never speak to anyone.

There is also online teaching, which, in theory, does not require much people contact—so long as the technology all works perfectly, everyone is dedicated, and everyone reads and follows all the rules and protocols.

Sigh. Ms. Mentor is running out of options for you.

She knows some of her faithful readers are thinking, "Get counseling already!" or "Get a personality transplant!" But Ms. Mentor will merely propose a few gimmicks you can use to protect yourself from chronic rage about the errors and inadequacies of others.

First, you must put on your cordial persona. Force yourself to smile and say, "Hi, how are you?" to everyone, including maintenance workers and students. (Ms. Mentor is appalled by university people who treat cleaning employees as serfs and students as vermin.)

Greeting everyone cheerfully makes you "collegial," which is essential to academic survival. "Scowler," for instance, was denied tenure at Left Coast U., because, although he published a great deal, "You never talk to anyone in the halls. People think you're a snob." If you cannot remember names or faces, all the more reason to greet everyone enthusiastically. Pretend you're running for mayor.

You can also practice—all by your lonesome—simple answers to the small-talk questions that Ms. Mentor knows have made you cringe with boredom. Begin by practicing your upbeat response to "And how are you?"

"Brilliant and beautiful" is one good answer. Another is "Life's treating me well" (even if it isn't, you'll feel less morbid). You can follow up with a complaint about the traffic, or a mildly inane comment about the weather ("Moist enough for you?") or sports ("How 'bout those Fighting Ferrets!").

Ms. Mentor warns you never to interpret "How are you?" as a medical question. Do not go into detail about secretions or itches.

Use the tricks for seeming adept at small talk. Learn to take compliments graciously ("Thank you! It's one of my favorite cudgels, too"). Inquire after family members ("I hope Beauregard's feeling perkier") and praise others' successes ("Hittite of the Year! That's awesome!").

Be careful about complimenting someone's appearance too aggressively, because that can come across as sexual harassment. And never say, "You've lost weight!" That suggests you thought your victim was oversized before—and it may also call attention to a deep private sorrow: anorexia, miscarriage, depression, cancer.

"But all that's office chitchat," you complain. "I still hate everybody."

Of course you do, and some of your colleagues deserve it. Longtime bosses know that every group will include four or five belligerents who demand special treatment, wail about being underappreciated, and want their enemies crushed this afternoon. You must smile, nod, and move on.

In truth, only one set of university employees routinely escapes human contact. At veterinary schools, the animal tenders do have to clean out the cages and stalls, but they also get to cuddle kittens and watch puppies being born. No one minds if they sometimes moo.

Many Americans, Ms. Mentor knows, would advise you to take whatever job you can tolerate, and then get on the right drugs. Ms. Mentor prefers to recommend meditation and swimming (but not yoga: the classes are with other people). She warns you against reading Jean-Paul Sartre's *No Exit*, with its chilling line, "Hell is other people." Try to smile, do your job, and purport to be contented—for doing so will get you a regular salary, health insurance, and a certain peace.

Cultivate an image of serenity, like the ornamental hermits of old. Look ethereal, feel superior, and sigh now and then. You will seem profound, mysterious, and—best of all—unapproachable.

Person's Best Friend

Q: New on the job and lonesome, I want to get a dog and take him to campus with me. But I'm told I can't, because of potential lawsuits over bitings and droppings. Do you have another prescription for my midwinter melancholy?

A: Meow.

I Know I Must Be Special

Q (from "Lenny"): I'm an ABD in linguistics and a traditional liberal, rather to the left of most of my students. But we're good-humored about it, I like this country, and I respect the majority religion, though I don't practice it. Yet it seems I'm almost alone among people in my field. I can avoid such subjects in interviews, but if I work somewhere for six years, people will find out where I stand—and then what?

Q (from "Ned"): I'm up for tenure this year, and my department is not supporting me. One of the issues is "unprofessional demeanor and appearance." I have been spoken to about teaching in jeans, but now that seems to be in print as if it's a defensible reason for my tenure outcome. What should I do?

Q (from "Philip"): I'm a successful freelance writer who's taught courses at Local U., where there's now a tenure-track opening. But Local has the lowest faculty salaries in the country, the students are dreadful, and the state is medieval in its treatment of education. I'm middle-aged and I can't pretend to be other than what I am: compassionate, honest, and generous. But I do speak my mind, am impatient with petty politics, and am driven to excel in my work—which threatens those who are insecure. Should I even bother to twist myself into a pretzel and apply?

A: Ms. Mentor is intrigued by the number of academics who consider themselves unique—almost all in the same ways. She is reminded of the hippies of the 1960s who flaunted their individuality by dressing alike and hiding behind their hair.

Likewise, every academic is a compassionate and generous soul who insists on honesty and deplores political infighting. All academics want to dress comfortably, and sometimes oddly, without any hootings in the hallways. All academics want bright students who are enthralled by the subject matter—the glory that was Greece, the beauty of a cone.

But since academics know that distinctions must be made, Ms. Mentor will now assign her sage readers to reread these three letters. Assume that all the candidates are equally qualified on paper, but you can hire only one of the three. Which one will you choose?

As you hum and twiddle and cogitate, consider: Will your new department-mate do committee work cheerfully and promptly? Will you enjoy lunch and sharing ideas? Will your new colleague be a good listener, communicator, and teacher?

Philip, alas, is convinced of his own superiority—which does not bode well for his interactions with colleagues. All jobs involve "petty politics"— egos, high horses, low blows. But to decide ahead of time that a college is mediocre, its students inept, and its faculty envious of your productivity seems to Ms. Mentor to be a recipe for depression, if not rage. It's rather like giving a student a preemptive F before the course starts.

Ms. Mentor, who has infinite generosity and compassion for students, advises Philip to stick to his writing career.

And then there is Ned, in his jeans, hoping for tenure despite his "un-professional dress and demeanor." (Ms. Mentor does wonder what that means.) Perhaps Ned is at Small Religious College, where the restrictions on dress, body language, and subject matter are stricter than at Large Public U. Ned was definitely warned (mentored) about not wearing jeans to teach in, yet he persisted. Was he protesting middle-class values and affirming himself as a free spirit? Or was he (as Ms. Mentor fears) taking a tough stand on a trifling matter and letting his career fall apart rather than wear nice slacks?

Ms. Mentor does not know what other "unprofessional" acts Ned may have committed. She presumes that they are the other "issues" he men-tions, and that he is not being junked simply for his jeans. If he has been denied tenure, he seems to have no recourse, especially if his university's tenure policies also mention "collegiality," a nebulous and dangerous criterion that may mean "doesn't fit in." Ms. Mentor advises Ned to decide what aspects of "professional behavior" do fit him, for he must get on with his life.

Lenny, finally, seems to be the only one who respects the opinions of others. He joshes with students, studies his professors, wants to know how to be a successful academic. Lenny will find some kindred liberal spirits. If his political opinions are not part of a course's subject matter, Lenny needn't express them—although he must, of course, use any instances of bigotry as opportunities for careful education.

Ms. Mentor is least worried about Lenny, and most likely to hire him—because he is neither obstinate nor wedded to his own worth. In his first year, Lenny will study the culture, and listen.

Ms. Mentor reminds readers that academe is not a world apart. It consists of people who've gotten excellent grades, yet have all the bad habits, misplaced ambitions, and saintly values of any other humans. (Some even have lusts.) Ideally, entrenched professors want to hire new people who are congenial and cooperative, but who have enough backbone and new ideas to add vitality to a department. And while senior profs like being venerated as sages, they were not always establishment pillars. Many of them didn't fit in either, at first.

Watching senior professors now will help you decide whether academe is for you, and whether you want to be part of one of the few professions in which you are paid to think and share ideas. Ms. Mentor would never let that slip away.

Oh, Botheration, Some More Awards for Me

Q: I'm just back from another awards ceremony in which I was cited for teaching excellence, or research achievement, or superior service, or something. So why am I grumbling?

Because such shows are mind-numbingly boring, and I'm not sure I can yawn and scratch through another. Do I have to start being a rotten teacher, a lousy researcher, and a do-nothing department citizen to escape?

A: Ms. Mentor will eschew calling you an ungrateful wretch, since she trusts that her readers have already done so. Rather, she will note that awards ceremonies need not be excruciating snoozers. Beauty pageants have singing and strutting and posturing, and the Olympic ceremonies have torches and swelling music. The Tonys have spectacular dancing, and the Academy Awards inspire great gowns and fabulous gaffes.

And then . . . there are the honors and awards convocations produced every spring throughout the land. Often they transpire in hot weather, and everyone's sweating even before the first of too many official welcomes. There may be a benediction, and a choir may dutifully sing. Audience members fan themselves.

Finally, a university official emerges to hand out the awards, which—in a just world—would be accompanied by banners, trumpets, and planes flying overhead in intricate and majestic formations. Ms. Mentor believes that university teachers should be lauded and honored for creating original knowledge, opening students' minds, and promoting campus tranquility, welfare, and pleasure.

But what usually ensues is a droned recital of too many facts and numbers and trivia. Book titles and scientific terms are hilariously garbled as each winner trots up for a handshake, certificate, quick smiley photo, and a round of dutiful applause. Sigh.

Ms. Mentor finds herself yearning for something more risky or extravagant or edgy. She longs for a better show, and she daydreams . . .

What if academic audiences really got to see how Excellent Estelle and Outstanding Otto made it to the pinnacle of academic stardom?

And then Ms. Mentor remembers *This Is Your Life,* one of television's earliest shows, in which real people—parents, best friends, teachers, bosses—were heard off-camera, praising the honoree ("She was the best pencil-sharpener ever"). Then they all came out onstage for a sentimental reunion, hugs and kisses, and tears. It was a mawkish delight.

But today's cynical audiences, Ms. Mentor knows, would rather hear it all from knaves and boors. And so there could be bursts of venom from Estelle's angry ex-partner, and vile aspersions from Otto's grad-school classmates. There could be spiteful snippets from diabolical department heads, and mewlings from students who wanted A's but didn't get them. Hostile neighbors and dogs could have their say, followed by a truly nasty encounter with a telemarketer.

Yet Ms. Mentor also knows that such a lively and candid show would never sell with academics, for it violates a host of unspoken norms. It would be undignified, it would be unserious, and it would probably be wildly popular—especially if, at the end of Estelle's toast and roast, university administrators broke out into a kick line and sang, "She's a Singular Sensation." How sublime. How impossible.

Still, schools can produce much better shows. At the annual New Orleans Jazz Colloquium, for instance, the lifetime honorees are introduced with slides of their childhoods, their first instruments, their mentors, their defining performances. It is an engaging show with a socko finale, when the honorees appear in all their mature glory.

But most of what scholars do can't be easily dramatized. Except for teaching, the drama is mostly in the mind: finding the best words, choosing the best books, deciding when and how to vary experiments. A video of hours spent at the computer would be worse than a video of committee meetings.

Well, you don't have to take part in any of this. You can decide to be such a terrible teacher, researcher, and colleague that no one will ever give you an award for anything. At universities where the award candidate has to do most of the paperwork, you can decline to write essays on such topics as "My Career Narrative" and "My Teaching Philosophy."

If you can't hide, you can deceive. You can fake sick. You can claim you have a domestic crisis. You can purport to be receiving another award at the same time, but in Bangkok or Banff.

Or you can do what Ms. Mentor does. You can devote your foot-tapping audience time to conjuring up alternatives, envisioning truly exciting awards ceremonies, full of risk and color, glory and gore. Imagine an awards competition as a hand-to-hand gladiatorial combat, held in a steel cage, after which the losers are slowly fed to hungry, waiting alligators who tear their flesh to bits while the audience hears, through special microphones, the terrific shrieking and blubbering.

Now wouldn't you rather be a winner?

Questions Great and Small

Who's Classier?

Q: I'm a teaching assistant at Rich Private Party U., where the decadent, spoiled undergrads make me want to puke. I worked two jobs to put myself through community college, and now I feel more empathy for the janitors than for the pouty young people I'm supposed to teach. And, yes, I feel jealous of their privilege and the ease of their lives. Will I have to stifle those feelings to be a professor eventually?

A: How vexed it is, the subject of social class in the United States. There are Ph.D. adjuncts who earn below the poverty level, and Ph.D. mathematicians who dress like refugees—while most Americans have trouble even defining what's meant by class. Income? Genes? Tacky or terrific taste?

Rich Republicans are rare among professors, for a Ph.D. isn't a good investment. It takes twice as long to earn as a degree in law or business, and fewer than half the Ph.D.'s in English (the largest field) ever get the tenure-track jobs they've been preparing to do.

But affluent adolescents—call them "Schuyler" and "Courtney"—can happily cavort at Rich Private Party U. Since they'll be in the 20 percent of college seniors who don't have off-campus jobs, they'll have leisure time for tennis, for taste-testing beers from around the world, and for studying the works of Oprah and Dr. Phil. When they need to get a paper in, they'll pull all-nighters, fueled by expensive drugs.

Not so with community-college students, who, on average, are older and have family responsibilities. They have to sandwich school in before or after their full-time jobs—which may be waitressing at Dot's Diner or scrubbing the toilets at Rich Private Party U.

No, it's not fair. And when the rich youngsters skip your "silly poetry" class for an impromptu sailing trip in Australia, you will feel like you've been stabbed in the heart. In your baser moments, you will chuckle over horrible scenarios: "Yachts That Eat Their Owners. Next on Springer."

As for grades, it's no secret that students at pricey colleges mostly get A's. If Schuyler doesn't get his A in economics, his parents will feel free to call up and rail at the professor, the department head, and the dean: "I'm paying $200,000 for my kid to go to your school. He deserves an A."

That's especially effective if Schuyler's father is a major donor. According to Ms. Mentor's spies, the strong-arming parent is most common at "Potted Ivies," the institutions that the fun-loving, low-grade-point average rich attend if they don't get into the genuine Ivies. But even Harvard is easy on the elite: some 90 percent of seniors graduate with honors. Yale won't release grade information at all.

Entitlement breeds entitlement. The hard-working poor do sometimes go to Harvard—but mostly as janitors and cooks. Ms. Mentor sympathizes with envy, fury, and yearning for a revolution.

Still, when you're teaching at Rich Private Party U., you have the chance to share life-changing knowledge. Your students will have gone to good high schools, many are good readers, all have computers, and many have a nascent intellectual curiosity. You can assign Michelle Tea's *Without a Net: The Female Experience of Growing Up Working Class* and Barbara Ehrenreich's *Nickel and Dimed: On (Not) Getting By in America*. You can get them to research difficult or unconventional questions ("Why are there beggars all over the world?").

You may also be able to persuade the professor in charge to include service learning. That means college credit for real-life work that benefits communities: sampling the water supply for contaminants, helping disabled people confront bureaucracies, building playgrounds and ramps. Students with cars can register voters and rescue battered women.

Service learning makes the professor in charge look good ("A town-gown partnership!"). It produces research data ("Hark! Oodles of questionnaires!"). And it appeals to the spirit of noblesse oblige ("We need to help those less fortunate"). Ms. Mentor believes that everyone can be taught, or shamed, into producing useful knowledge. Those who've seen real poverty before they join Dad's business firm or political dynasty are less likely to let babies die for lack of medical care. With any luck, your students' consciences will gnaw at them.

But will your righteous rage gnaw at you if you're the professor in charge of wealthy students? You probably won't have the chance, since rich and elite colleges hire only their own kind. Of the twenty-seven tenured professors in Harvard's English department, for instance, twenty-three have Ivy League or European Ph.D.'s. Only two hold degrees from state universities.

You'll be hired at a lower prestige level, but your students will be more diverse, juggling school and jobs. They'll have goals and strategies, and you can lead instead of grumbling.

If Ms. Mentor were in charge, academe would be a thorough meritocracy, the one green place where lads and lassies from humble beginnings could rise to full professorships at the finest universities in the land, through pluck and intellectual might. But the United States actually has very little economic mobility: According to economist Gary Solon's research, only 1 or 2 percent of those born poor will ever become rich.

You're reaching the rich right now, spreading knowledge and the spirit of charity. There are also many rich and beautiful people encouraging activism (Oprah Winfrey, Susan Sarandon, Angelina Jolie, Brad Pitt, Denzel Washington), and you can tell your students that it's cool to help out others.

In fact, it's more than cool. It's classy.

—

Reader Response: This column attracted several outraged letters from those who feel that Ms. Mentor "discriminates against the rich." Oh, dear.

What Should I Wear?

Q (from "Renee"): I'm a female biologist, an adjunct in a department where the male science profs dress like standard academic geeks (T-shirts, baggy pants, running shoes), but the women dress more formally. I try to blend in with them, but a three-hour lab in a skirt and heels is killing me. I also hate having to wear expensive clothes while I dissect a frog. But I'd rather get on the tenure track than foment a revolution. Is there anything I can do?

Q (from "Zena"): I'm a grad student in management, aiming for an academic career. I'm also a butch dyke (my preferred term), and I absolutely refuse to wear makeup, skirts, or any other "ladies' wear" endorsed by the patriarchy. Thus I wear my one custom-tailored, double-breasted suit, oxford button-down shirts (but no tie, except on dates), and loafers. Will I have job problems?

Q (from "Mrs. Hobo"): My hubby, back in grad school after fifteen years, is a sartorial horror. He teaches in faded jeans with torn knees, or bloodstained hockey jerseys, or smelly Motley Crue T-shirts. He won't believe that image and "fit" matter. Someone who's too scruffy to be brought to dinner with bigwigs won't make it, and I know this isn't the time for "I'm messy, disheveled, and don't look professional, but get over it, I gotta be me!"

A: Right now, while Ms. Mentor is writing this, someone, somewhere is agonizing over what to wear. Whole industries thrive on that. And yet the fashion questions that real people ask ("Do I look fat?" and "Does this make my butt look big?") are simple, compared with the academic desire to be employed, comfortable, and scholarly, without selling one's soul.

Most new and wannabe academics have settled the "what to wear" question for job interviews. At the Modern Language Association convention, everyone gets sucked into a swamp of graveyard green, deadly black, and toad brown. Job candidates dare not be risqué or extravagant, and if they spill coffee, they don't want it showing on their clothes. But Ms. Mentor wonders if creativity can survive among people who look like they are cloning each other.

Ms. Mentor no longer believes, as she once did, that women candidates will do better if they wear dresses or skirts—preferably long, so that they needn't worry about revealing Victoria's secrets. But women interviewing at conservative religious institutions may assume that pants will be frowned upon. Piercings, except for women's earrings, may also be turnoffs, but a spot of color—yellow on a tie, a turquoise pin, a red scarf—makes a candidate memorable. Senior professors sometimes sport electric-blue polyester suits or skirts made of men's ties—but those are only for the eccentric and very secure.

Ms. Mentor's correspondents don't yet qualify for that.

Renée, however, has good sartorial instincts. She knows to take her cue from those in the job she'd like to have, and she knows that a fashion revolution can't be started from below. She may be worrying too much—for high heels are risky in labs, and most science bosses (mostly men) wouldn't notice whether a woman's suit is vintage, chic, or cheap. But lucky Renée needn't really start a revolution, for the dignified, professional, and always-in-style garment already exists. "Wrap thyself in a lab coat," Ms. Mentor advises, "and worry no more."

Zena also knows that clothing can make the woman. Can she wear her tailored man's suit everywhere? Probably, in the Northeast and the West, and especially in big public institutions. But if her job nibbles come from smaller schools or the more conservative Midwest and South, then Zena may have to choose: "My clothes—or my career?"

Hobo, meanwhile, seems to be traveling down a rapidly narrowing road, for people do make snap judgments based on clothes. Hobo, oblivious about campus culture, will come across as unserious, undisciplined, and uncooperative—deadly deterrents to getting good recommendations and mentorings. His unmade-bed look may also harm his teaching, for if students are whispering about his attire, they're not listening to him. He is catering mightily to himself.

Ms. Mentor does not mean that anyone should slavishly follow the fashion sense of the entrenched faculty, but "I gotta be me" can mean "My self-esteem, which is dependent upon my clothes, is far more important to me than getting hired in a career for which I've been training for twenty years or more."

Ms. Mentor thinks that is a strange fashion statement.

Deans

Q: What, pray tell, does a dean do?

A: In academia, a dean is middle management, the connection between departments and "the upper administration." The dean funnels money up or down, follows directives, and constantly reconfigures numbers. (The role is described in greater depth in A. Leigh DeNeef and Craufurd Goodwin's *The Academic's Handbook* and in the classic text, Van Cleve Morris's *Deaning: Middle Management in Academe*.)

Ms. Mentor's readers like to chat about deaning. Some deans pride themselves on being paragons of fairness, looking at "big pictures" and carving up "budget pies." Some are supremely self-congratulatory, while others see themselves as martyrs. (One likes to exercise on his personal treadmill.) They agree that the proper adjective for "deanly" is "decanal," and not "diaconal," which refers to deacons. Perhaps there's confusion because, as one dean wrote, people in their heart of hearts know that the deanship is "somehow sacred."

But must deans be tall, as is commonly claimed?

Ms. Mentor's readers praise one ultra-competent female dean who is five-foot-two, while others insist that male deans must be "very athletic and charismatic." One five-foot-seven dean reportedly compensates by appointing a fierce six-foot-four assistant dean, known as "The Enforcer." Another man, dean for over a decade, admits to being five-foot-eight, but declares that it is "the majesty and power of the office that makes those of us who hold it seem more imposing than mere mortals."

How Dysfunctional Is My Department?

Q: If your workplace calls itself a family, is that a sure sign that it's dysfunctional?

A: Ms. Mentor, like most of her flock of a certain age, grew up with happy family images: Scrabble tournaments by the hearth, Dad with pipe, Mom with apron. But literary study introduced her to such outlandish characters as the Snopeses, Oedipus, and Medea. She read about authors who ignored their spouses, despised their children, and flew the coop. "All happy families are alike," Tolstoy wrote in the first line of Anna Karenina—but he later deserted his family, reinvented himself as a prophet, and died wandering around in the Russian snow.

He did not want to be ordinary—and even in academia, there are those who find happiness dull. They need to act out and drum up adventures.

A department is a faculty member's home. Some are havens in a heartless world, ruled by benevolent patriarchs or Mama Bears, with dedicated staffs. Maybe your department has harmonious brown-bag lunches, productive meetings, and lively end-of-year parties with delectable treats. Maybe you never have food snits over Atkins vs. vegan, or hear someone whispering, "How can you eat something that once had a face?"

Or maybe your department is a nest of vipers, and every time you move, someone bares fangs. You listen for hissing.

"Dysfunctional," Ms. Mentor notes, does not mean malodorous or corrupt, but "impaired in its functioning." Many dastardly departments actually work very smoothly—for those who are entrenched, socially challenged, and power-mad.

The malcontents and the victims are the ones who write to Ms. Mentor, who knows that all happy academics are alike in one way: they love gossip.

And so, to Ms. Mentor's mail:

- From "Annie": Our bellowing pontificator ("Rex") butts in on lunch conversations and tyrannizes us at department meetings. When I apologized once after a small misunderstanding, he responded with loud, filthy language and a threat to turn my husband into "raw hamburger."
- From "Brenda": At department parties, "Professor Priapus" drinks like a walrus, strips, and flings himself on fully clothed graduate student women.
- From "Caligula": Our hated chair hosted a party for a new job candidate, and only three people (adjunct wimps) showed up. They need to be punished for their disloyalty.
- From "Desmond": The top three administrators in my department ("The Unholy Trinity") all live together, sexual arrangements unknown, but we're sure their pillow talk is about ways to yank our chains, cancel our raises, and sentence us to vacuous committees.
- From "Eve": In our latest faculty job search, as in all previous ones, the men voted to hire the OK man over the much more accomplished and energetic woman.

- From "Fabian": At my small private religious college, one colleague was jailed for child molestation, faculty members attacked each other in hallways and classes, alumni phoned in death threats, and people were mysteriously fired over weekends. I quit and moved to New York City, where they'll never find me.

Ms. Mentor sighs. Some of these scenarios are achingly familiar. Rex, the boom-voiced pontificator, is the drunken uncle whose perfect wisdom about football and politics will ruin everyone's Thanksgiving dinner—after which Priapus, a different drunken uncle, will harass anyone remaining. The peacemaker siblings who tune out the yelling and praise the turkey will be savaged by someone like Caligula, who sees them as traitors. Desmond is the cousin who knows that everyone is picking on him, Eve protests when the boys gang up on the girls, and Fabian, fed up, runs away from home.

And all of them, or their ilk, inspired the British literary magazine *Granta* some years ago to do a special issue called "The Family: They Fuck You Up," in which writers declared that family dynamics had given them a lifetime's worth of material.

Which does not, of course, solve the problems of Ms. Mentor's correspondents. Fabian is right to flee. Annie, Brenda, and Eve should seek out allies and report bad conduct if anyone is receptive, but should also quietly look for other jobs where women are more valued and protected. (Yes, they could sue, but that would consume their lives for years and steal time from their own families, research, and teaching.) Desmond might put together a well-rehearsed cabal of his own allies to combat the Unholy Trinity at department meetings—though Ms. Mentor does wonder who put the Trinity in charge, anyway. What goes up can be brought down.

There are other avenues for beleaguered academics. Threats should be reported in writing to administrators and campus security; sex discrimination can be reported in writing to human-resource and equal-opportunity offices; faculty unions may help; and victims should seek friends outside their departments and outside academe. Sometimes mediators have to be brought in. You cannot force people to be warm or clever—but most can be taught to be civil.

Ms. Mentor's columns have been forwarded, anonymously, to miscreants who become convinced that the world is talking about them. Student grapevines can pass along knowledge that administrators want to overlook. Tips to newspapers or alumni may inspire investigations. Yet some villains genuinely do not know that their behavior is illegal, immoral, and frightening to the horses. Ms. Mentor feels it is her duty, and that of all right-thinking individuals, to inform, cure, or expel sinners.

But just as in families, not all problems can be solved with a cudgel, a tabloid exposé, or a generous spirit of sharing our differences. Sometimes low expectations simply fulfill themselves, as with the reader who wrote to Ms. Mentor: "In our department we've got shouting matches, profanity, bullying, torture, sadism, paranoia. Doesn't everyone?"

The Secretaries Hate Me

Q: Our hateful department secretaries won't make my phone calls or straighten my office, and sometimes they don't even answer me (I can't be bothered to learn their names, since they all look alike). I've complained and complained, but their attitude never improves. I don't want to photocopy my own materials, but will I have to?

A: Yes.

I'm Getting Married in the Springtime

Q: I'm in a very collegial department, but there are thirty faculty, and I can't afford to invite them all to my wedding if we have the splendiferous pageant that his mom and my mom want to have, with the cathedral and the flowers and the ice sculpture and the sit-down dinner and the live music and the videos, all at a local plantation that we have to reserve a year ahead of time. I'm an academic, not a Bridezilla, and I'd be much happier inviting everyone to a picnic in the park, with hot dogs and hamburgers and kicking around a soccer ball. May I have the wedding I want to have?

A: Yes.

Loose Lips

Q: If I tell my office mate a juicy secret about my surprise pregnancy, new job offer, kidney stone, or Professor Z's odd little adventure with the goat, can I rely on him/her to keep the secret?

A: Ha ha.

This Project Will Outlive Us All

Q: I've been drafted to work on "Project M," a university-wide research program that is an embarrassment (in all senses) of riches. More than one hundred faculty members have accomplished nothing meaningful despite five years of substantial foundation support.

The project leaders are forever worrying about securing more money (which supports faculty lines), but not about actual findings. Although the grant has been renewed, the best efforts of the few lucid participants have met only cold rebuke. I want to be a good campus citizen, but do not wish to be stigmatized by association with the project. It's bad enough that I have to invest valuable time and energy in something certain to fail; I would hate for the foundation to think less of me later.

A: Ah, yes. Ms. Mentor knows how soul-searing it is to be a lone voice of truth crying in the wilderness. She feels your pain. But you may be fretting inordinately.

First, you have been chosen to work on a richly rewarded project, where your presence will be noticed and appreciated. Other participants may later vote on your tenure, your promotion, or your travel money. They may write glowing references if you are seeking another job. Everyone will become aware of your talents, and it could be a fine opportunity—except that you think it stinks.

Which is the most intriguing part of your communication.

Ms. Mentor does know slow-moving projects. Her work of reforming the academic world—getting it to rely on merit, openness, and justice—sometimes seems hopelessly stalled on a grimy railroad track at midnight, while owls hoot mournfully.

But your midnight assignment, should you accept the mission, is more mundane and achievable. You can begin by doing the homework that few vociferous objectors ever do: You can read every word of the grant proposal. Read it aloud, slowly and carefully. (Try out your stentorian James Earl Jones voice.) Notice the typical rhythms of academic prose. If you find a typo, allow yourself a brief chortle of superiority. Note the vague generalities ("to facilitate awareness"), but seek out what sounds innovative or specific ("to increase participation of . . .").

That should be the core, the jewel, the overt purpose for which the foundation is willing to pay. It is usually a magnificent and mildly utopian aim. But academic projects always have more than an overt purpose—and that is why they are so frustrating to young and eager participants.

And so Ms. Mentor urges you not to believe everything you read. Projects also exist to bring together like-minded people who will create social and scholarly networks. Your friends, "the lucid participants," now have allies, with whom they can achieve smaller goals. They are now a community with some stake in the project, and their interest in one another will keep them coming to meetings. It will make them more loyal to the university. They may even brag about their association with the foundation.

Sometimes more than friendship blossoms from long-term, slow-moving projects. "Althea" and "Hengest," for instance, were first dragooned onto a mini-subcommittee to revise a tiny corner of the curriculum. But their post-meeting gripe sessions segued into coffee, and then drinks, and then intimate dinners . . . and on the day that the huge committee report was finally delivered, and immediately filed with all the other huge committee reports . . . their daughter was born. (They resisted suggestions to name her "Curricula.")

Very few project outcomes are so final, dramatic, or welcome, and there is an air of melancholy when a grant ends—especially since, as has always been the case, most projects do not achieve their long-range goals (transmuting base metals into gold; finding a passage to India). Nowadays, a project just needs to make some kind of headlinable progress ("Mentoring may cure cancer, study shows").

It is not truly in anyone's interest to solve major problems, Ms. Mentor has long noted, for armies of people, in and out of academe, would then lose their jobs. A weight-loss pill that really worked, for instance, would throw millions of people out of work. And who would absorb all the scientists, beauty editors, exercise mongers, diet gurus, and charlatans who are now kept busy making people hate their own bodies? Ms. Mentor imagines them all on the streets, begging for bread. She snickers and then feels guilty.

But you should not feel guilty or tormented about joining Project M. The foundation will not "stigmatize" you, since it obviously supports the project. It will welcome you, and so will the caucus of lucid malcontents. If the project cannot be redesigned to produce more "findings," at least you will get to do colorful wailing with friends and allies. (That will be defined as work time, too, so you needn't fear the classic academic refrain in your head: "I should be working on . . .") You and the Lucid Caucus will bond. You'll have in-jokes. You can blog together under secret screen names that everyone will secretly know.

Will Project M achieve its overt purpose, whatever that may be? Maybe. Maybe not. Will it continue to create more faculty lines? Ms. Mentor hopes so.

Will it annoy, bore, and amuse you to be part of it? Indeed it will.

Will it also teach you about human idiosyncrasies, jargon, and posturing, while showing you, with bad examples, how a meeting or class should *not* be organized and run? Will it give you a peek into how academic administration works, should you be inclined in that direction? Or teach you enough so that you will flee, shrieking, blanket over your head, if anyone ever says "committee"?

Being part of Project M can be a "learning experience," even a baptism by fire, although Ms. Mentor knows you will not be grateful to her for saying so. (No one has ever gotten a grant to write an "Ode to Ms. Mentor.")

Still, solving problems, or at least explaining what academicians really mean, is Ms. Mentor's life work and her overt purpose. If there were no problems, and everyone were always righteous, well paid, selfless, noble, and thoroughly competent—she knows what would happen.

She would be out of work.

Portrait of the Artist as a Young Academic

Q (from "Delilah"): Because I play in a rock band in my nonschool time, my professors claim I'm "not serious," and have threatened to yank my assistantship. I think what they're doing is a gatekeeping mechanism used by the socially retarded to maintain their awkward priesthood.

Q (from "José"): I'm a Spanish instructor (with an M.A.), an academic and cultural adviser with a student-services center, and a writer, genealogist, and photographer. And a flamenco dancer. What kind of university teaching job can I get?

Q (from "Barry"): Well, I finally got what every M.F.A. dreams of: a tenure-track job that'll support my writing. But it's at "Mediocre U.," in the middle of nowhere. Since I write for major magazines with tight deadlines and picky editors, I'm commuting two days a week to Mediocre City, and living the rest of the time in New York. But my department keeps scheduling stupid little meetings on days when I'm not on campus, and then people carp and backbite about my absences. Why don't they have some consideration? I've got much more important stuff to do.

A: Ms. Mentor sighs. So many people, so many talents, so much fussing.

It is not easy to be an artist in academia. Creative spirits often feel unloved and unrewarded. Their inspirations and their divine madnesses can't easily be shoehorned into fifty- or seventy-five-minute blocks, fifteen weeks at a stretch, midterm in the middle, final at the end. Nor is it easy for creative spirits to assign a grade. What if a student practices assiduously but plays the piano without heart or feeling?

And then, many traditional academics mistrust enthusiasm and inspiration. One of the unspoken purposes of graduate school is to socialize students into a cool, detached style—an aura of objectivity.

Teresa, for instance, used to be an exuberant English major who told everyone, "I just love to read!" But by the end of her first semester in grad school, she'd learned that such effusions were horribly gushy and naïve. Now Teresa praises, soberly, "work that is theoretically sophisticated."

Now when she talks about literature, Teresa never smiles.

In Teresa's department, her role models are a rather stuffy crew ("pencil heads") who went through school without any particular passion except a strong sense of duty and a driving urge to accumulate A grades. As adults, such nose-to-the-grindstone academicians are haunted by the fear that someone, somewhere is having fun.

Delilah, the rocker, is especially suspect. Not only does she have an outside passion, but it's one that's loud and sensual. She may even get paid for it. She's not a monomaniac, tethered to lab or laptop, devoting her life to studying one author, one compound, one cockroach. And so—though Delilah is also an outstanding student—she makes traditional academics very nervous.

José, similarly, doesn't fit into a neat slot (traditionalists would call him "scattered"). He is a strange bright bird in a world where people are supposed to be monochromatic. If he chooses one field, and gets a Ph.D. in it, and narrowly directs his teaching and research toward that field—he may be able to get a tenure-track job, five or six years from now. That will credential him to continue teaching and writing in the same fairly narrow groove.

Will that make José happy? Ms. Mentor doubts it. But if he tries to follow all his pursuits, he'll undoubtedly burn out. He will also make traditional academics very nervous.

Barry, though, will make them angry. When he doesn't show up for meetings to discuss requirements or hiring, Someone Else will wind up doing his work for him. Someone Else will have to handle advising his students while Barry is commuting or communing with his Muse. Someone Else will have to be cooperative and hard-working, while Barry is the prima donna.

That Someone Else—who will be many people—will resent Barry's failure to be "collegial," to share the workload and do the whole job for which he's been hired. In Ms. Mentor's blunt opinion, Barry is asking to be axed.

Another problem for artistic types in academia is their reputation. Racy stories abound about visiting artists who drank too much and groped everyone in sight, or the famous visiting writer who crouched for hours, naked, in the elevator (Beat poet Gregory Corso was notorious for that). But those are one-timers.

Artsy academics who want permanent jobs need to, somehow, "fit the institutional mold" and not go astray.

"Brett," for instance, held his playwriting classes in local bars ("a more relaxed atmosphere"), not noticing that students under twenty-one could not attend. And students who couldn't afford to buy drinks—or who preferred not to drink—were the victims of malicious stares from the management.

"Michael" and "Paul," sculptors and painters, made a point of encouraging their students to "free themselves" from their clothes and their sexual inhibitions. "Phyllis," a performance artist, was arrested by campus police when she led her class into the middle of a busy street and urged them to flap their wings: "I know we can fly!" "Horace," a poet, was so overcome while reading an experimental poem that he mooned his class—whereupon students gleefully took cell phone pictures and sent them to the local papers. Horace had to take his poetry elsewhere.

Sexual misconduct and peculiar behavior are not unique to "creative types," but artists seeking permanent jobs in academia do need to take a few mundane steps:

- Be aware of the "institutional culture" and what's tolerated. Are there others who dress strangely, use cuss words, or discuss intimate personal experiences in class? If there aren't, do not be the first.
- Read the faculty handbook, especially for the rules about teacher-student interactions, and especially if you're in a church-related school.
- Try to get a clear, written job description—what you're expected to teach, what or how much you're expected to publish, and what kind of committee and department service work is expected of you. Will you be evaluated as an academic (who must publish) or as a practitioner (who must create or perform)?
- Find out what level of artistic success and visibility is expected. "Valerie," for instance, knew that she had to have her prints exhibited, but no one told her that only juried shows "counted." At tenure time, her small regional shows were tossed aside, and she was said to lack a "serious professional reputation."
- Be aware of others' egos. If your department colleagues are known only locally, they may be embittered souls who won't be pleased if you brag that you've been invited to read, perform, or exhibit in Japan or Brazil or South Africa. Watch out for envy and revenge.
- Have an adult social life. Never have sex with students.

- Don't be caught in orgies of self-pity. It is a sad truth that the world does not really care whether you ever compose a concerto or paint a work of genius. You must generate your own drive and your own supports.

As for Ms. Mentor's correspondents: Barry may decide that academia is not the best way to support his writing career. Delilah may get a recording deal, and José may decide that academia is too narrow a floor for his dancing feet.

Tenure is a great prize, but for some artistic souls, it can be a prison. If you dread your job . . . and if you never laugh . . . and if, when you try to clear your mental pathways for the Muse, you imagine yourself in a never-ending committee meeting discussing six intricate and slightly different possible course-requirement lists for a fifteen-credit minor in aesthetics, philosophy, and critical and cultural theory . . . Ms. Mentor has only one piece of advice for your artistic soul:

Flee.

Artist's Revenge

Q: Do you have a computer program that would enable me to break into my nemesis's computer, get at his new novel, and put in clichés every few paragraphs?

A: Um, not yet.

Does Your Voice Make Them Scream?

Q: Having never heard you speak in person, Ms. Mentor, I can only assume that like 99 percent of successful female academics, you have a nice low voice. I can count on one finger the number of successful professional women I have met who speak in a high, piping voice. Heaven forbid that we should sound "shrill"! Yet my female students have voices all over the range. Do the men who still dominate most academic fields weed out the high pipers and reward those of us who can almost sound like guys?

A: Ms. Mentor does indeed have a mellow contralto voice, a supple instrument that can be stately, soothing, or sensual. But one needn't be born with an excellent voice to develop a good, serviceable one.

Ms. Mentor knows that high-pitched voices are considered sweet and demure. But like so much that is classically feminine (hats, frills, the extended pinky at tea time), high soprano tones are now a career minus. Ms. Mentor sighs. So much of female life, in our transitional time, is taken up with role questions: Am I playing a woman now? Am I playing a professional role? And how do I dress, sit, and sound?

Of course, both genders use high voices to speak to babies and cats, and "nightingale voices" used to be considered the pinnacle of sexiness in Japan. But now university lecturers have to project confidence and knowledge to large groups. High-pitched voices are harder to hear, and not all academics are the souls of patience.

The irascible "Dewey," for instance, had hired "Julianne," a shy graphic designer, as his assistant in an arts program. Dewey was losing some of his upper-register hearing, as many men do in middle age. Whenever he barked orders, Julianne became flustered, her throat muscles tensed, and her voice grew so shrill that her boss could not understand her tumbled words. "Lower your voice!" he would scream.

"Kari," similarly, found that her dissertation director routinely ignored questions she asked him in the lab. She tried calling his name first, and then pulling his sleeve to get his attention. But he simply could not hear her soft, high-pitched voice (nurtured by her Asian-American home training). Kari's confused students also complained that "We can't understand her English"—but Kari was born in California. It was her tentative voice that they could not hear.

And "Tara," who'd never outgrown her breathy, teenage-sounding voice, was simply dismissed by faculty members and students alike: "Ditzy," they concluded.

Is voice discrimination, like racism and sexism, a prejudice about qualities one is born with—a way of keeping out those who don't fit a white male standard? Does anyone ever vote against a promotion case because "If I have to listen to her screech until 2030, I'll fall on my sword right now"?

Ms. Mentor thinks it unlikely to come up. High-voiced women who get that far are ones who've assimilated, who conform to a lower-voiced academic norm—like immigrants learning the native language.

Lower voices gain respect. "Gloria," a poet, has such a rich alto voice that it can be midsemester before students realize she's only five feet tall: "You don't sound short," they marvel. Gloria also projects her voice as a matter of manners—for it is rude to make others strain to hear you.

Women's voices do get lower with age, and the usual vices—smoking, drinking, late nights in bars—can produce a gravelly tone. But Ms. Mentor would encourage high pipers to consult voice coaches instead, just as graduate students on the job market sometimes hire coaches to rid themselves of pronounced regional accents. (Yes, they are contributing to the homogenization of American life, Ms. Mentor admits—but unless they get jobs, they'll have no opportunity to show that Louisianians are as smart as Minnesotans.)

Coaches can teach speakers to sound more engaging, varied, and resonant. Coaches can train people with unpleasant nasal voices to open their mouths wider. Women with artificially high, anxious voices can relax their throat muscles by practicing such sentences as "I don't think it is going to snow."

And, as always in our media-saturated culture, there are celebrity role models: "The Best and Worst Voices in America," as determined in a 2001 poll by the Center for Voice Disorders at Wake Forest University. The women's "worst" were Fran Drescher (nasal) and Roseanne Barr ("screechy")—both of whom, Ms. Mentor notes, are comedians whose natural voices are much more pleasant. The "best" women were Julia Roberts, Katie Couric, and Barbra Streisand. Roberts's voice ("melodious") is the lowest of the women's, with a speaking pitch only slightly higher than Sean Connery's.

Ms. Mentor encourages women to rent Roberts's films, to sing along with Streisand, to harken to Couric—but not to give up on the unique expressive range of the female voice. Shrews and witches have high voices that can scare away demons, and while feisty yelling is Just Not Done in academe, at times a loud, shrill, mean voice can win battles, as notes one correspondent to Ms. Mentor. "When I haul my landlord to court, I don't want to make nice. If they think I'm emotionally unstable and maybe dangerous, they'll be sure to listen to every word, even if it makes their ears bleed."

Ms. Mentor does like the world to listen to women.

Thank Them for Sharing

Q: As a new administrator, I'm stunned by the tenured colleagues who are not only irascible, but also narcissistic, brutal, and wacky. Do these people write to Ms. Mentor?

A: Nearly every day.

Adjuncts

The situation crept up in academe. Two decades ago, some English departments already had a cadre without a name. Some called it a "shadow department."

By the late 1980s, half of the teachers in English departments belonged to this shadow cadre, and they'd gained a name. They were "adjuncts," also known as "contingent faculty"—people who might be teaching a full-time load, but who were paid by the course, hired or let go at the last minute according to enrollments, and had no official permanent status. Some had health benefits and desks and file cabinets in department offices; some had none of those. The adjuncts had various titles—visiting assistant professors, instructors, lecturers, graduate students, teaching assistants, and part-timers—but the commonality was no security, little respect, and invisibility.

"Nobody knows my name," one of the adjuncts told Ms. Mentor in 1985. By 1997 the future president of the American Association of University Professors, Cary Nelson, had published a book about the adjunct situation called *Will Teach for Food*.

How did it happen? First there was the glut of Ph.D.'s, especially in the humanities, since the Vietnam War. Then there was the mood of stinginess in state legislatures. Then there were voters who thought professors were overpaid and underworked ("twelve hours a week and they call that a job?"). Administrators seized on the chance to get more "flexibility" in hiring, firing, and course offerings. Community colleges hired part-time professionals to teach skills courses. Everyone seemed to be emphasizing job preparation, not intellectual growth.

By 2007, over 70 percent of the courses in American universities and colleges were being taught by adjuncts. Many have Ph.D.'s and cannot get fulltime jobs because there are none; some barely have bachelor's degrees. Some teach as many as eight courses a semester at four different schools. Some teach online as well. They have no time to meet with students, to do research, to sleep.

Students are shortchanged. In 2007, it was possible for a psychology major at Florida International University to get a bachelor's degree without ever encountering a full-time faculty member—someone who might have the clout to be a mentor, or the status to write recommendations for graduate school. The chair of that department, Suzanna Rose, resigned in protest, but the situation remained.

Americans are starving their educational system, and the adjuncts are the walking wounded. Many teach brilliantly and with whole hearts, but they know that next semester they may be unemployed.

The majority of them are women.

Ms. Mentor wishes she had a solution. At some schools, especially in Michigan, adjuncts are now unionized. Rutgers University agreed in a labor settlement in 2007 to add one hundred tenured or tenure-track positions, and in 2008 George Washington University agreed to pay adjuncts a minimum of $3,800 per course. The American Federation of Teachers was pushing for state laws requiring that 75 percent of classes be taught by tenured or tenure-track teachers.

But right now there are many victims. Students whose teachers are part-timers are less apt to graduate. They cannot get extra help or even a friendly wave from someone who's perpetually driving from one campus to another. The adjuncts also know how they're regarded, as the cofounder of the Washington State Part-Time Faculty Association, Keith Hoeller, told the *New York Times* in November 2007: "It's a caste system, and we are the untouchables of academia."

This chapter is Ms. Mentor's collection of portraits from the adjunct world.

Scarlet "A" for Adjunct

Q: I am one of many Ph.D.'s who have fallen into the longtime adjunct trap. I received my degree from a top institution in 1998 and have been adjuncting ever since. I have published my first book, and am editing a second, and continue to be able to find research money and give papers at top conferences. And I am an effective teacher. But because of family geographical mobility issues, I have had to restrict my job search and have been unable to land a full-time tenure-track position. And yet I continue to try.

Here is the question: When my CV comes across a search committee member's desk, does it appear to them to have a big giant scarlet "A" on it? If so, how might those of us in this predicament present ourselves in our CVs and cover letters in a light that might dim the stain of our shameful status?

A: Of course there is no shame in adjuncting, but search committees do sometimes favor candidates they see as having "a continuous work history," which they (wrongly, in Ms. Mentor's opinion) define as full-time work.

Moreover, there can be a prejudice against someone who's "been out too long," no matter the reason and no matter the record. "Everyone wants a virgin" is sometimes true in academic hiring (though much less so in community colleges).

The system is not just, and it is not fair, and women who have "family geographical mobility issues" may not be able, ever, to find tenure-track jobs. Twenty years ago, Nadya Aisenberg and Mona Harrington found that following a male partner to his job was most apt to destroy a woman's own tenure-track possibilities and make her a "deflected woman."

"As far as I know," wrote one of Ms. Mentor's recent readers, "no one is working on the cause and cure for what I've come to call 'Followers' Disease.' "

The only individual cure, right now, may be to seek a position outside academe. Susan Basalla and Maggie Debelius's book *"So What Are You Going to Do with That?" Finding Careers Outside Academia* tells how to do it, as does Richard Nelson Bolles's classic, *What Color Is Your Parachute?*

And yet . . . Ms. Mentor mourns.

My Friends Are Adjuncts

Q (from "Merv"): A friend of mine has been an adjunct composition instructor at the same school where his wife is a full-time tenured professor. He applied for the full-time, tenure-track position that opened up in his department, but they hired someone else. Even worse: The part-time job he's held for seven years is being given to the spouse of the new hire. I know things are bad in academe, but this strikes me as the height of injustice. Is there anything my friend can do?

Q (from "Susie"): My circle of friends includes Über-Adjunct, a generalist who teaches in more than one field at several local community colleges. Her "plan" is to spread herself around until some department is so taken with her that it offers her a full-time position. I take great discomfort in talking shop with her, because I am working on my dissertation and am keenly aware that the use of adjuncts erodes my future prospects. Do I try to enlighten her?

A: Being an adjunct can be a pleasant diversion—or it can be soul killing.

Some adjuncts are visiting stars, politicians, or artists who swoop in to teach one course a week. They are highly lauded and fawned over. But the world of adjuncting is different for those who teach, say, English composition for less than $2,000 a course. Sometimes they are hired just a week before classes start, whereupon they scramble to get texts, plan lessons, and find the buildings—to which they will wheel everything in a luggage cart, because few have their own desks or offices. Many teach at more than one college, and some teach in two countries (United States and Canada or Mexico). Their lives are measured out in freeway miles.

Adjuncts are among the most dedicated and skilled teachers in academe, but they are rarely rewarded. "This is a great plaque," said "Rowena" when she won her teaching award, "but it won't buy food."

Ms. Mentor knows that she was not called upon to rant about the plight of adjuncts. Nor was she asked to denounce the faculty members who still blithely steer their most eager students to graduate school ("You'll make a great professor")—even though there's been a tenure-track job shortage in the humanities for thirty years. In 1983, when the Modern Language

Association held its centennial celebration in New York, a large group of dissidents threatened to stage a "Parade of the Adjuncts" to protest the plight of the underemployed.

But Merv and Susie were not asking for a description of "Mentorland," the ideal society in which all great minds would be cherished, employed, well paid and well fed.

Instead, Merv's friend has lost his job—and unless someone promised him, in writing, a full-time job or a continuing adjunct slot, he would seem to have no legal rights. Does he have a moral right? Maybe, but Merv hasn't said so.

Merv has not, in fact, made a strong case for Friend. Does Friend have stellar teaching abilities, important publications, or extraordinary talents? Did Friend teach classes no one else could handle, such as conversational Arabic? Did Friend create enticing new courses ("YouTube and Mine," "Eat or Be Eaten") that students clamored to take? Was Friend irresistibly charming when he and his wife held scrumptious dinner parties for all the powerful people who might be doing the hiring?

Friend needed a unique niche and needed to be loved—but now he must, like thousands of other adjuncts, consider leaving academe, trying a commuter marriage, or lobbying his spouse to change jobs. Humanities Ph.D.'s do fare well in the "real world," because they have exceptional research and writing skills and a strong work ethic. The world needs educated people outside the ivory tower, and what seems like a wall may turn out to be a door.

Friend needs to look ahead, not pine for what is behind him.

Über-Adjunct, meanwhile, has been busy currying favor, seeking the love that Friend did not find. Her efforts to charm powerful people may work, if she's seen as "collegial," bright, fun to have around. She presumably has the academic credentials, and community colleges are less wedded to the idea that the perfect job candidate must be from Somewhere Else (a delusion common among research universities, especially if Somewhere Else is an elite university with a slightly snooty reputation).

But Über's friend Susie has a moral objection—that the use of adjuncts as cheap labor is killing the tenure-track posts that offer security. If a tenured full professor retires or dies, universities can hire three or four adjuncts for that salary, and call it "flexibility." If there's less money, the new adjuncts can be "pruned."

Ms. Mentor hisses along with her readers: "Exploitation." She would like all would-be teachers to refuse, on principle, to be adjuncts. She would like them to stage a general strike, demanding full-time jobs with benefits, which would lead to . . .

Unemployment, Ms. Mentor fears. Academics aren't known for their solidarity as workers—or as Susie's comrades might argue, ungently, "The halls of ivy are covered with scabs." This is not Mentorland.

In the absence of utopia, Ms. Mentor exhorts full professors to notice the adjuncts among them, and honor and pay well the toilers whose work allows the senior faculty to teach their specialties. She would like voters to harangue their legislatures for more money to hire full-time faculty members. She would like the rich parents of students in wealthy institutions to demand full-time salaries for those who teach Grayson and Muffy.

But she would also like Merv to write good recommendation letters for Friend. She would like Susie and Über-Adjunct to continue to be friends, enlightening one another about ways to burrow from within, ask impertinent questions, and nudge and lobby for change.

Obedient cringers and meek mice will not be welcome in Mentorland.

—

Reader Response: Several letter writers said Ms. Mentor painted too rosy a picture of life in Adjunctland. One reported earning just $1,000 to teach an English composition course that included diligent preparation and mounds of paper grading—so that the adjunct, Ms. Mentor calculates, may earn as little as five dollars an hour.

One correspondent said he once taught an entire semester-long course in an expensive Texas city for $300. "I did it to keep my hand in," he says.

Another correspondent wrote that health insurance, bought independently, would cost 75 percent of his salary. Still others live in boardinghouses, buy secondhand clothes, and eat uncooked ramen noodles. Ms. Mentor knows that we are supposed to admire the dedication of Chaucer's Clerk in *The Canterbury Tales*, a skinny, threadbare young man who spends all his money on books. But more than six hundred years later, forcing teachers to live in poverty strikes Ms. Mentor as nothing but shameful.

He's Making Me Work on My Teaching

Q: I'm a recent Ph.D. in a temporary, one-year job where I was unlucky enough to receive bad teaching evaluations in my first semester. Now my chair is piling on punitive measures—making me do lesson plans every week, turn in lists of student projects, keep a teaching portfolio, etc., etc. I filed a grievance. Should he be allowed to do this to me?

A: Ms. Mentor thinks you're confusing guidance with punishment. Asking for lesson plans is a thoughtful, tactful way to say, "You are screwing up. I could fire you, but this way you'll learn what you need to know." The chair is trying to work together with you, so that you may have an academic life after this year.

Filing a grievance makes you seem petulant and ungrateful. You should have written a thank-you note.

How to Make the Most of a One-Year Job

Q: In great grief and high dudgeon, I'm ending my year as a replacement prof at "Top Drawer University." When the old fart in this slot retired, opening a tenure-track position, I was ecstatic. Top Drawer has smart students, a world-class library, and a great location—and they'd already hired me. I wrote my pro forma application letter, didn't apply anywhere else, and began hunting for the ideal apartment.

And then the hiring committee didn't even interview me. When they brought in other candidates to interview (for "my" job), some of the faculty members (those who'd bothered to learn my name) even expected me to go to the candidates' talks and rate them (I hotly refused).

So now "Alex," who doesn't have any more experience or publications than I do, will get the tenure-track job that was my life's dream. I feel like the little match girl, allowed to press my nose against the glass to see the favored ones laughing and playing and eating and drinking—while I perish outside in the cold.

How can they be so cruel? And what do I do now?

A: Ms. Mentor agrees that one-year jobs can be bittersweet peeks at paradise. She also knows that too many academic departments hire thoughtlessly, even recklessly, for replacement posts. When circumstances change, new academics have their hearts broken.

Most new Ph.D.'s, especially in the humanities, have few options. Most will never be considered by Top Drawer University—which offers not only the salary, the students, and the library, but also the glamour of its name. Anyone who's taught at Top Drawer University has a mighty lifetime credential, especially if it's coupled with top recommendations ("We were so sorry we could not keep someone so splendid as Muriel").

And that's where Ms. Mentor thinks you may have blundered.

Your letter mentions students, city, and library, but says nothing about department colleagues—except that they either ignored or bedeviled you.

What did you do with them?

Were you like Frances, who was always "too busy" to have lunch or coffee with anyone? (Frances should have assigned less written work, because it was consuming her life.) Were you like Abbott, so in-the-clouds with your research that you looked right through people and never said hello to anyone in the halls?

It is indeed difficult to insinuate yourself into the lives of people you may never see again. But that is the only way to convert a one-year job into a tenurable one.

You have to make them cherish you.

"Daryl," for instance, hadn't quite finished his dissertation when he landed a one-year university postdoc. He immediately joined the faculty basketball team. Although his teammates were old enough to be his dad, Daryl knew that hanging out with people his own age—grad students— was useless professionally.

Thanks to the team, Daryl met people all over campus. He learned who in his department was powerful and worth cultivating, and he took those people to lunch. He dropped into colleagues' offices to schmooze. He faithfully attended every department meeting and introduced himself to everyone. He made small talk, he laughed at others' jokes, he cheerfully volunteered for committee work, and he talked about how "cutting edge" his research was.

Before he gave a department presentation, Daryl asked every full professor for advice and acknowledged them all. He brought homemade apple pie to department picnics. He made himself loved. And so, though he still hadn't finished his dissertation, the department overwhelmingly voted to offer Daryl its one tenure-track slot.

"But that's not fair!" you say. "What an ass kisser!"

Maybe—but every job candidate offers brains, grades, degrees, and great promise. Daryl also offered his colleagues the pleasure of his company. You presumably pleased the students and enjoyed the town and library, but you neglected the decision makers. You were not "collegial." You didn't focus on your potential teammates.

Also, some academics get wildly excited when they have the power to hire. They become impossible to please. They're sure that the bird in hand can't possibly sing as well as that unknown lark from Yonder University who's just applied. Especially at mid-level schools, academics are always comparing and worrying (Ms. Mentor calls this "Whose Is Bigger"). And too many academics can't get beyond pigeonholing: If you were once a temporary, you can't ever ascend to the tenure track.

Sometimes clever academics who yearn to work at Elite U. go off and teach at Medium U., planning to "write their way out" and get back to Elite U. Some—a few—do succeed. But most, Ms. Mentor thinks, would do better to settle at Medium U. and make real lives for themselves. Pining and yearning can be corrosive to the soul.

And so Ms. Mentor advises you to apply for every remaining job in your field and study how to be an upbeat, cooperative colleague. When you were asked to rate the visiting candidates, you should have swallowed your bile and done so. Good sports go further than snarlers do, for they get top recommendations, they network superbly, and they can make their new colleagues feel honored to have someone with such brilliance and charm.

But as a P.S., you may be pleased to learn that Daryl never did finish his dissertation. He bounced from job to job, mooched off friends, moonlighted as an exotic dancer, and finally found his calling as a taxi driver whose customers adore him.

His old job's now open again.

Goldilocks Disappears

Q: In my first semester as an adjunct, I had that "Dreaded Youthful Glow." I looked young, had long, luxurious blonde hair, and while it was beautiful, I gradually realized it spelled "bimbo" to many of my elders. So I had it cut and dyed to a sophisticated shade of mousy brown. And now I have a four-course load and three summer courses, as opposed to the piddly single class I taught while I was a blonde. Maybe now I can start paying off those student loans.

A: Ms. Mentor began to write a congratulatory note in her column . . . but a few months later, Goldilocks reported: "I'm pregnant. No more adjuncting for me. Hubby's career comes first from now on."

Why I Quit Adjuncting—or Wanted To

- They gave me an extra class on a separate day of the week, and I couldn't afford the extra train fare.
- They promised me an assistantship, yanked it away under murky circumstances, and left me ineligible for student loans. I'm now semi-homeless, living in the library and in my car.
- The chair, who has a violent temper, took my assigned courses away and gave them to a grad student he was screwing.
- I got a tenure-track job, but my partner, who's an adjunct, no longer has a sex drive.
- My boss made life hellish for me because I'm middle-aged, chubby, frumpy, and worst of all—Southern.
- I'm one of those exploited adjuncts who is choosing between poverty and teaching, and I'm losing. My class size has doubled (from thirty-five to seventy students), my grader's been yanked, and my copy card has been taken away because we were going over budget on copying costs.
- My college is in a city oversupplied with able and eager young people with degrees. Just to get hired as adjuncts, we have to go through a peer review, supply three letters of recommendation from academics at other schools, and pass a dean's review. There's an off-the-record

way to get tenure as an adjunct, but it still doesn't mean a full-time salary. There's no such thing as a full-time salary for adjuncts in these parts.

- I'm retiring and offered my services as an adjunct to some thirty colleges in my new city. I'm well-published and a big name. I got only four replies, all brush-offs. There's no respect in Adjunctdom.

I'm Not Supposed to Speak

Q: I teach at two colleges as an adjunct, and I get outstanding reviews from students at both schools. One is a university (massive and bustling); the other is a community college. My university colleagues have embraced me (but let me know that there's no hope of tenure as they gesture toward twenty-year adjuncts).

My colleagues at the community college shun me as if I trailed streamers of plague in my wake (I have a higher degree than my boss). One tenured member of my department has taken pity and encouraged me to attend staff meetings, promising that they "hire from within."

At a recent staff meeting, the dean was asked about adding a tenured position to the department. I am paraphrasing here, but the response was, "There are adjuncts in your department who mentor students, create new curricula, and basically perform full-time duties. Adjuncts in biology and chemistry barely show for their classes and don't hold office hours. The funding will go to the science departments before English. Don't even ask."

Another adjunct at this community college refers to the environment as "toxic."

What should I do?

A: Ms. Mentor, in her perfect wisdom, doubts that you have the power to do anything—except wait, publish if you can, apply elsewhere, and decide whether you want to be treated this way.

What Will You Sacrifice?

Q: I've been working my ass off as an adjunct for two years, teaching, publishing, advising, kissing any ass that condescends to present itself—and yet, no interviews. Should I let someone surgically remove my left arm for a tenure-track job? Is it worth it?

A: No.

Is It the Same Old Song?

Q: I've been a professional musician my whole life, and I am old. This year I'm a full-time adjunct at a nearby university—but next year, they promise me, I'll become a tenure-track assistant professor. That would make me eligible for tenure in my late sixties, and I could be a full professor before I'm eighty. But the new university administration says I have to publish. I've never published in my life, and wouldn't know a refereed journal from a refereed boxing match (which I might prefer).

Does this seem to be another one of those scenarios in which one hand says, "Do this," and the second says, "Do that," and then third and fourth hands come in, slap the first two, and change the rules again?

A: Yes.

I'm the Inside Candidate, But . . .

Q: I am currently in a visiting position that is going to become a permanent tenure-track job next year. Although I've been told that I am a strong candidate, I am afraid that being on the inside might work against me.

Like most academics, my colleagues have grandiose ideas about landing a "star." I am not, by any stretch of the imagination (or padding of my CV) a star in my field, but I am diligent and my diligence is paying off. I'm earning high student evaluations and good, though modest, research opportunities. Also, the department is highly dysfunctional, and anyone who is truly a shining star would merely use it as jumping-off point for something better. I, on the other hand, plan to stay, if hired. On a few occasions my colleagues have jokingly asked why I would want to continue here.

I have my reasons (mostly personal, plus I need a job), but I want some advice on how to "play the job game" when I'm already a colleague to these people. Should I keep a low profile or use this opportunity to assert my presence (nicely, of course) in the department? Should I advertise my publications and student approval, or let the hiring committee read it on my CV? Should I socialize with my colleagues or avoid faculty gatherings altogether? Should I try to network with faculty in other departments at the university? Should I try to teach new classes? Or should I devote what spare time I have to more research and writing?

A: The single most important thing in academia is "collegiality." If you want to stay, you must butter up first, while slyly letting everyone know about your publications and the students who love you. Orchestrate a campaign to make yourself adored. Only you (and perhaps a significant other) can say what's most adorable about you.

Ms. Mentor can only speculate.

Fury

Q: Sometimes my situation as an ignored and abused adjunct makes my blood boil—giving me high blood pressure, anxiety attacks, and heart palpitations. I need to quit, yes?

A: Yes.

The Tenure Trek

Tenure, or lifetime job security, is the crown jewel for professors. Ms. Mentor will tell nonacademics that tenure does not make you rich or beautiful, but it makes you secure—and academics as a group are not great risk takers. The Harvard philosophy department does not field a bungee-jumping team.

What academics want—besides a paycheck, classes, and colleagues—is the assurance that they'll be able to devote the rest of their lives to cultivating their minds.

That is a rare and wondrous opportunity, earned through five or six grueling years of stellar teaching, research, and service.

It is also a matter of doing your homework precisely and meticulously, one more time. Unless you're blessed with an exceptional clerical staff, it's up to you to put your dossier together: piles of material, in color-coded folders or tabbed binders, to demonstrate your prowess at teaching, research, and service. There may be outside letters, which a tenure committee has to fetch and then hide from you (confidentiality), but you're responsible for everything else.

Of course, you've followed Ms. Mentor's advice and kept everything in your Tenure Diary, so that you'll have no trouble hauling it out now. (Yes, Ms. Mentor, who knows all, knows you can't put your hands on everything right away, and you must have powerful enemies who've misfiled stuff. She forgives you. Carry on.)

You may need to find and turn in: copies of syllabi; copies of exams; copies of the best student papers; copies of teaching evaluations (quantitative and qualitative); copies of your publications; copies of soon-to-be published articles; copies of grant proposals and reports; copies of any articles about you; copies of your vita; copies of award citations; copies of notes praising you from the chancellor, the mayor, or other important people; and any other papers attesting to your effectiveness at whatever you're doing. Some schools also require that you write essays about your philosophy, your goals, your future research plans, your future contributions to your university, and the good of society and the universe as we know it . . .

Ms. Mentor advises you to allot several weeks for this clerical torture.

You might even want to have a dossier party and offer beer and pizza to friends who'll help you assemble everything and croon appropriate melodies (YouTube.com has several tenure songs).

Your dossier circle can also be part of your vigil, which can take up to nine months, in which you wait and wait while the department, the college, the dean, the university, the regents . . . all presumably read everything and perform some kind of deliberations in secret, and communicate to you vaguely, sometimes with dropped hints or with unsubstantiated rumors.

This all starts in August, and by May, you'll get the official letter giving you tenure.

In the meantime, even if you've done everything right, you'll worry and fuss (while quietly keeping track of any procedural errors). If you think your school is more apt to tenure a white male rather than you, you're right—but you're the one who has to be the watchdog.

Maybe you'll notice that someone else, hired when you were, seems to be the department Golden Boy or Girl, who dances around, being ingratiating and flattering everyone. You're sure that the old faculty will fall for charm (theirs) and ignore stolid accomplishment (yours).

This is the time to gather 'round your mentoring team, and all the people who adore you. Significant others, loving friends, doting moms and dads, cousins, children, dogs, and cats—tell them about your greatness, and make sure they recite it back to you. Cheer their efforts as a cheering section—and have a fabulous party when you get the good news.

When another good person gets tenure, Ms. Mentor believes, somewhere in the universe a kitten purrs.

Threats and Temptations

Q: Oh, how I long to send my two-faced, libidinous adviser something dead and wet through snail mail. But then I get all compassionate and guilty about endangering the beleaguered souls who work in the Post Office. Must I resist this thrilling temptation, smile through gritted teeth, and get my revenge through the long, slow process of achieving tenure?

A: Yes.

What's Really Confidential?

Q: The proceedings of tenure committees are shrouded in mystery, it seems to me. Different judgments are made at different levels (according to the faculty handbook, which I've memorized), but is it possible to find out how things are going? Is confidentiality really kept on most campuses?

A: When asked about secrecy, Ms. Mentor quotes a famous sage: "Can two academics really keep a secret? Yes, if four of them are dead."

People who rate themselves by their brain power do have ecstatic fits when they know something no one else knows: a literary theory, a mathematical proof, or the news that priapic Professor Dirk has been canned for chronic sexual harassment. By the end of the day, everyone in town, from janitor to judge, will know what's up with Dirk.

In truth, one such "Dirk," in a small Ohio town, was stunned to learn that he had been denied tenure—especially because he first heard about it from Adriana, the dental hygienist, while she was poking about in his incisors. Adriana murmured sympathetically while Dirk roared in pain.

Ms. Mentor, in her perfect wisdom, would abolish the charade of confidentiality. When things go really awry—when courts intervene—confidential references, including embarrassing e-mails, do always come to light, making academicians seem less than forthright, sometimes comical and occasionally perverse.

Ms. Mentor believes that smart adults should be able to discuss hiring, job performance, and money face-to-face. Millions of real people do it every day, and hardly anyone goes postal.

A Hint of Tenure in the Air

Q: In my first semester on the tenure track at my small college, I am summoned into the office of a venerable but crotchety professor, who tells me he's sure I'll get tenure. And while it might seem rather soon, he is completely confident of his declaration. Tenure decisions, he says, shouldn't come as a surprise to anyone.

So, Ms. Mentor, who Knows All, are tenure decisions really made in the first three months? And if so, what can they be based on, beyond my smile? And is it true that if you're not told that you're going to get tenure, you should assume that you won't? And if you're told that you shouldn't be surprised by your tenure decision, does that mean you won't be getting tenure, or that you will?

And who makes up these crazy rules?

A: Ms. Mentor agrees that few things are more vexing than hints. What is a threat, and what is a promise? What is a danger signal, and what is a paranoid musing? Is a sigh ever just a sigh?

Some fundamental things do apply. If, for instance, your disgruntled colleagues have left a horse's head in your bed, take that as serious evidence that you may not get tenure.

But most other signals are open to interpretation. If the maintenance people don't empty your wastebasket, are you the only one? If your mail gets lost, are you the only one? If Professor Mega Grouchy snarls at you, are you alone? (Unlikely.)

Overeducated people will always seek out dire portents and morbid interpretations. Consider "Havelock," a lifelong New Yorker who arrived for his first teaching job at Deep Southern U., only to find that he hadn't been assigned an office. Sure that everyone hated him because he was a Yankee, and equally certain that his career was dead, Havelock took to slinking about with his huge black briefcase, and holding office hours with students in random doorways and alcoves (or, if they were over twenty-one, in bars).

"Man, that guy's creepy and furtive," said one student who'd just wanted advice for his paper on slime molds.

But then, in early November, "Florence," the department's newly tenured star, accosted Havelock and whispered, "Are you a secret smoker? Is that why you're always skittering about and hiding?"

Once she knew what truly ailed him, Florence laughed, then cleared out some space in her own office for Havelock until the next semester, when his office and desk abruptly materialized. "Another bureaucratic screwup," everyone assured him.

And yet . . . when one is new, academic communications all seem a tad Machiavellian. Information is sometimes garbled, or concealed under code words. "A fine mind" means "many friends but few publications." "Brilliant but . . ." can mean "is abrasive" or "harasses students." "Flexible" is good. "Rigid" is bad. "Traditional" may be either.

Confidentiality as a tradition may be baffling. In business, employees routinely read their own performance reports. But in academe, dossiers and recommendations are supposed to be sealed away. Ms. Mentor wonders if teacher-scholars are considered more delicate than other working souls.

And then there are tenured faculty members who like to amuse themselves with bons mots that can be misunderstood, or taken far too seriously, by newcomers. "I feel like I'm being held captive in a very lengthy game of Clue," one anxious visiting instructor wrote to Ms. Mentor. "One colleague claims there are 'big plans for you,' while another says, 'They just brought you in as a brain for their ship of fools.'"

Who should be believed? The wise newbie listens to everyone, smiles, files away the information, and applies Ms. Mentor's Trusty Guide to Informants:

- Does your informant gossip regularly with at least one knowledgeable clerk or administrative assistant?
- Does your informant belong to a powerful promotion, tenure, or personnel committee where decisions are made?
- Is your informant a department administrator, such as chair/director/head, associate chair, or director of graduate studies?
- Is he or she a recovering dean? (They always have special knowledge.)

- Is your informant related to anyone in a significant position, such as a member of the board of regents?
- Does he or she hang out at the Faculty Senate, or play poker, golf, or squash, or drink with powerful people who know things?
- Does your informant sleep with anybody important?

If your informant has none of these connections, you may consider him or her a lively gossip or a dreadful crank, but not an apt interpreter of reality.

But, Ms. Mentor, you are howling, Will they really decide my fate in the first three months?

Well, sometimes they will, although the official tenure criteria (teaching, research, and service) have barely kicked in. The unofficial tenure decider—"collegiality" (whether They like you)—can indeed be checked off in your first semester, if you alienate everyone.

"Stone," for instance, challenged every curriculum decision, invaded private meetings, disdained the food, despised the students, and loathed the town. He was friendly only to the youngest assistant, whom he'd grab around the neck while crooning, "Got any lately?"

But Stone, the man without a hint or a clue, is a rarity. Because new faculty members are more apt to be edgy and hypersensitive, Ms. Mentor urges their elders not to spin out conspiratorial musings: Do not make drama out of molehills. Resist the temptation to present yourself as an oracle. Instead, tell the youngsters that the "crazy rules" for promotion and tenure don't come from Mount Olympus. They're in the faculty handbook, and often they're even online.

Ms. Mentor also urges entrenched professors to pay more attention to newbies. Be sociable, treat them to lunch, and help them with unwritten rules (how do you get your office computer repaired?) Don't carp or prance, but do what Kenneth Blanchard and Spencer Johnson suggest in *The One Minute Manager*: "Catch someone doing something right."

Praise the untenured, and watch them blossom. That's what educators do.

That's what mentors do.

My Friends Are Failing

Q: I'm on my way to tenure, with publications, good teaching evaluations, and good relations with my older colleagues. But I'm losing friends my own age, who are falling off the tenure track.

They have mental problems, or they haven't finished their dissertations, or they spend too much time on teaching and not enough on writing, or they're tied up with family obligations. What can I do to help them? And what happens when I'm on a tenure committee, reviewing people who haven't pulled themselves together?

A: Ms. Mentor sees in your letter a bit of the anhedonic academic—the professorial type who cannot accept pleasure. Those are the people who seem to be forever looking over their shoulders, just waiting for the signal so they can drop to their knees, flail their arms, and moan: I am unworthy! I am unworthy!

Or, I'm worthy, but my friends aren't!

And if my friends aren't, it's my responsibility!

And it's probably my fault, too!

Ms. Mentor thinks you're suffering from a kind of survivor guilt. You got through grad school, you got hired, and now you're trying to figure out how you lucked out. After all, a big purpose of graduate and professional schools is to make you feel vulnerable, ignorant, and inadequate. You can never know enough, never read enough, never do enough experiments. There are always flaws in your logic, holes in your data. They are always going to judge you and find you wanting, because you are a worm.

After the final oral defense, everyone thinks, "I got by again."

And yet, somehow, some of the worms find jobs. They burrow out of their holes, blinking, into a new world where—at least in the classroom—they have to purport to be top worm. They even grade the wormettes in their care.

What power! What fear!

And now you're really sure that some day, They'll find out that you're bogus. They'll yank your degree, confiscate your underthings, and send you to some cell where the only things to read will be in Bulgarian.

And so you'd better appease Them—which brings Ms. Mentor back to her correspondent, who seems unable to rest on her laurels. (Yes, the letter writer is a she.)

Her kind of guilt especially flourishes in the humanities, where people are accustomed to reading novels about depression and suicide and applying them to their own troubled lives. And, of course, apparent failures are real. In a typical year in English, for instance, there are about a thousand new literature Ph.D.'s, but only about four hundred tenure-track jobs.

Some new academics, especially young women with Catholic consciences, want to atone for being winners. They self-deprecate ("it was all luck"), or they insist on crediting others ("I owe it all to my dog"), or they become responsibility magnets ("I have to do everything to show I'm worthy"). They volunteer to redo the lab, redesign the Web site, re-deck the halls. They join every committee, seek out troubled students, offer to teach new and extra courses for no money ("I live to serve"). They cannot say no, even to the most blatant requests: "We've got to have a woman on this committee. Guess you'll do."

But Ms. Mentor's remarkably successful correspondent seems to have risen above much of this. She has managed to be ambitious, intelligent, and kind—yet she cannot sit still and enjoy her own greatness. She feels somehow responsible for her peers' ills.

Ms. Mentor gently advises that there is little she can do for her friends' family and health problems—besides listening, providing tea and casseroles, and referring them to the Family and Medical Leave Act and the Americans with Disabilities Act.

For the publishing-challenged, she can create a writing group to meet regularly and evaluate each other's work. Stringent deadlines and the risk of public humiliation always spur academics, and unless the group is too gentle or unstructured, most members will come through with something. One bad page a day adds up to a book-length manuscript in a year, and shaping and editing is much easier than confronting a blank screen. Even a word a day adds up to an op-ed piece. And when the word is "a," "an," or "the," the writer can quit early.

Still, there are those souls who really do not want to be academics. It's said that half of ABD (all but dissertation) types never do finish, and Ms. Mentor thinks the actual figure is higher. She believes that people who are not self-motivated or intellectually engaged are better off moving on down the cafeteria line of life, selecting a different entree, and sitting at a newer, cleaner table.

Once you quit the dissertation struggle, you'll have a surge of self-confidence: "I'm not a worm after all. I can make it in the Real World."

Academic misfits, especially the more gregarious ones, can become superb museum directors and mavens, writers and reporters, politicians and players, advertisers and activists. If talented people feel out of water as tenure-track academics, they are probably right—and if you're on the committee judging them, you are not being their friend if you vote to tenure them. You'll be strangling them with security.

While Ms. Mentor often scoffs at hippie-like sentiments, she does believe that if you love someone—including yourself—you should set them free.

Women on the Edge

Q (from "Doreen"): As the only ethnic minority faculty member at my college, I'm an assistant professor of psychology, Asian studies, gender, culture, and two or three other things I'm too tired to remember. I'm on diversity committees and status-of-everybody commissions, and every troubled student comes to me for advice. Yet I'm also supposed to publish as much as my white male colleagues who come to campus twice a week and play tennis every afternoon.

Q (from "Eileen"): After I was hired to develop a new arts program at our college, the schedule was changed. I couldn't do the planned work and wouldn't be paid for the summer. So I had to hustle grant money to live on, and that meant long commutes to Larger City. And now I'm labeled "uncollegial" because I haven't done what I was hired to do.

Q (from "Kathleen"): As an adjunct, I teach four different courses and have been told not to do research or work on curriculum design, which is my field. Is this a fast track to nowhere?

Q (from "Maureen"): I'm up for tenure soon, with more graduate students and research money than any other professor in my department. I've done it despite a painful divorce, no child support, and serious bouts of depression and exhaustion. I've never mentioned any of this at work, but should I include it in the personal statement for my tenure dossier?

A: Ms. Mentor's sage readers will note that all these letters come from faculty women—who, like clerical, staff, and maintenance women, are overworked and underappreciated. Even Ms. Mentor, in all her majesty, is not worshipped sufficiently.

And now Doreen, in the classic minority bind, finds that she's expected to represent everyone who is "other," be a mentor to everyone who is "other," and devote her time to "otherness" instead of to the research and writing that feed her. She goes home depleted, while her white colleagues frolic on the tennis court.

Someone's also playing with Eileen, whose schedule mysteriously "was changed." And now her job, apparently, is to rise above it all, do without rest or money, be several places at once, and be cheery ("collegial") at the same time.

Ms. Mentor doubts that anyone could do that without serious drugs.

Kathleen, meanwhile, has been whomped by "institutional needs." If she does what she's told—and most women do want to be good citizens— she'll never have the publications or administrative experience that can lift her onto a tenure-track line. And she may be paid as little as $12,000 a year for her pains.

Brave and stoic Maureen, though, is about to land the golden prize, tenure. Ms. Mentor wishes that Maureen could brag in her tenure statement about every accomplishment in her life ("I raised a child on my own! Hear me roar!")—and yet, Ms. Mentor knows the patriarchs of academe. There may be traditionalists who'll suddenly decide that Maureen's not professional enough ("She takes things personally"). A few may even decide, suddenly, that Maureen is a braggart and a whiner, and who wants someone like that around for the next quarter-century?

And so Ms. Mentor reluctantly advises Maureen to write up only her professional achievements. But once she's tenured, Maureen must speak about inequalities: tenure clocks that compete with biological clocks, assumptions that women needn't be paid well, and beliefs that no one has a home life more important than round-the-clock Pushing Back the Frontiers of Science.

Ms. Mentor insists that women seize control of their work lives.

Doreen should plump for a reduced teaching load. She should write down how many hours a week she spends on service (committees, advising, mentoring), and write her department head a memo requesting equivalent release time. She should also ask in writing that service be listed as part of her job description, which governs how she'll be evaluated for tenure.

Ms. Mentor also thinks that Doreen should look quietly for another job where she will not be a martyr.

Women need to self-promote. Eileen should ask that her job description include grant writing, and Kathleen should tout her own expertise in curriculum design—and wouldn't it benefit everyone if she worked on that in lieu of one of her courses? She could also share her findings in a spectacular public presentation.

Doreen, Eileen, and Kathleen must be tough women, not docile girls. They must go after the best deals for themselves, and not warp and starve themselves to fit someone else's notions of quiet self-sacrifice. Ms. Mentor recommends Linda Babcock and Sara Laschever's *Women Don't Ask: Negotiation and the Gender Divide* for tips on growing a healthy selfishness. It's good for the goose.

As for the gander, Ms. Mentor recommends that male readers peruse Arlie Hochschild and Anne Machung's *The Second Shift: Working Parents and the Revolution at Home* for the truth about who's doing what in the house. Women still do some two-thirds of household tasks and child care—and they are the ones who sacrifice their careers, not always willingly. They are the ones who are always tired.

Maureen is a superwoman, but all academics deserve opportunities to use their talents. Scholars rarely get rich, but they can nourish their souls and teach the young to love knowledge and appreciate smart women.

There are no better lessons.

Is Your Book Really Coming Out?

Q: What does "forthcoming" really mean? Suppose somebody coming up for tenure had a book manuscript being considered by a publisher for over a year. And suppose the author ("Wally") put the book on his

CV as "forthcoming." But suppose someone powerful in the department ("Professor Peevish") got very angry, said the listing was deceptive, and threatened to take steps.

Who is right? Is there an official rule? I would tend to say "under review" or "in the final stages of review," but that's more because I worry about the evil eye than because I'd find it actually dishonest. We have several tenured colleagues whose books have been "forthcoming" for years, and one suspects that if one called their alleged publishers . . . but that is not the sort of thing a good person does, really.

When does "forthcoming" begin, at conception or at birth?

A: As a schoolgirl, little Ms. Mentor never spitballed or squealed, and if a class discussion degenerated into a mosh pit of diverse learning styles, she would be the one shrieking, "Define your terms! Define your terms!" Ms. Mentor has noted in the ensuing years that "Define your terms" has a quieting effect on expressions of rage and controversy. And so she has become a Definer, whose sacred task it is to reveal the lurking real meanings of such terms as "forthcoming."

And yet Ms. Mentor knows that the issue isn't really whether a book is a zygote, or gestating, or incubating. "Forthcoming" can mean "at the idea stage" or "inchoate." It can be a mote in the mind, a song on the wind, a glimpse of the ineffable not yet reduced to the dry mundanity of words.

The key point is whether the people in charge want to give you tenure.

Outsiders may believe that academics write books solely to advance the frontiers of knowledge, with nary a thought for sordid material gain. Indeed, a love for the esoteric is supposed to be a *ne plus ultra* and *raison d'être* of the *mundus academicus*. But if that were solely the case, scholars might spend years—indeed, generations—exploring the really fundamental questions: What is the meaning of life? Who are the good, the bad, and the ugly? Why do they still serve clam chowder on Fridays?

Instead, a newly hired Wally at a research university has five or six years to get his first book published. If he fails, he's unlikely to get tenure, which means that he's fired, and he may have to go out and get a job in the Real World. (He need not shudder or quail, says Ms. Mentor. Thousands of recovering academics are delighted to abandon footnotes and sophomores forever.)

Meanwhile, back in the ivory tower: If Wally's book is accepted by a publisher, he's met the research criterion for tenure in the humanities at most institutions. (Literature and history departments traditionally require a book; other fields want significant articles.) His colleagues will presumably vote to tenure him, and enjoy the fruits of his knowledge for the next twenty-five years or so. Everyone will be secure and happy.

But it appears that Wally's book is not quite accepted, and the liminal stages before the actual physical book appears can be dangerous for an untenured scholar. The rules vary. The definitions waver.

Some departments think it sufficient that a book be under serious consideration by a publisher. (For the intricacies of academic publishing, Ms. Mentor recommends William Germano's *Getting It Published.*) If Wally is considered a "fine mind" by his colleagues, they may vote to tenure him even if the book is undone (brilliant but latent). But other universities may want a publisher's letter saying that Wally's monograph is accepted, pending revisions. Still others may want to see a final contract, with tentative publication date (the classic definition of "forthcoming").

There are also those who insist that by tenure time, Wally's book should be "in press." (Ms. Mentor envisions huge, shaking machines churning out copies, while committees shout about Wally's merits as teacher, researcher, and department citizen.)

Some years ago, an Ivy League university refused to tenure an up-and-coming scholar who later became one of the stars of queer theory. When the committee was voting on his tenure, though, his book was only in galley proofs. It was not yet a bound volume, and so it "doesn't really exist yet," the senior professors reportedly sniffed.

Self-styled "stringent" departments have denied tenure to scholars unless their books have been reviewed in academic journals (even though that may be a year after publication). Some very bright people have been denied tenure for a book's bad reviews, or no reviews ("Your work isn't important").

And yes, all of that smacks of injustice, and while Ms. Mentor assures up-and-coming scholars that stinginess and meanness are not rampant, senior faculty's egos do sometimes come out and play over definitions of a term. Professor Peevish may have high and honorable standards. Perhaps he's a bit of a pedant. It's unlikely that he's read Wally's manuscript, and he may simply be fussing over a procedural point. He may think Wally is deceptive rather than confused. But late in the day, with tenure vote coming up, Wally has one thing he must do, besides propitiating all gods and hoping for an actual contract from a publisher:

Wally must placate Peevish.

Ideally, Wally has discussed his book all along, from the time he arrived at his university. It may have been the subject of the job talk that got him hired; he may have given university presentations about it; he may have gotten media attention. He should have talked frequently about his book—to get feedback, but also to self-promote. He should have chatted about it amiably with senior professors and asked their advice. That always wins fans.

Now it is incumbent upon Wally to take Professor Peevish to lunch, praise the Peevish oeuvre, and do whatever he can to make nice, to curry favor, and to win support for tenure (and the votes of the Peevish clique, if there is one). Yes, he is buttering up, and Ms. Mentor knows there are hotheads in her audience who will condemn Wally as a toady and a lackey of the system. But being chronically oppositional and ornery nowadays in academe is a sure ticket out the door. Wally wants to stay inside, where it's warm—and where the real intellectual riches of academe become available.

Besides, once tenure is no longer just "forthcoming," and your first book is in your hand, all those people who thought you were a nerd in high school will be cursing their own shallowness and wishing they were a swan like you.

Well, that's what they should be doing.

All right, that's still forthcoming.

Will They Promote a Viper?

Q: I am in my third tenure-track year at Wannabe Ivy U., where I'm the only woman in a mostly tenured department of very career-oriented men. "Roscoe," who shares my same general teaching area, goes up for tenure this year. He has never once willingly discussed his research with me, and when I asked him to read a draft of mine, all he said was, "Fine. I wish I found writing as easy as you do." I've invited him for dinner, and it's been pleasant, but he still won't treat me as a peer.

I'm willing to accept that we won't be academic buddies, but now he's seriously trying to undermine me. When he planned a meeting for all of us who teach the survey course, he somehow forgot to notify me (my TA told me). Students in my grad seminar say he's been belittling the topic I'm teaching this semester. And at a recent faculty meeting, he denounced my exam as poorly designed and unimaginative. If I can't get him to play nice, or even play at all, how do I at least keep him from throwing sand in my face?

A: Ms. Mentor is pleased that you are not confusing Roscoe with Mother Teresa. She also applauds your vision of an ideal academic department: kindred souls, shared research, pooled teaching ideas, food and friendship. Like Ms. Mentor, you believe in generosity. But Roscoe evidently believes in the Udder Theory, that the world is like a big cow with limited milk—and if one person grabs hold of a teat, there's nothing left for anyone else. Roscoe wants you to starve.

He may truly believe that there is a quota—one tenured prof per subject area. Some colleges do have quotas. But Wannabe Ivy Universities can always grant tenure to someone who fills a unique niche. You, a woman who can mentor other women, can do something that Roscoe can never do.

That may be what's irking him, turning him into a playground bully who won't share his toys.

Ms. Mentor is reminded of "Fletcher," a forever-in-motion assistant professor at Large East Coast U., who could be spotted cantering past the department office, hair flapping: "I'm late—no time to chat, no time for that . . ." He was always jetting off to Cambridge to give a paper. He alone was in close communication with the Great Expert in the field, who had once spoken to Fletcher at a Major International Meeting. The rest of Large's faculty, Fletcher told his students, consisted of "barely satisfactory minds." (By the time the story snaked its way through the grad student grapevine, Fletcher had called his colleagues "dolts and dorks," and they all knew it.) Meanwhile, Fletcher said that even having coffee with his colleagues was "a waste of research time," and that he would not deign to join a writing group: "I send my drafts to Dr. Expert," he declared. Junior professors who met to edit and encourage each other were "the blind leading the half-cocked."

When Fletcher came up for tenure, no one had to mention his boor-ishness to women, especially department staff. Nor did anyone say that students thought him arrogant and unprofessional. No one could praise his teaching innovations, because he never came to teachers' meetings. As for his much-vaunted book, the one that would "change the complexion of discourse" in his field—it wasn't finished. With all his hithering-and-thithering, Fletcher had not made desk time every day, as productive writers must. "I know others write more facilely and superficially," he conceded. The meeting to vote on Fletcher's tenure was short, and not even nasty or brutish. His career died.

Ms. Mentor thinks that Roscoe may not be a Fletcher, but when he rants about your exam, which he should have discussed with you privately, he is telling future tenure voters that he is uncooperative and rude. When they vote, the tenured professors will surely wonder: "Do we want to hear this kind of yammering for the rest of our professional lives?"

No one wants to promote a viper.

Nor should you be devoting your energies to taming him, says Ms. Mentor. You must give up the hope—common to women—that everyone will like and appreciate you. You must write off Roscoe and devote your-self to the senior professors. Invite them to lunch or coffee or dinner, visit their offices, and ask for advice.

You may, with an air of naïveté, ask about teacher meetings: "Shouldn't everyone who teaches a course be invited?" You are so sorry that Roscoe somehow didn't notify you about his meeting. Always appear puzzled and frustrated at these mistakes that happen.

Word will get around that Roscoe is being less than civil to his female colleague, who is always pleasant and gracious to her elders. Roscoe will seem even more churlish. When you do see Roscoe, always smile broadly, but do not even invite him for coffee. He will be befuddled and anxious. He will be sure that you know something he doesn't know, and you do.

You know how to be a great colleague.

I Was Dedicated When I Should Have Been Decadent

Q: I should have written to you before I got fired, but then I didn't know I was in such trouble. I was hired to teach English literature to future teachers in a college in a Mediterranean country ("Tiberia"). I was given an official syllabus and told I had to follow it carefully, because of accreditation.

But I found that the only English books in the library were trashy old novels, and like an idiot, I nagged the librarian about where the course books were. "They have to be here, because they're on the official list," I insisted—inadvertently making bitter enemies throughout the library. Soon, and without notifying me, the administration canceled one of my two courses.

I threw my energy and enthusiasm into my tiny remaining class, but I had serious problems with absenteeism, tardiness, and a general refusal to do homework (I later discovered I was the only English teacher assigning any). Several students failed because of poor attendance and no homework, and because their spoken and written English were so poor that they couldn't understand the literature we'd studied. I offered to give them incompletes and tutor them during the next semester.

You won't be surprised that I was sacked days before the beginning of the second semester. My crime was "not fitting in," and obviously I didn't. I'd seen this job as a chance to improve the level of English teaching in this country, and it took me far too long to realize that anyone who paid tuition and had a pulse was assured of getting a degree.

I've taught before, and I know I'm a good teacher, but how could I have avoided this debacle?

A: Ms. Mentor is glad that you are not claiming to be wildly superior to those about you, as many disgruntled Americans do. Nor are you humming, "I'm too savvy for my spot." Instead you're wondering—wisely— how you might have salvaged your job.

Some hotheads would advise you to fight the system—to demand higher standards, to publicize the sins and lies of the students and professors and librarians, to beat your little fists against the tide of mediocrity surging in . . .

But Ms. Mentor will not do so, for she is a realist who does not like to see bloodied fists. The current Tiberian system evidently satisfies most of the people who've designed it. It protects their jobs and turns out enough English teachers to satisfy whoever needs to be satisfied.

It does not satisfy you, and that's often true for outsiders. Ms. Mentor's mailbag always has letters from arts professionals—directors, singers, painters—who are appalled at what they consider the low level of accomplishment among the college students they are hired to teach. The professionals threaten, cajole, bully, and scream as they try to elicit "professional-level performances" from their charges—most of whom don't want to be pros. They just wanna have fun.

And so the professionals wind up being fired for "not fitting in," for demanding too much.

Ms. Mentor does feel that you deserve praise for having standards. In your one semester, you may have aided or even inspired some students. Some will see you as heroic. And yet . . .

It's obvious that the Tiberian students and faculty members have other priorities. Possibly they prefer to spend their time in cafes—flirting, drinking, and solving (in their own way) the problems of the world. They may be discussing intellectual issues or fomenting revolution, as cafe-goers do in Paris. Or they may just be experimenting with new genres of sex, drugs, and rock 'n' roll.

Whatever their agenda, you—with your assignments and your expectations—were an annoying little gnat. You had to be squashed.

And so, what might you do, when in Rome? Rather than fuming, you might have decided that you, too, would prefer to while away your time in cafes, enjoying the Mediterranean atmosphere, drinking wine and feasting on cheese and olives—instead of grading ineptly done papers. You might have decided to teach good oral English to those who attended class, and put the others out of your mind.

Also, if you had in mind some research and writing projects of your own, you would have had much more time for them. Knocking one's head against a wall does sap one's concentration.

Your real choice was simple: Did you want to have fun, or did you want to get fired?

Next time, Ms. Mentor trusts you to do . . . well, whatever works for you.

When It Looks Like You Won't Get Tenure

Q (from "Gregory"): As a junior faculty member at Ivy League Elite University, I am not supposed to be "campaigning" for tenure. One recently rejected candidate was described as a suck up. Yet I know that getting the full professors to like me is crucial. If I invite them to lunch, will I seem like a sycophant? Is it safe to give drafts of my unpublished work to senior colleagues and risk their criticism? What about a particularly neurotic colleague who is said to have spoken ill of me at those senior-faculty-only meetings where we—the untenured—seem to be the main subject of discussion?

Q (from "Amanda"): I am a second-year assistant professor at an Ivy League university and love my job, though the department is chaotic and dysfunctional. Many full professors tell junior faculty members that if we write two books, we will get tenure, but the actual tenure rate in our department is about one out of six—and so I expect to be moving on. I love this city, where I have nonacademic friends who keep me sane, but I'm also a graduate of fancy Ivy League institutions with equally low tenure rates. I want to avoid the despair, bitterness, and low self-esteem that I've seen others fall into. Some who do get tenure end up as psychically deformed as the ones who don't. How soon should I apply for other jobs? Should I conceal my job search? Should I apply for undesirable jobs that I probably would not take? And how should I explain wanting to leave an Ivy League job?

A: Ms. Mentor sees Gregory and Amanda as stars in one of academia's more painful dramas. Smart and accomplished, they have been allowed to dwell, briefly, at the Pinnacle—but the gates will almost certainly be shut on their noses. There is already a sadness in their epistles, and Ms. Mentor deplores the waste of talent when young people are thrown out of what seems to be paradise—just because it's always been done that way.

Ms. Mentor asks her readers to imagine, instead, that Gregory and Amanda have been hired in tenure-track jobs at Midlevel University. Full professors warmly invite them to dinner; department parties and meetings always include them. They join pedagogical circles where no one is afraid to describe teaching ideas that don't work. Their partners are helped with jobs and child care, and invited to clubs, movies, and concerts. Because Midlevelers know that hiring is time-consuming and frustrating ("so many good people"), search committees nurture those they hire, wanting them to get tenure and be able to spend their careers happily teaching what they love and enhancing Midlevel's growing scholarly reputation.

Of course, Midlevel Universities are not prestigious. Their libraries are small, and their faculty lists do not include Nobel Prize winners. Their students get all kinds of grades (not just A's) and rarely grow up to become members of the ruling class. And Midlevel Universities do have their own feuds and factions. Academics everywhere tend to be highly verbal people who value their own opinions inordinately.

But what happened to Gregory and Amanda?

Well, while Ms. Mentor was musing about Midlevel U., Gregory and Amanda were chewing their fingernails, stocking up on anti-anxiety medicines, interpreting every senior professor's frown or smile as a judgment, and worrying about how to stay and where to go. Gregory cannot have lunch with a senior colleague without its taking on a Symbolic Weight, while Amanda needs nonacademic colleagues as a reality check.

Ms. Mentor can certainly tell Amanda and Gregory how to impress their senior colleagues. She can suggest that they apply for other jobs a few years before they might have to move. They needn't explain why they're on the job market, because it's widely known that Ivy League schools woo Big Names—while assigning most teaching to junior faculty members and graduate students, who are used relentlessly before they're spit out.

Ms. Mentor can advise Gregory and Amanda to be charming to neurotic senior colleagues—smile, though your jaw is breaking. She can also tell them that full professors do not spend all their time conspiring against the young. She will encourage Gregory and Amanda to get feedback on their works-in-progress from senior scholars, who are often flattered to be asked—and who may be willing to write future recommendations.

But Ms. Mentor would also like Gregory and Amanda to use their intellects for research, not for scheming and self-preservation. Worrying about whether you should suck up—or whether you've sucked up enough, or how well you've done it—is rarely as soul-satisfying as teaching, writing, or feeling appreciated.

Right now, Gregory and Amanda's stories seem headed toward the same poignant conclusion. They may do everything right, publish one or two books before the tenure deadline, impress several senior professors, teach with verve, and do dedicated committee work. But unless they are like the late Stephen Jay Gould, who spent his whole career at Harvard, they'll most likely be turned down for tenure.

If they do beat the odds, Ms. Mentor hopes they will be kinder than the powerful seniors who are, apparently, untroubled about using and throwing out a rolling cohort of bright, ambitious young people. Surely Ms. Mentor is not the only one who observes all this and wonders who benefits.

—

Reader Response: Ms. Mentor is delighted to report that Amanda and Gregory were both awarded tenure at their Ivies. There is some justice in this world.

The Tenure Gloat

Q (from "Cora"): I'm up for tenure. I've published a reasonable amount, am a good teacher, and have created a new interdisciplinary program. My faculty colleagues publicly assure me that they're for me—except the one ("Nemesis") who has not talked to me in two years. But I'm confident that my department will vote yes, and usually the other levels fall in line after that. (Yes, I've asked everyone I know.) So, when should I celebrate? When should the drinking start?

Q (from "Wilbur"): This is my up-or-out tenure year. I'm a top-notch teacher, do more than my share of service, and have a reasonable research record—but my department committee voted to deny me both tenure and promotion. My chair, in an unprecedented move, wrote a strong dissent and recommended both tenure and promotion. The college committee agreed unanimously, and that committee head assured me things are OK, though "someone on your department committee must have been out to get you." My question: How much overt gloating is permissible? Obviously, my department committee looks foolish, when every other person involved has supported my tenure. How much can I rub their (committee members') noses in it? Or should I just stay all friendly and nice, bide my time, and wait for a chance to get even?

A: Ms. Mentor will admit that her favorite football performances are the little gloating leaps and pats in the end zone after a big play. She likes to see big men shake and shimmy when they celebrate.

When their good news comes, Cora and Wilbur need to smile humbly and thank everyone—*everyone*—for their support. If they gloat, they must do so secretly. But their questions are premature. Right now, Ms. Mentor wonders if Cora and Wilbur will get tenure. Danger signals abound.

Cora's Nemesis is one, and Ms. Mentor cannot fathom why an entrenched senior professor would make a point of shunning a youngster. If theirs is a male-dominated field, Nemesis and his long-term buddies may resent Cora as an interloper and vote against her, no matter her academic record—unless they like her socially (she doesn't say). Collegiality often outweighs the three official criteria—teaching, research, and service—when academics decide on tenure.

Should Cora celebrate now, halfway through the tenure process? Ms. Mentor recommends a glass or two of wine, but cautions against premature victory dances.

Cora needs to mend fences with Nemesis. She can stop by his office, bring him a news clip, offer him candy, ask his opinion—anything to recharge the conversational muscles. He may be more shy than snarly, and Cora needs to win him over if she's to have a pleasant future. If and when she does have a tenure celebration party, she wants no boycotts and no mourners.

Meanwhile, poor Wilbur did not know he had naysayers in his department—and it seems that Wilbur himself has a bit of a hostile streak. Once it's all over, he wants to gloat. He wants revenge.

But academe is not the NFL, where you can be rich and famous right away, even if everyone hates you. Academic careers last much longer, and youthful brashness is rarely forgiven. Wilbur must remain silent until the regents deliver their verdict, at which point he should behave like a good winner, shaking everyone's hand and vowing to work harmoniously with all. He may smirk inwardly, but Ms. Mentor exhorts him not to plot revenge or harbor grudges. That will steal time and energy from his teaching and his intellectual work; it will eat him up inside. Instead, he should sail through the halls, doing a few invisible leaps and pats, while proclaiming his long-term research plans. Gracious condescension is far more powerful than back- or front-stabbing—because it makes your opponent feel guilty.

Ms. Mentor, who has seen it all, knows that if you habitually gloat, brag, or taunt "I told you so," you will make people shun you, even if you've managed to get tenure. Your colleagues can still warn students against you, undermine your research, crowd your lab space, refuse to share resources, deny you travel money, ignore what you say in department meetings, abolish courses in your specialty, and hiss when you walk by. A civilized veneer of camaraderie and bonhomie will make your path to full professorship smoother and sweeter smelling.

———

Reader Response: Wilbur, who wanted to gloat and taunt but didn't, now has his tenure. "I can take pride in having taken the high road," he brags. Ms. Mentor does not know whether Cora drank up or drowned her sorrows.

How Shall I Behave for My Public?

Q: If I get tenure, will I feel (a) ecstatic, knowing They do love me; or (b) sad, fearing I'll lose all ambition forever; or (c) relieved that I got by again, and They still don't know I'm a total fraud and incompetent ninny?

A: Yes.

What Is Life After Tenure?

Ms. Mentor has a very large cabinet filled with the musings, threats, fantasies, and prankish questions devised by academics before they came up for tenure. Some have spent decades imagining what they'll do.

Here are their comments, along with a homework assignment from Ms. Mentor.

Academics Think About Getting Tenure

- "I plan to wave a two-bird salute to the self-promoting, self-important, truth-bending director of our program."
- "I've always done my homework, and gotten A's through twenty-five years of school, spent every second at my desk, taught herds of students, attended every meeting ever called, and published half a hundred articles. Now I want to eat junk food, sign up for match. com, and watch *Desperate Housewives*."

Query

Will you ask your readers to explain why tenured professors are, in my humble opinion, such a bunch of miserable whiners?

Thinking About Life After Tenure

- "I have a chance to switch from being a topnotch medical researcher, with grant money and prestige up the wazoo, to being a medical school teacher-director, which will make me 'deadwood' to my research peers, but will turn me (I hope) into a hero in my own heart. Knowing that life is finite, research is glacial, and mentoring future doctors can change the world, should I commit what some call professional suicide and follow my heart?"
- "I've been invited to apply for a fancy job at an elite school that will give me a 30 percent raise, higher-caliber students, and a better library. But it will also mean colder weather, chilly manners, and icy colleagues who hate each other. Do I dare stay at my midlevel state university, where everyone works together harmoniously? And if I do, will people laugh at me for turning down a prestigious plum? And if they do, should I say, 'So what?' "

Homework

Ms. Mentor has an assignment for you. Now is the time to write those long-overdue letters of thanks and appreciation to past teachers and mentors. Too often the people who change our lives with wisdom, sympathy, humor, and encouragement go unrewarded. Do not be an ingrate.

Gratitude

- "I'm grateful that my father and my graduate adviser both lived long enough to see me get tenure. I feel that I'm now fully grown up and fully responsible for myself, and I have to take on responsibilities for others, including mentoring grad students and new hires. This is in the natural order of things, but there's also something very sad about knowing that you're not a 'young scholar' any longer. I'll do my best not to be an arrogant jerk or to fuel (let alone start) factional disputes or departmental hissy fits."
- "It's true that academics today have higher workloads, more admin-

istrative work, slower students, less time to publish, smaller labs, and more ignorant colleagues. But they also get paid for living the life of the mind, they have flexible hours, they can wear decrepit shoes, and they rarely have to submit to drug testing."

- "From your column and your contributors I've learned many things, including the correct plural for CV (curricula vitae) and the term for the letdown after one finishes writing a book (postlibrum depression)."
- "I've outpublished the young turks and will outlive the old goats."

I'm Still Stuck

Q: Because of political factions in my department, it looks like I'll never be promoted to full professor. I've published more than most of the full professors, I've been an officer in national organizations, and I'm a nationally recognized expert in my field. CNN even calls me for comments.

Yet it seems I'm mired in the muck, forever, as a tenured associate prof.

I can't move to another job, even if one were offered. And so I find myself fuming in department meetings, grinding my jaw at night, and accumulating stress symptoms during the day. All this makes it harder for me to write my next book, too, or to teach with gusto.

What should I do?

A: Ms. Mentor agrees that the road from associate to full professor should be a wide and clear path. But for some academics, it is more like a swamp with mosquitoes, strange cawings, and things that fester.

Few universities provide a timeline or a road map for what it takes to get to the top.

What, really, is "outstanding performance?" What is "distinguished achievement?"

Perhaps you've produced super papers, won prizes, and dazzled students with your pedagogy. And yet "Amos"—a so-so researcher and teacher who plays tennis with the powerful professors in the dominant faction—got promoted to full, and you didn't.

Could it be—oh, dear—that the academic world is not truly objective?

Of course there are those who do zoom up the ladder, but others . . . well, if they are wise, they write to Ms. Mentor, who will remind them about their colleagues, and about themselves. To wit:

Academics are people who have been successes in school. They've followed a linear model of upward striving. They've aced tests, graced the honor roll, filled up the dean's lists. They've survived the graduate-school rite of passage, landed a job, and triumphed to tenure. Always, they've moved up to the next level.

Some do plateau for a while after tenure ("Is this all there is?"). Some finally opt for a balanced personal life. They marry, divorce, come out, have children, or devote themselves to elder care. Some really daring ones buy boats, take trombone lessons, or even develop hobbies.

Of course, they do risk being gossiped about in the halls and called "senior juniors." If they buy new cars, especially red ones, everyone knows they're having midlife crises.

Still, the academic culture gnaws at them—and you. You're laggards, you've derailed yourselves. You must push onward and upward to the last stop, to the Mount Everest world of full professordom.

But, Ms. Mentor asks, do you need to reach that pinnacle now? And what will it take to do so?

If your feuding colleagues are stumbling toward retirement, you may need only to lie in wait. But if you're in a hurry, you may have to take your colleagues to coffee or lunch, and smile at what strikes you as inane or absurd. You may have to enlist as a foot soldier in a powerful faction trying to make tiny changes in the curriculum. You may have to serve on endless gnat-picking committees to demonstrate your diligence.

Ms. Mentor does not recommend the strategy adopted by "Fleur," a legendary figure in a small humanities department in the Midwest, who decided to sleep with (or at least put the moves on) every one of her male colleagues. Ms. Mentor, who has a very intense imagination, shudders.

Rather, she asks you to consider what you will get if you are promoted to full professor. Besides knowing that you have reached the pinnacle, what else is there?

Will you get an enormous raise? At most schools nowadays, No.

Will you get glory and honor in your field? Probably not. If you're already well-known nationally, most people will assume you've been a full professor for years. If they find out you're not, they'll figure you must be a terrible teacher or a vicious colleague.

Will you become a different kind of teacher, better or worse? Probably not.

Will you get perks, such as a better teaching schedule or newer equipment or a better parking space? Maybe, but that's iffy.

Will you get more respect from your hostile colleagues? Not a chance.

On the other hand, what if you remain a department pariah?

You may find that people forget about you for long-term committee assignments, so you spend less time wrangling over trivia. You will have blocks of time for meeting students, class planning, thinking, and research, especially if you can do it away from campus. You will have much more energy for teaching and mentoring students. You might offer a service learning course. Teaching is the only part of your job that can give you immediate gratification. It can also give you joy.

If you opt out of climbing the ladder, you will not be giving your time and energy to unworthy causes. You won't be sacrificing your health, nor tormenting your friends with your anger and pain.

Since September 11 and Hurricane Katrina, thousands of Americans have wept and grieved and brooded about what they really want to do with their lives. Many realize they do not want to sacrifice their souls to be rewarded by people they do not respect.

And so, Ms. Mentor gives you permission to give up the futile, soul-crushing effort to be respected by bozos.

If the ladder isn't going to a loft where you want to be, stay on the ground. And whip up a soufflé, cook up a mess of greens, gather up your friends, walk in the sun, and drink in the rain.

Insistent Query

Q: What about your column on tenured whiners?

I'm Still Stuck, Too

Q (from "Adele"): Another summer, and I'm in the same spot. I earned my Ph.D. at twenty-five, got a tenure-track job, published two books, made full professor. I teach at Very Respectable U. with excellent research grants and teaching opportunities, and I've won fellowships and awards.

I'm also socially isolated. I have no partner, am older than the interesting new hires, and have a rather pathetic tendency to answer simple questions with, "Let me explain why it works that way . . . in the early 1990s . . . then at the end of the decade . . . and the latest innovation . . ." I make people's eyes glaze over.

Most jobs advertised at my level are for administrators, but I'm somewhat disorganized, less socially adept than many, and don't have a mentor. Things aren't awful, but I've been here fifteen years and I'm afraid if I stay, I'll feel more and more trapped. Is there any way to improve my job mobility?

A: Ms. Mentor hears the usual reader grumblings ("Just let me at 'em. I could handle *those* troubles"). But unhappiness dwells at every level of the human condition, and Ms. Mentor, in her infinite wisdom, recognizes the real, classic questions that we all ask at midlife: "Is that all there is?" "What do I do for my next trick?"

You needn't do anything at all, of course, and many tenured academics do not move from where they've been planted since their twenties. As a lifelong academic, you've marched in a neat, laid-out groove—but there must be more than menopause, retirement, and death.

Administration is the usual way to move. Be a dean or department head for a few years, and then fold back smoothly into a department at Your Newer U. But to do that, you'll have to change your ways. You'll need to go to conferences and cultivate schmooze buddies who'll tell you about job openings, who's really in power, and what they're looking for (hatchet man? visionary leader? caretaker? toady?).

If you want to move as a full professor, you also need to schmooze, for senior hires are most often made by targeting particular people. ("We need Adele to round out our program. What will it take to get her?") Hirers may know your publications, but unless they know you—especially in the humanities—you're unlikely to be on their mental recruiting screens.

You need friends in high places—and you get them by smiling, remembering everyone's names, and working the room at conference receptions, with intense mini-conversations full of ambition and gossip.

To move in academe, you have to work on your charm.

You can do that by being a dutiful scholar, reading biographies of famous charmers (Cleopatra, Bill Clinton). You can study canonical texts (*How to Win Friends and Influence People*) and furtively buy *Relationships for Dummies*. (Ms. Mentor is not making that title up.)

You can watch talk-show guests, promoting their latest movies with well-structured, engaging anecdotes. You can try out seductive personalities ("Lusty Southern Belle," "Randy Rosalind") in Internet chat rooms—and if you get crude overtures, at least you'll learn new words.

You can also practice people chat in creative-writing groups, wine-tasting classes, bird-watching outings, activist circles, group therapy, or dinners you host for visiting celebrities (take off the store tags and claim you cooked everything yourself).

And after a few years of this self-inflicted charm school, you should be ready to Take On the World and Grab a New Job.

Or not.

Ms. Mentor, herself a loner, does not enjoy the social jangle of mindless chitchat. Too many faculty-senate meetings and receptions, in fact, drove her to the splendid isolation of her ivory tower, from which she now watches the scene—and then closes the door. She would rather be a reclusive Emily Dickinson, dwelling in the richness of her own mind, than a strutting Madonna, cheered by millions. Academe is the most congenial profession for motivated and intelligent people who work well by themselves.

Adele, too, may be a loner by nature, as celebrated in Anneli Rufus's *Party of One: The Loners' Manifesto*, a tribute to the independence and imagination of solitary souls. Money and power are less important if you do not seek the world's approval—and Adele may realize that she most loves the pursuit of knowledge, of any kind.

People who don't need people for entertainment will never wind up like the actor George Sanders, who wrote in his last note in 1972: "Dear World, I am leaving you because I am bored. I feel I have lived long enough. I am leaving you with your worries in this sweet cesspool—good luck."

To loners, the world is a carnival and not a cesspool, and Ms. Mentor hopes that Adele will eschew the rat race and learn to enjoy, fully, her sweet solitude and the pleasure of her own company.

After September 11 and After Katrina

- "I'm taking more time to smell the roses and be selective about what I choose to spend my time on."
- "Academic life demands that we ponder what is truly of value to us and what we want to accomplish. Promotions are nice. But in the larger scheme of things, those strokes are buried with you. Whatever is permanent in one's academic history is likely to reside in the students (and their students and their students) and in the writing one leaves behind."

Still . . .

Q: Come on already. Will you ever publish your column on tenured whiners?

Are You the Retiring Type?

Q: When I started out in this profession, during the Vietnam War, I was young and brash and knew you couldn't trust anyone over thirty. I was the same age as Janis Joplin, and I somehow thought I'd die before I grew old. Instead I'm nearly sixty-five, just like Mick Jagger. My contemporaries are retiring, and I'm wondering if I should also be heading toward the glue factory. How do I know when it's time?

A: Ms. Mentor's readers may think she gets many letters like this from mature academics wanting to know when to hold and when to fold. But Ms. Mentor admits that she created this letter herself, so that she could pontificate about retirement. Not one of her sage correspondents has ever brought it up.

Still, it crouches like an elephant in the middle of the floor at countless faculty meetings about five-year plans and "the future of the department." Thanks to buyouts, phased retirements, and other ingenious fiduciary maneuvers, many departments are now heavy with those who are half-in, half-out—still teaching, still holding tenured slots, but not committed to the future. Some are dedicated; some are grumblers ("Didn't we do all that in 1972?"); many are invisible.

But those curmudgeons are not Ms. Mentor's subjects. Nor are those who retire for health reasons, or because their bank accounts are exceptionally healthy. The Caesars (the precise planners) are far less interesting to Ms. Mentor than the Cleopatras (queens of denial).

Ms. Mentor believes that her fictitious correspondent should retire right now if she has a passionate pursuit. Many retirees want to travel, or grow their own herbs, or find eighty-five ways to cook eggplant, or spoil their grandchildren. Some who were geeky stay-at-homes in high school become full-time rock 'n' roll fans at last, lining up for Led Zeppelin's reunion concert or the Rolling Stones' latest farewell tour. Many mild-mannered academics make mischief on the Net, luring romantic partners with their literate wit and provocative screen names ("Hot Babe Dulcinea" and "Great Expectations").

There are also academics with long-postponed research projects, set aside for any number of reasons, that they could finish if they retired. Many an academic has a half-written biography on a favorite figure, such as Supreme Court Justice William Brennan or playwright Lorraine Hansberry. Ms. Mentor well remembers Frederick Jackson Turner, the historian who created the influential "frontier thesis" in the 1890s—but never wrote "the book" setting out his argument in all its glory. Many graduate students have heard the story (perhaps apocryphal) that on his deathbed in 1932, he whispered to a younger colleague, "Finish the book, Max."

Turner may not have truly wanted to finish: What would he do next? Happier retirees tend to be those with plenty of plans and plenty of changes to make.

"Marshall," who always resented wearing a coat and tie, now revels in his round-the-clock ratty bathrobe. "Matilda" gave up makeup, and her hair is its natural color. Both belong to a retirees' group that meets weekly at their local Barnes & Noble to hash out "the meaning of life." They yell a lot about "responsibilities" and "rights," and they guffaw and high-five each other every time they scare younger people.

Indeed, it's students who are sometimes the reason that academics hear an insistent little voice urging them to "Flee! Flee!"

Some kinds of students do drive their teachers out the door. "Harry," a physics professor, quit in his early fifties, tired of trying to get lusty teenagers to care about particles instead of private parts. "Ted" decided teaching political science was a hopeless cause when more than half of his students admitted they hadn't registered and didn't plan to vote. (Ted ran for public office himself and is now a vocal city councilman, inveighing against waste and corruption.)

"Claudia," a literature professor, had an epiphany one day when half a dozen students who'd earned B's on their term papers staged an in-class protest, marched to the department head's office, and got their parents to bombard the dean with telephoned complaints. They demanded the "right to rewrite," so they could get A's.

Claudia told them they could rewrite till they were blue in their hearts, and some did. She read none of the rewrites, gave them all A's, and filed papers to retire. "I couldn't stand the whining anymore," she says.

There are also retirees fleeing from their colleagues. The late Carolyn G. Heilbrun retired from Columbia University after decades of sexism and lack of appreciation for her pioneering work in feminist criticism. "Walter" hid in the men's room so as not to have younger colleagues ask "your generation's opinion" on current events.

Many would-be retirees no longer care about what's new in their professions. Some, in science, lose interest in new computer gizmos. "Georgia," a generation ago, dutifully learned the jargon of literary theory but never liked it, and eventually could not bring herself to read it at all. It gave her migraines.

But what is the number-one reason for healthy, solvent academics to retire? Ms. Mentor, querying her usual sources, got some version of the same answer: "Administrative baloney."

Many do come to dread the memos: more forms, more reports, more questionnaires, more ballots. They despair of regime change in hostile departments; they suffer from chronic turnover in the dean's office. They hate their legislatures and wish they could find a way to shred their e-mail messages.

They wake up scowling.

Yet all academics have learned from their years of teaching and committee service. They know how to make an agenda, move decisions, find out who really has power. They know how to lobby colleagues and how to rig a meeting through strategic rumors, changes of site, lost mail, and misplaced information. They know how to be Gandhi or Genghis Khan.

Ms. Mentor, who is of an age herself, believes that those who can teach with vigor and enthusiasm should never stop. Especially when they're able to teach new things, academics of any age can learn from their students. Those who can produce research that's humanly valuable should keep at it. Committee work whizzes should do all that work and save others.

But Ms. Mentor is also delighted when vital academics retire and move into the "real world" of politics and activism. They've defended abortion clinics, sometimes escorting their former students past picket lines. They vote actively and are vocal on school boards. They fight for health care and other rights that will come only when articulate, committed citizens write convincing letters, use their lecturing skills to sway audiences, and yell a lot.

All ye who've pontificated from a podium, says Ms. Mentor, can just as easily pontificate to the world and make it better than it was when you began. Retired or not, we owe that to ourselves and to our posterity.

Daring to Create Your Own Life

Q (from "Lawrence"): During my four years as a part-time adjunct teaching composition, I've struck out every year on the job market. How much longer should I keep trying for a full-time, tenure-track job?

Q (from "Yvette"): I'm tenured at a college that I've hated since the first day. My colleagues do nothing but teach: no research, nothing truly intellectual. I have some friends, but our book club flopped after a few months. I've applied fruitlessly for other jobs (I'm in English), but with my heavy teaching load, my first book's still not done. I'm drowning in a sea of mediocrity in "Ruralville," where there isn't even a museum. How can a tenured associate professor move to a new job?

Q (from "Sally"): My spouse was a loved and admired professor at the university where I'm also tenured. But after he was diagnosed with Alzheimer's, he retired, and has been lingering in late-stage dementia in a nursing home for the past four years. I continue to work and pay his bills (no long-term insurance) as well as mine. In the past year, I've reconnected with a college sweetheart, and after considerable soul-searching, we've decided to make a go of it, together. I've started bringing him to campus events and introducing him as "my friend" to those who knew my husband. It's awkward, but I'm over seventy, and life is short. Am I wrong to introduce him as "my friend," or should I use a more generic "acquaintance" or "neighbor?" Or should I not introduce him and let people wonder?

A: Ms. Mentor is reminded of morbid poets like Thomas Gray, who described a "mute inglorious Milton"—one who never did get his writings published. She also thinks of Edwin Arlington Robinson, whose "child of scorn," Miniver Cheevy, found daily life far too crass for his refined romantic tastes—and so he "kept on drinking."

Which brings Ms. Mentor to her correspondents, two of whom have unfulfilled dreams, and all of whom have kept on thinking.

Lawrence, pondering his options, is also plundering his wallet. On an adjunct's salary, which may be as little as $1,500 a course, Lawrence cannot pay back loans, raise a family, have a health crisis, travel outside his immediate vicinity, or do very many things that adults ought to have the right to do. A couple of lattes at Starbucks could wipe out his book budget.

How long should he wait for that elusive tenure-track job, while his degree grows older? Ms. Mentor wonders if he has unusual accomplishments: a book on the verge of publication? A prestigious national award? Lawrence could still get lucky by networking with community colleges. He could win the lottery—or become notorious for something. But he needs a flair factor to lift him above the herd.

Otherwise, adjuncting becomes more like an expensive hobby. Lawrence's teaching and writing talents would be better rewarded in public relations, advertising, nonprofit jobs, activism, tutoring, editing, technical writing, speech writing, or ghostwriting. Or his adjuncting could suffice if it's just a day job, shoring up what really matters to him, such as music or filmmaking.

But long-term adjuncting means losing self-respect. Friends and family rarely know the odds, that only 40 percent of English Ph.D.'s will ever get tenure-track jobs. Nonacademics rarely know that one has to be able to move anywhere, to strange and unknown locales, to land a semipermanent, reasonably-paying job. Since the average Ph.D. in English takes ten years to get the degree, Lawrence may be fortyish by now, very angry and very worried.

Ms. Mentor grieves for Lawrence of Academia, and knows that adjuncts will spit and hiss about Yvette: "I wish I had her tenure," they'll say.

Yet if Yvette stays in Ruralville, she will never find the joy in learning that she yearns for. She can change her criteria ("I've discovered quilting, and I love it"), or find an intellectual community online—or spend the rest of her days in quiet desperation, as an academic Miniver Cheevy.

Meanwhile, unless it proves to be a best seller, Yvette's book will not propel her into a new, wildly desirable category. Most departments with tenure lines hire new assistant professors or multi-published superstars—and her book won't make her any more enticing to community colleges, the growth area where teaching is most important.

Yvette might get a job elsewhere as an administrator, if she can run a composition and rhetoric program, or has the experience to be hired as a dean.

Or she can take a big risk, and push herself away from Ruralville for a year.

It may be a sabbatical, or an unpaid leave, or a faculty exchange—but she can try moving to a city where she would like to live. She can be a temporary office worker, as a way to meet "real world" people. She can devote each day to networking and schmoozing, making herself known, visiting the real-world places where an "English person" might work. It may turn out to be grueling, and she may discover that Ruralville is a pleasant womb after all.

But if it still sickens her, she should be bold, and quit.

Yes, that is a frightening thought, for academics—as the late Leslie Fiedler wrote—have a great tolerance for boredom and an enormous fear of risk. Yet if Yvette accepts stagnation, that will be her life. There is no second life coming; there is no vista of unlimited years in which to make a change, suddenly grow wings, or live in Paris. Yvette must seize the time—as Sally has.

Sally could have immured herself—spending her days at her beloved husband's nursing home and telling herself, against all reason, that enough loving care will somehow heal the broken synapses in his brain. The world is full of expectations that women will sacrifice themselves. Like adjuncts whose contracts are renewed only if they please and amuse adolescents, young women too often move to the rhythms of others. Only later in life, when most of the hurly-burly's done, do women get to ask themselves, "What do I *really* want?"

That is what the late Carolyn G. Heilbrun called "the last gift of time," and Sally's gift to herself is the man she has chosen, the partner she deserves to call publicly, with all affection and respect, "my friend."

Miniver Cheevy spent his life railing against fate, and Lawrence and Yvette could do the same. Or they could refuse to wallow in the winter of their discontent, and instead follow Sally's example, knowing that for everything there is a season.

Ms. Mentor's Exemplary Bibliography

Note to Sage Readers: Ms. Mentor continues to be an eclectic and indefatigable reader of all that is great and wise, especially in book form. She also whizzes about on the Internet, where she reads many excellent blogs. But she shall not recommend any here, lest she inspire jealousy, wrath, and grade appeals.

For extra credit, Ms. Mentor directs eager readers to the bibliography in her first tome, *Ms. Mentor's Impeccable Advice for Women in Academia*. This bibliography continues that noble work, together with a similar warning that if a book is not listed here, it may not have made itself known to Ms. Mentor. Or it may be no good.

Aisenberg, Nadya, and Mona Harrington. *Women of Academe: Outsiders in the Sacred Grove.* Amherst: University of Massachusetts Press, 1988.

Allitt, Patrick. *I'm the Teacher, You're the Student: A Semester in the University Classroom.* Philadelphia: University of Pennsylvania Press, 2005.

Amis, Kingsley. *Lucky Jim.* New York: Penguin, 1993.

Babcock, Linda, and Sarah Laschever. *Women Don't Ask: Negotiation and the Gender Divide.* Princeton: Princeton University Press, 2003.

Bain, Ken. *What the Best College Teachers Do.* Cambridge: Harvard University Press, 2004.

Barreca, Regina, and Deborah Denenholz Morse, eds. *The Erotics of Instruction.* Hanover, N.H.: University Press of New England, 1997.

Basalla, Susan, and Maggie Debelius. "*So What Are You Going to Do with That?" Finding Careers Outside Academia.* Revised edition. Chicago: University of Chicago Press, 2007.

Basow, S. A., and K. Howe. "Evaluation of College Professors: Effects of Professors' Sex Type and Sex, and Student Sex." *Psychological Reports* 60 (1987), 671–678.

Basow, Susan A., and Nancy T. Silberg. "Student Evaluations of College Professors: Are Female and Male Professors Rated Differently?" *Journal of Educational Psychology* 79, no. 3 (1987), 308–314.

Bechdel, Alison. *Fun Home: A Family Tragicomic.* Boston: Houghton Mifflin, 2007.

Behrendt, Greg, and Liz Tuccillo. *He's Just Not That Into You.* New York: Simon and Schuster, 2006.

Belenky, Mary Field, Blythe McVicker Clinchy, Nancy Rule Goldberger, and Jill Mattuck Tarule. *Women's Ways of Knowing: The Development of Self, Voice, and Mind.* New York: Basic Books, 1986.

Berkin, Carol, Judith L. Pinch, and Carole S. Appel, eds. *Exploring Women's Studies: Looking Forward, Looking Back.* Upper Saddle River, N.J.: Pearson–Prentice Hall, 2006.

Bernard, Robert. *Deadly Meeting.* New York: Norton, 1970.

Bestor, Dorothy. *Aside from Teaching, What in the World Can You Do?* Seattle: University of Washington Press, 1977.

BlogHer Discussion Guidelines: http://www.ashleyrichards.com/2005/08/06/blogher_discussion guidelines.

Bolker, Joan. *Writing Your Dissertation in Fifteen Minutes a Day.* New York: Holt, 1998.

Bolles, Richard Nelson. *What Color Is Your Parachute? A Practical Manual for Job Hunters and Career Changers.* Berkeley: Ten Speed Press, 2007.

Bombeck, Erma. *I Lost Everything in the Post-Natal Depression.* New York: Random House, 1995.

Boufis, Christina, and Victoria C. Olsen, eds. *On the Market: Surviving the Academic Job Search.* New York: Riverhead, 1997.

Boylan, Jennifer Finney. *She's Not There: A Life in Two Genders.* New York: Broadway Books, 2004.

Caesar, Terry. *Traveling Through the Boondocks: In and Out of Academic Hierarchy.* Albany: State University of New York Press, 2000.

Carnegie, Dale. *How to Win Friends and Influence People.* New York: Pocket Books, 1936. Revised edition, 1982.

Center for Voice Disorders, Wake Forest University. "Best and Worst Voices in America," 2001.

Clark, VéVé, Shirley Nelson Garner, Margaret Higgonet, and Ketu H. Katrak, eds. *Antifeminism in the Academy.* New York: Routledge, 1996.

Clydesdale, Tim. *The First Year Out: Understanding American Teens After High School.* Chicago: University of Chicago Press, 2007.

Coiner, Constance, and Diana Hume George, eds. *The Family Track: Keeping Your Faculties While You Mentor, Nurture, Teach, and Serve.* Urbana: University of Illinois Press, 1998.

Cornell University. Program on Employment and Disability.

Daniell, Rosemary. *Secrets of the Zona Rosa: How Writing (and Sisterhood) Can Change Women's Lives.* New York: Owl Books, 2006.

Davis, Lennard, ed. *The Disability Studies Reader.* Second edition. New York: Routledge, 2006.

DeNeef, A. Leigh, and Craufurd D. Goodwin, eds. *The Academic's Handbook.* Third edition. Durham: Duke University Press, 2007.

Dobson, Joanne. *The Northbury Papers.* New York: Bantam, 1999.

Drago, Robert. *Striking a Balance: Work, Family, Life.* Boston: Dollars and Sense, 2007.

Ehrenreich, Barbara. *Nickel and Dimed: On (Not) Getting By in America.* New York: Holt, 2002.

Fiedler, Leslie A. *What Was Literature: Class Culture and Mass Society.* New York: Simon and Schuster, 1982.

Filene, Peter. *The Joy of Teaching: A Practical Guide for New College Instructors.* Chapel Hill: University of North Carolina Press, 2005.

Finder, Alan. "Decline of the Tenure Track Raises Concerns." *New York Times,* November 20, 2007.

Findlen, Barbara, ed. *Listen Up: Voices from the Next Feminist Generation.* Seattle: Seal Press, 1995.

Freedman, Estelle B. *No Turning Back: the History of Feminism and the Future of Women.* New York: Ballantine, 2002.

Fulghum, Robert. *All I Really Need to Know I Learned in Kindergarten.* Fifteenth anniversary edition. New York: Random House, 2004.

Germano, William. *From Dissertation to Book*. Chicago: University of Chicago Press, 2005.

———. *Getting It Published: A Guide for Scholars and Anyone Else Serious About Serious Books*. Chicago: University of Chicago Press, 2001.

Giddings, Paula. *When and Where I Enter: The Impact of Black Women on Race and Sex in America*. New York: Morrow, 1984.

Gilligan, Carol. *In a Different Voice*. Cambridge: Harvard University Press, 1982.

Gladwell, Malcolm. *Blink: The Power of Thinking Without Thinking*. Boston: Little, Brown, 2007.

Goodman, Allegra. *Intuition*. New York: Dell, 2007.

Gravois, John. "Growth in Part-Timers Slowed in Past Decade, Education Department Finds." *Chronicle of Higher Education*, January 20, 2006.

Greenhill, Pauline, and Diane Tye, eds. *Undisciplined Women: Tradition and Culture in Canada*. Montreal: McGill-Queen's University Press, 1997.

Hamermesh, Daniel S. "Beauty in the Classroom: Professors' Pulchritude and Putative Pedagogical Productivity." National Bureau of Economic Research Working Papers no. 9853, July 2003.

Hart, Jack. *A Writer's Coach: An Editor's Guide to Words That Work*. New York: Pantheon, 2006.

Heiberger, Mary Morris, Julia Miller Vick, and Jennifer S. Furlong. *The Academic Job Search Handbook*. Fourth edition. Philadelphia: University of Pennsylvania Press, 2008.

Heilbrun, Carolyn. *The Last Gift of Time: Life Beyond Sixty*. New York: Random House, 1998.

———. *Writing a Woman's Life*. New York: Random House, 1989.

———. Academic mystery novels under the pen name of "Amanda Cross."

Heller, Zoe. *Notes on a Scandal (What Was She Thinking?)*. New York: Picador, 2006.

Hirshman, Linda R. *Get to Work: A Manifesto for Women of the World*. New York: Viking, 2006.

Hochschild, Arlie Russell, and Anne Machung. *The Second Shift: Working Parents and the Revolution at Home*. New York: Penguin, 2003.

Hume, Kathryn. *Surviving Your Academic Job Hunt: Advice for Humanities Ph.D.s.* New York: Palgrave Macmillan, 2005.

Hynes, James. *Publish and Perish.* New York: Picador, 1998.

Jaschik, Scott. "Age Bias or Anti-Adjunct Bias?" Insidehighered.com, August 15, 2006.

Jones, D. J. H. *Murder at the MLA.* Athens: University of Georgia Press, 1993.

Jong, Erica. *Fear of Flying.* New York: Holt, Rinehart and Winston, 1973.

Kincaid, James R. "Eroticism Is a Two-Way Street, and I'm Working Both Sides." In Barreca and Morse, eds., *The Erotics of Instruction,* 81–93.

King, Stephen. *On Writing: A Memoir of the Craft.* New York: Simon and Schuster, 2002.

Klein, Laura Cousino, Shelley E. Taylor, et al. "Sex Differences in Biobehavioral Responses to Threat." *Psychological Review* 109, no. 4 (2007).

Kolodny, Annette. *Failing the Future: A Dean Looks at Higher Education in the Twenty-First Century.* Durham: Duke University Press, 1998.

Koppelman, Susan, ed. *The Strange History of Suzanne LaFleshe and Other Stories About Women and Fatness.* New York: Feminist Press, 2003.

Lamott, Anne. *Bird by Bird: Some Instructions on Writing and Life.* New York: Knopf, 1995.

Lang, James M. *Learning Sickness: A Year with Crohn's Disease.* New York: Capitol Books, 2004.

———. *Life on the Tenure Track: Lessons from the First Year.* Baltimore: Johns Hopkins University Press, 2005.

———. *On Course: A Week-by-Week Guide to Your First Semester of College Teaching.* Cambridge: Harvard University Press, 2008.

Lima, Marybeth, and William Oakes. *Service-Learning: Engineering in Your Community.* Wildwood, Mo.: Great Lakes Press, 2006.

Lodge, David. *Changing Places.* New York: Penguin, 1979.

———. *Small World: An Academic Romance.* New York: Penguin, 1995.

Looser, Devoney, and E. Ann Kaplan. *Generations: Academic Feminists in Dialogue.* Minneapolis: University of Minnesota, 1997.

Lurie, Alison. *The War Between the Tates.* New York: Random House, 1974.

Magnan, Robert, ed. *147 Practical Tips for Teaching Professors*. Madison, Wis.: Atwood Publishing, 1990.

Malamud, Bernard. *A New Life*. New York: Farrar Straus Cudahy, 1961.

Marsh, Nigel. *Fat, Forty, and Fired*. New York: Andrews McMeel, 2007.

Martin, Judith. *Miss Manners' Guide to Excruciatingly Correct Behavior*. Freshly Updated. New York: Norton, 2005.

Mason, Mary Ann, and Eve Mason Ekman. *Mothers on the Fast Track: How a New Generation Can Balance Family and Careers*. New York: Oxford University Press, 2007.

McCarthy, Mary. *The Groves of Academe*. New York: Signet, 1963.

McCloskey, Deirdre. *Crossing: A Memoir*. Chicago: University of Chicago Press, 1999.

McKeachie, Wilbert, and Marilla Svinicki. *McKeachie's Teaching Tips: Strategies, Research, and Theory for College and University Teachers*. Twelfth edition. Boston: Houghton Mifflin, 2006.

Miner, Valerie, and Helen Longino, eds. *Competition: A Feminist Taboo?* New York: Feminist Press, 1987.

Morris, Van Cleve. *Deaning: Middle Management in Academe*. Urbana: University of Illinois Press, 1981.

Mullen, Laura. *Murmur*. New York: Futurepoem Books, 2006.

Nathan, Rebekah. *My Freshman Year: What a Professor Learned by Becoming a Student*. Ithaca: Cornell University Press, 2005.

Nelson, Cary, ed. *Will Teach for Food*. Minneapolis: University of Minnesota Press, 1997.

Nietzsche, Friedrich. *Untimely Meditations*. Trans. R. J. Hollingdale. Cambridge: Cambridge University Press, 1997.

Olson, Lynne. *Freedom's Daughters: The Unsung Heroines of the Civil Rights Movement from 1830–1970*. New York: Touchstone, 2001.

Orenstein, Peggy. *SchoolGirls: Young Women, Self-Esteem, and the Confidence Gap*. New York: Doubleday, 1994.

Parini, Jay. *The Art of Teaching*. New York: Oxford University Press, 2005.

Parker, Dorothy. "The Banquet of Crow." *The Portable Dorothy Parker*. New York: Penguin, 2006.

Plotnik, Arthur. *Spunk and Bite: A Writer's Guide to Punchier, More Engaging Language and Style*. New York: Random House, 2005.

Rhode, Deborah L. *In Pursuit of Knowledge: Scholars, Status, and Academic Culture*. Stanford: Stanford University Press, 2006.

Robbins, Alexandra. *Pledged: The Secret Life of Sororities.* New York: Hyperion, 2004.

Rosen, Ruth. *The World Split Open: How the Modern Women's Movement Changed America.* New York: Penguin, 2000.

Roughgarden, Joan. *Evolution's Rainbow: Diversity, Gender, and Sexuality in Nature and People.* Berkeley: University of California Press, 2005.

Ruffner, Sara. *A Liberal Education.* Santa Barbara, Calif.: Fithian, 1991.

Rufus, Anneli. *Party of One: The Loners' Manifesto.* New York: Marlowe, 2003.

Russo, Richard. *Straight Man.* New York: Vintage, 1997.

Sarton, May. *The Small Room.* New York: Norton, 1976.

Sexton, Anne. *All My Pretty Ones.* Boston: Houghton Mifflin, 1962.

Showalter, Elaine. *Faculty Towers: The Academic Novel and Its Discontents.* Philadelphia: University of Pennsylvania Press, 2005.

————. *Teaching Literature.* New York: John Wiley, 2002.

Sittenfeld, Curtis. *Prep.* New York: Random House, 2005.

Smiley, Jane. *Moo.* New York: Random House, 1998.

Smith, Zadie. *On Beauty.* New York: Penguin, 2005.

Solon, Gary. Economic Mobility Project. Pew Charitable Trust.

Spender, Dale. *Women of Ideas and What Men Have Done to Them.* Boston: Routledge and Kegan Paul, 1982.

Stone, Douglas, Bruce Patton, and Sheila Heen. *Difficult Conversations: How to Discuss What Matters Most.* New York: Penguin, 2000.

Syfers, Judy. "Why I Want a Wife." In *Radical Feminism,* ed. Anne Koedt, Ellen Levine, and Anita Rapone. New York: Times Books, 1973, 60–62.

Tannen, Deborah. *You Just Don't Understand: Women and Men in Conversation.* New York: William Morris, 1990.

Tea, Michelle, ed. *Without a Net: The Female Experience of Growing Up Working Class.* Seattle: Seal Press, 2004.

Thomson, Rosemarie Garland. *Extraordinary Bodies.* New York: Columbia University Press, 1997.

Tokarczyk, Michelle M., and Elizabeth A. Fay. *Working-Class Women in the Academy: Laborers in the Knowledge Factory.* Amherst: University of Massachusetts Press, 1993.

Toth, Emily. *Daughters of New Orleans*. New York: Bantam, 1983.

―――. *Inside Peyton Place: The Life of Grace Metalious*. New York: Doubleday, 1981; Jackson: University Press of Mississippi, 2000.

―――. *Kate Chopin: A Life of the Author of "The Awakening."* New York: William Morrow, 1990.

―――. *Ms. Mentor's Impeccable Advice for Women in Academia*. Philadelphia: University of Pennsylvania Press, 1997.

―――. *Unveiling Kate Chopin*. Jackson: University Press of Mississippi, 1999.

Toth, Emily, ed. *A Vocation and a Voice: Stories by Kate Chopin*. New York: Penguin, 1991.

Toth, Emily, with Janice Delaney and Mary Jane Lupton. *The Curse: A Cultural History of Menstruation*. New York: Dutton, 1976; Urbana: University of Illinois Press, 1988.

Toth, Emily, ed., with Per Seyersted and Cheyenne Bonnell. *Kate Chopin's Private Papers*. Bloomington: Indiana University Press, 1998.

Ulrich, Laurel Thatcher. *Well-Behaved Women Seldom Make History*. New York: Knopf, 2007.

Vincent, Norah. *Self Made Man: One Woman's Journey into Manhood and Back*. New York: Viking, 2006.

Wachs, Kate M. *Relationships for Dummies*. New York: For Dummies, 2002.

Wann, Marilyn. *Fat! So?* Berkeley: Ten Speed Press, 1998.

Weinstein, Debra. *Apprentice to the Flower Poet Z*. New York: Ballantine, 2004.

Weissmann, Heidi. "Insults and Injuries." *Women's Review of Books* 13, no. 5 (February 1996), 21–23.

Whicker, Marcia Lynn, and Jennie Jacobs Kronenfeld. *Dealing with Ethical Dilemmas on Campus*. Thousand Oaks, Calif.: Sage, 1994.

Whicker, Marcia Lynn, Jennie Jacobs Kronenfeld, and Ruth Ann Strickland. *Getting Tenure*. Thousand Oaks, Calif.: Sage, 1993.

Wolf-Wendel, Lisa, Susan B. Twombly, and Suzanne Rice. *The Two-Body Problem: Dual Career Couple Hiring Practices in Higher Education*. Baltimore: Johns Hopkins University Press, 2003.

Woolf, Virginia. *A Room of One's Own*. New York: Harcourt, 1991.

Zinsser, William. *On Writing Well*. New York: Collins, 1976. Revised and expanded edition, 2006.

—

Ms. Mentor also recommends that eager scholars and sage readers become regular perusers of the *Chronicle of Higher Education*'s columns and forums (chronicle.com/jobs) and of insidehighered.com. There may be a test later.

Index

Acknowledgments

Most of Ms. Mentor's contributors cannot be acknowledged.

They dwell among us, nameless and faceless—thousands of them, plotting their e-mails in their garrets and grottoes, and trembling as they entrust them to the ether and Ms. Mentor. A few brave souls sign their real names, but many crouch behind meaningful pseudonyms, such as "Ornithologist" or "Barbara Stanwyck" or "King Rear."

Ms. Mentor answers as many of their plaintive cries as she can in her columns and books, but she has pledged never to reveal their names. Nor can she name those she has met in person, such as the sly author of the missive about "Dr. Hissy" (in the chapter on "Working and Playing Well with Others"). But Ms. Mentor decorously thanks all her correspondents for sharing their woes, their wit, and their original and thoughtful queries. The world of academia is better for having them.

Others whose names may safely be uttered have contributed to this book, in addition to those acknowledged in Ms. Mentor's first tome, *Ms. Mentor's Impeccable Advice for Women in Academia*.

Ms. Mentor's advice giving—or that of her channeler, Emily Toth—was first nurtured by Dorothy Ginsberg Fitzgibbons, John Fitzgibbons, and Sara Ruffner. Dennis and Ellen Fitzgibbons continue family traditions.

At the *Chronicle of Higher Education*, Liz McMillen and Scott Jaschik are responsible for the creation of Ms. Mentor's column in 1998. Denise K. Magner has been a deft and adept editor through most of the column's existence. Ms. Mentor thanks Philip W. Semas for his support, and thanks Jeanne Ferris, Piper Fogg, Jennifer Jacobson, Alison Schneider, Michael Solomon, and Jean Tamarin for good conversations.

The stalwart and pseudonymous contributors to the *Chronicle of Higher Education*'s forums have contributed more than they know (or might want to know).

Mary Jane Lupton and Janice Delaney were among the first to recognize Ms. Mentor's talents and peculiarities. Their book written with Emily Toth, *The Curse: A Cultural History of Menstruation*, has been in print for thirty-two years, and its original readers have all reached menopause and beyond.

Ms. Mentor's life's work—uplifting the huddled masses of academia—has been greatly aided by the courageous and sophisticated Louisiana State University graduate students who have taken Emily Toth's course in Women's Advice Writing: Nicole Donald, Tamika Edwards, Marie D. Goodwin, Syd Hart, Tena Helton, Kerri Jordan, Thomas Maul, Kristine Plukarski, Michael Redmond, Rachel Roubique, Jennifer Walker, and Clay Weill.

Ms. Mentor's columns have been enhanced by perspicacious critiques from her writing group members in Baton Rouge and New Orleans: Kathleen Davis, Elora Fink, Charles Gramlich, Steve Harris, Dorothy Jenkins, Rosan Jordan, Candice Proctor, Laura Joh Rowland, and Gerilyn Tandberg.

At Louisiana State University, Marybeth Lima has been a model for persistence, excellence, wry observations, and constant surprises. Laura Mullen is a singular and exemplary colleague, poet, diner, and sage. Both have made unacknowledged but highly welcome contributions to Ms. Mentor's wisdom.

This book owes its existence to Ms. Mentor's able, energetic, and good-humored editor, Jerome Singerman of the University of Pennsylvania Press; to the precise, diligent production editor, Noreen O'Connor-Abel; and to the other members of the Penn Press staff, including Chris Bell; Will Boehm; Sandra Haviland; John Hubbard; Mariana Martinez; Ellen Trachtenberg; Laura Waldron; and Eileen Wolfberg, copyeditor extraordinaire. Patricia Reynolds Smith and Bruce Franklin abetted the original incarnation of Ms. Mentor's advice in book form.

Only Nicole Hollander could capture, in her brilliant cover drawing, the essence of Ms. Mentor as advice giver, lover of cats, and incessant ferreter-out of difficult problems.

For advice on publishing, Ms. Mentor thanks Carole Appel, William

Germano, Elaine Markson, Seetha Srinivasan, Geri Thoma, and Ken Wissoker.

Bernitta Berniard, Pamela Roussel Fry, and Dr. Shaoqing ("Ching") Guo keep Ms. Mentor in healthy fighting shape.

The felines Beauregard, Bunkie, Foxy, and Mr. Fussy have all contributed ideas, aplomb, and smug indifference to human struggles.

Susan Koppelman deserves special acknowledgment as a long-time friend, muse, critic, and fellow satirist.

Bruce Toth deserves kudos for practical wisdom, eccentric theorizing, clever scheming, and marvelous laughter.

Others who have contributed include Janet Allured, Debra Andrist, Martha Baker, Lynn Bartholome, Rexanne Becnel, Alison Bertolini, Pablo Bigasso, Cheyenne Bonnell, Patricia Brady, Pat Browne, Ray Browne, Eva Bueno, Bethany Bultman, Terry Caesar, Jane Caputi, Jennifer Cargill, Anne Coldiron, Rita Culross, Mary Darken, Barbara Davidson, Cathy N. Davidson, Frank de Caro, Carmen del Rio, Robert Drago, Ken Dvorak, Barbara Ewell, Linda Gardiner, Carol Gelderman, Deborah Gonzales, Angeletta Gourdine, Suzanne Disheroon Green, Pauline Greenhill, Mary Hamilton, Kay Heath, Diane Long Hoeveler, Amy Hoffman, Kristen Hogan, Dominique Homberger, Fred Isaac, Jackie Jackson, Ron Javorsky, Jill Jones, Annette Kolodny, Bernard Koloski, James M. Lang, Andrea Lapin, Susan Larson, Jeanne Leiby, John Lowe, Andrea Loyola, Michelle Masse, Carol Mattingly, Deirdre McCloskey, Sally Mitchell, Janet Montelaro, Anna Nardo, Dana D. Nelson, James Nolan, Bonnie Noonan, Lisi Oliver, Darlene Olivo, Abigail Padgett, Margaret Parker, Stephanie Paul, Mary Perpich, June Pulliam, Marjean Purinton, Michael Radis, Susan Radis, Malcolm Richardson, Robin Roberts, Becky Ropers-Huilman, Meg Schoerke, Elaine Showalter, Leah Smith, Woollcott Smith, David Sokol, Judith Stafford, David Starobin, Catharine Stimpson, Susan Sullivan, Susan Swartzlander, Bette Tallen, Helen Taylor, Linda Wagner-Martin, Marilyn Wann, Martha Ward, John Waters, Janet Wondra, Beth Younger, and Joyce Zonana.

Ms. Mentor finished proofreading this book as Hurricanes Gustav and Ike washed over her ivory tower.

She endures.